CHILD LABOUR AND RIGHTS ISSUES
A STUDY OF MIGRANT LABOURERS

CHILD LABOUR AND RIGHTS ISSUES
A STUDY OF MIGRANT LABOURERS

By

Dr. Robin D. Tribhuwan

M.A., M.Sc., PGDM, Ph.D.

&

Dr. Jayshree V. Kharche

M.A., M.Phil, Ph.D.

DISCOVERY PUBLISHING HOUSE PVT. LTD.

NEW DELHI-110 002

Published by:
Tilak Wasan

DISCOVERY PUBLISHING HOUSE PVT. LTD.
4383/4B, Ansari Road, Darya Ganj
New Delhi-110 002 (India)
Phone : +91-11-23279245, 43596064-65
Fax : +91-11-23253475
E-mail : discoverypublishinghouse@gmail.com
sales@discoverypublishinggroup.com
parul.wasan@gmail.com
web : www.discoverypublishinggroup.com

***First Edition:* 2014**

ISBN: 978-93-5056-444-8

Child Labour and Rights Issues
A Study of Migrant Labourers

Printed at:
Aditi Fine Art Press
Delhi

Preface

The subject of movement of populations has occupied a prominent place in social as well as biological sciences. The shifts of physical space and their consequences – economic, social, political and biological – has been the focus of enquiry of many studies (Malhotra K.C., 1976:3). The term migration means movement of an individual, a family, a group or a community from one place to another.

The concept of migration is as old as human civilization. Migration is a process through which people move from one place to residence to another. The change in residence results in redistribution of population, both at its place of origin and place of destination. The process of migration changes the size and structure of population.

Social scientists have defined the concept of migration differently. According to Everett Lee, "permanent or semi-permanent change of residence is migration." Tripathy and Das, define migration as the flow of people over shorter or longer distances from one origin to a destination, either for temporary or permanent settlement. Winberg (1961) defines migration as the change of place permanently or temporarily for an appreciable duration as in case of seasonal labourers.

Concept of migration has been classified in to several types namely: *(i)* permanent or temporary migration; *(ii)* Forced or voluntary migration; *(iii)* External or Internal migration.

Social science studies on migration reveal that people migrate from one place of residence to another for following reasons;

1. *Economic Reasons* – For economic reasons such as jobs, business, trade, barter system, collection of Minor Forest Produce etc.
2. *Educational purpose* – For attaining higher education in cities, towns or even abroad.
3. *Political Reasons* – Those who elected has political representatives in the State or National Governments migrate to the capital of the State or to the country to represent the concerned Government.
4. *Due to natural and manmade calamities* – People migrate due to natural calamities such as earth quake, flood, eruption of volcanoes, storm, epidemics etc. and manmade calamities such as riots, wars due to development projects etc.

As aptly pointed out by Panjiar Smita (2007), while the booming Indian economy has provided tremendous opportunities of growth for the top 20 percent of its population, those at the bottom have been further marginalized. This situation has given rise to new challenges that need to be continuously grappled with. One such challenge is the rising trend of distress seasonal migration, that is, millions of families being forced to leave their homes and villages for several months a year in search of livelihood. These migrations mean that families are uprooted, and their children forced to drop out from school. At work sites migrant children are inevitably put to work. The phenomenon of seasonal migration is highly complex, largely unsearched, and more or less ignored by all- be it the Government, Academia, the development sector or the media.

In the case of Katkari brick kiln labourers and Bhil sugarcane cutters who migrate seasonally (temporarily) to place of destination, are forced due to certain push and pull factors identified through this research study. On the basis of pilot study conducted before the fieldwork and the data collected by administering 200 interview schedules and documenting 50 case studies of respondent, supported with review of literature, a conceptual model was developed and proved scientifically through the data collected analyzed and interpreted.

The child labour and child rights conceptual model is the main contribution of this study. A conceptual model has been evolved through this research, with the help of which comparative studies can be conducted on other occupational group belonging to unorganized labour. Secondly, the research study has also developed an appropriate methodology to study the concept of child labour and child rights issues of two tribal communities. Thirdly, the recommendation given in the study will surely be useful to policy makers for developing appropriate and culturally acceptable programs for the children of communities that form part of the unorganized labour.

The present research study focuses on one such un-researched area namely, "Child labour and rights issues among the Katkari brick kiln labourers and Bhil sugarcane cutters". Emphasis of the study is to explore the socio-economic background of the Katkari brick kiln labourers and Bhil sugarcane cutters. Secondly, to unveil the impact of distress seasonal migration on the lives of the migrant labourers and their children. The child labour and rights issues of the Katkari and Bhil migrants have been explored through this research. The study also highlights the various schemes that Government and NGOs implement for the tribal children. Lastly, it provides recommendations for the development of the Bhil and Katkari migrants and their children.

Dr. **Robin D. Tribhuwan**

Dr. **Jayshree Kharche**

Acknowledgement

We take this opportunity, to put on record our sincere gratitude and thank all those who have helped us in completing this study.

We express my deep gratitude to Dr. Anupama Keskar, Prof. Vijay Karekar, Dean, Department of Social Sciences, Dr. Jagan Karade, Dr. Vishal Jadhav of the Department of Sociology, Tilak Maharashtra Vidyapeeth, Dr. Swati Shirwadkar, Head, Department of Sociology, University of Pune for their inspiration and academic support.

This study would not have been completed without the cooperation of the brick-kiln owners and sugarcane factory contractors and more importantly our respondents, the migrant Katkaris and Bhils. The officers and staff of Commissionerate, Sugar, Pune were kind enough to furnish relevant details.

We thank Mr. Pravin Mahajan of Janarth and Shri. Vivek Pandit of Shramjeevi Sanghtana, NGOs for furnishing valuable information. We are indebted to Vijaya Kulkarni, Librarian, TRTI, Pune for her help.

Last but not the least we thank Dr. Jyoti Gagangras, Vice-Principal, Modern College, Ganeshkhind, Pune, for her support and good wishes.

Dr. **Robin D. Tribhuwan**
Dr. **Jayshree Kharche**

Contents

CHAPTER 1

Child Labour and Child Rights Issues Among Katkaris and Bhils

The Brick Kiln and Sugarcane Cutting Labourers

INTRODUCTION

The social problem of child labour and rights has been researched by Economists, Anthropologists, Social Work experts, legal experts as well as Sociologist world over. The International Labour Organization (ILO) and UNICEF have published few reports on the issue of child labour and child rights.

Sociological studies by Breman Jan & Das Arvind (2000), Breman Jan (1996), Tribhuwan Robin & Patil Jayshree (2008), Shende Sadashive (2011), Tribhuwan Robin & Rgnahild Andreason(2003) although have conducted research studies on various labourers belonging to informal sector such as the sugarcane cutters, brick kiln workers, hawkers, salt pan workers, stone quarry works etc. very few studies have made reference of the child labour and rights issues. In fact there are hardly any studieson the child labour and child rights issues among the Katkari brick kiln labourers and Bhil sugarcane cutters. The Katkaris who work as labourers at the brick kilns and sugarcane cutters migrate seasonally to their respective places of destination for survival.

Furthermore, studies by Naik T.B. (1965), Singh K.S. (2004), Tribhuwan Robin and Sherry Karen (2004), Tribhuwan Robin and Kulkarni Vijaya (1999), Gare G.M. (1982) in their studies on the Bhils have not made any reference of child labour and child rights among the sugarcane cutting Bhil labourers.

Similarly studies by Heredia Rudolf & Srivastava Rahul (1994), Singh K.S. (2004), Tomar Y.P.S. and Tribhuwan Robin (2004); Gaikwad Nancy (1995); Sachidanad and Prasad R.R. (1996), Tribhuwan Robin (2004), Enthoven

R.E.(1925), Russel and Heeralal (1916), Tribhuwan Robin and Others (2008), Tribhuwan Robin and Others (2009), Tribhuwan Robin and Peters P. (1994), Tribhuwan Robin and Patil Jayshree(2008) on the Katkaris have not highlighted the issue of child labour and child rights.

The above mentioned studies reviewed by the researcher indicate and are substantially evident to prove that the child labour and rights issues of the Bhil children whose parents work as sugarcane cutters as well the children of Katkari brick kiln labourers have not been researched. After reviewing secondary literature a pilot study was conducted by the researcher to assess the gaps in the existing Sociological research on the target population. Fifty respondents from each tribe were informally interviewed during the pilot study. Besides the parents, children involved in labour were too interviewed, including contractors, Sugar School and Bhonga School teachers and NGO representatives working for the Bhils and Katkaris.

Informal interactions with the brick-kiln Katkari workers and Bhil sugarcane cutters as well as other respondents during the pilot study, supported by review of literature put forth following facts to the notice of the researcher about the labourers of both the informal sectors. These facts are:

1. ***Seasonal Migration:*** Both, the Katkari brick kiln and Bhil sugarcane cutting labourers are seasonal migrants.
2. ***Economic, Food and Debt Crisis:*** Both groups are victims of economic, food and debt crisis.
3. ***Landless or marginal farmers:*** Majority of these families are landless or marginal farmers. Although landlessness has been identified as one of the key push factors that is responsible for pushing both the Katkaris as well as Bhils into brick making and sugarcane cutting labour. It was observed that some Katkaris do own cultivating land, the quality of which is poor. In the case of Bhils it was observed that although 71 per cent of them own land, it was revealed through in depth interviews that the land owned is divided among three to four brothers and hence the agriculture produce shared by three to four families is hardly sufficient for 2 to 3 months. In their study Bhatia Arun and Tribhuwan Robin (2004) conducted in Nandurbar revealed that the food grains produced by the Bhils are hardly enough for 2 to 4 month. This certainly indicates that the meager share of cultivable land, and agriculture produce that is shared by 3 to 4 families is insufficient and hence push the victims to the place of destiny.
4. ***Unskilled Labourers:*** They are unskilled labourers.
5. ***High Illiteracy Rate:*** Illiteracy rate among the parents is high and very high among the women in particular.
6. ***High rate of unemployment in their place of origin:*** There are no jobs in their native place and hence seasonal migration.

7. ***Push Factors:*** Poverty, bonded labour, landless status, poor housing, unemployment, illiteracy, unskilled labour, food, economic and debt crisis push them to seasonally migrate to brick kilns and sugar cane fields with their children to work as labourers for long hours day in and day out for very less salaries.*Kharchi* (Weekly expenses) and *Uchal* (loan) are two powerful pull factors take them to the sugarcane factories and brick kilns. Brick kiln owners and mukadams are like banks for them. In fact they are like ATM machines for the labourers.
8. ***Heavy Work Targets:*** Yet another feature observed among the Katkari brick kiln workers and Bhil sugarcane cutters was, the heavy work load targets given them either daily, weekly or monthly forces them to work for long hours, along with their children. For example, one Katkari family is expected to make 1,00,000 bricks a month. The cost of one brick is Rs. 4/-, hence the owner gets Rs. 4,00,000/- per family, per month. However in return they get only Rs. 3000/- to 5,000/- per month as kharchi. If the target is completed, they get the desired amount.
9. ***Economic Exploitation:*** This brings us to another feature of these families and that is they are worse victims of economic exploitation. They are exploited by the brick kiln owners as well as the contractors and Mukadams of sugar mills. In fact, when they return back to their villages to work as agricultural and daily wage labourers even there they are exploited by their employers. For example, the Katkaris are given two meals comprising of rice and dal and 20 to 40 rupees a day. They work for 10 to 12 hours a day. Besides this they get rice grains i.e. 30 to 40 kg for two months per family.
10. ***Temporary and Weak houses with few belongings:*** Last, but not least feature of the brick kiln and sugarcane cutters is the condition of their houses back home. Their houses are small having an area of 150 to 250 sq. ft. Given below is a brief description of their houses.
    (a) **Katkari House:** A small house with a thatched roof, walls made up of karvi sticks smeared with clay and cow dung. The floor is earth, smeared with cow dung. The house is usually without a plinth. There are few vessels, clothes, bed sheets and a hearth in the house. A family of Katkaris can make and break these temporary houses within one day's time. The doors are small and the roof is low. The shape of the house is squarish. The area of the house varies from 150 to 200 sq. ft.
    (b) **Bhil House:** The shape of a Bhil house is rectangular. The area of a typical Bhil house varies from 250 to 1500 sq. ft. The walls are however made up of bamboos; the roof is a thatched one. The floor is of earth, smeared with cow dung. More or less Bhil houses of sugarcane cutters are with less belongings and temporary in nature. These houses are better off as compared to the houses of Katkari brick kiln workers.

Both the groups live in worse houses while at work. The Katkaris live in very small houses thatched with rice sheaves and the walls form arranged bricks. The Bhils on the other hand live in peculiar huts made up of bamboo sheets called *Khopis*. They live at the work site for a period of 6 to 8 months.

THE CHILD LABOUR – CHILD RIGHTS: A CONCEPTUAL MODEL

Informal interviews with Katkaris working at the brick kilns and Bhils working as sugarcane cutters, the contractors, the owners, NGOs and Activists working for these groups etc. during the pilot study and after conducting review of literature helped the researcher to develop a conceptual model and the hypothesis of the study. The model was tested and proved by collecting, analyzing and interpreting primary data.

Before getting into understanding the research problem and review of literature, it is appropriate at this juncture to discuss the conceptual model developed on the basis of facts collected during the pilot study and after reviewing secondary literature.

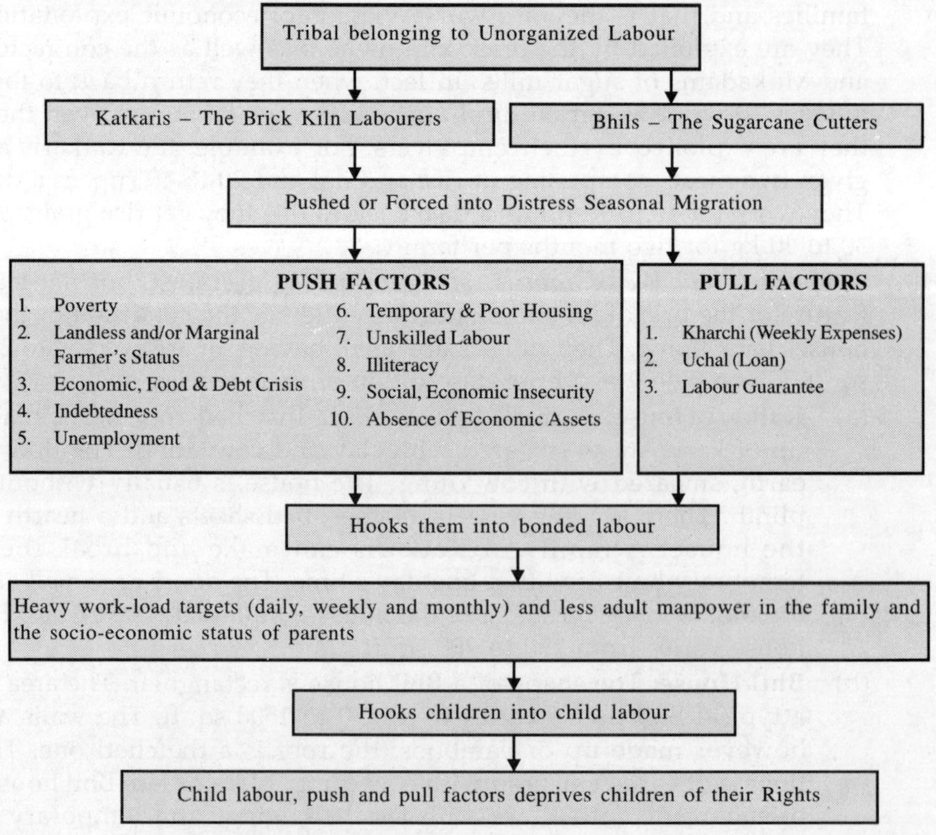

Child Labour and Child Rights: A Conceptual Model

Tribals belonging to Unorganized Labour Sector

Salient Features of Informal/Unorganized Sector

The term unorganized sector is also termed as informal sector by certain social scientists. Given below are salient features of the concept.

In an overview of unorganized labour by Press Information Bureau (18th September 2001) Government of India, classification of unorganized workers and characteristics of unorganized labour have been given, which are as follows.

Classification of Workers

Unorganized workers may be categorized under the following four broad heads, in terms of:

- Occupation
- Nature of employment
- Specially distressed categories, and
- Service categories

Small and marginal farmers, landless agricultural labourers, share-croppers, fishermen, those engaged in animal husbandry, in beedi rolling, beedi labeling and beedi packing, building and other construction workers, leather workers, weavers, artisans, salt workers, workers in brick kiln and stone quarries, workers in saw mills, oil mills etc. may come in the first category.

Attached agricultural labourers come under the second category.

Toddy tappers, scavengers, carriers of head loads, drivers of animal driven vehicles, loaders and unloaders, belong to the especially distressed category. Midwives, domestic workers, fishermen and women, barbers, vegetable and fruit vendor, newspaper vendors etc. come under the service category. (Tribhuwan Robin& Patil Jayshree;2009:22)

Some of the other categories of labourers and workers that are included by the researcher in this category are:

1. Farm house maids
2. Small and marginal farmers
3. Farm house watchmen
4. Brick kiln labourers
5. Sugarcane cutters
6. Daily wage labourers
7. Tendu leaf gatherers
8. Gatherers of minor forest produce
9. Toddy tappers
10. Mauha liquor sellers
11. Tribal artisans
12. Mango and chickoo grove workers

13. PWD and forest labourers working for contractors
14. Herders
15. Fuel wood sellers etc.

1. **Katkaris - the brick kiln labourers**

According to the All India Brick Kilns and Tile Manufacturers' Federation, there are around 50,000 brick kilns in India. Taking a conservative estimate of five members per family, a staggering figure of 25 million is obtained as those dependent on brick sector for their livelihood, a third of which are likely to be children. (Panjiar Smita, 2007:33). Tribhuwan Robin (2004) has stated that, out of the 45 tribes in Maharashtra Katkari is the poorest, backward and most needy tribe in the state. Despite of 63 years of independence the members of this tribe are below the poverty line, landless, jobless, victims of poverty, debt, food crisis and social stigma. The rate of illiteracy is very high among the Katkaris and so among women. The bench mark survey conducted by the TRTI (2001) states that the illiteracy of Katkaris in Maharashtra T.S.P area is 83.62, with 89 per cent among males and 78.30 per cent among females. Tomar YPS and Tribhuwan Robin (2004) in their book captioned 'Development of Primitive Tribes in Maharashtra' have shown that the illiteracy percentage of Katkaris studied in two villages was 97.13 per cent, with 91.66 per cent among males and 90 per cent among females.Tribhuwan Robin (2010) in his report captioned, 'Human Development Indicators among Scheduled Tribes of Maharashtra' has stated the illiteracy percentage of Katkaris as 83.62 per cent.

Given above is just a brief socio- economic and educational profile of the Katkaris, but the fact remains that despite of their hardship and insecurity they are forced to become victims of economic exploitation at the hands of scruples brick kiln owners.

2. **Bhils - the Sugarcane cutters**

A study commissioned byJanarth, Aurangabad based NGO, estimates that about 6,50,000 labourers migrate from central Western Maharashtra for sugarcane cutting each year. Of these around 2,00,000 are children in the age group of 6 to 14.

Out of the 45 tribes 3 to 4 tribes are known for working as sugarcane cutting labourers. These tribes are Bhils, Pawaras, Thakars, Mavchis and Koknis. Bhils and Pawaras work as sugarcane cutting labourers the most, followed by the Thakars of Kannad Block in Aurangabad. These families are mostly landless, marginal farmers and daily wage labourers. Thus, poor families belonging to the above tribes are forced to take up sugarcane cutting labour. Bhils are the most poorest of the above mentioned groups. According to TRTI'S benchmark survey (2001) 91 per cent of the Bhils are below the poverty line.

Push Factors

The model conceptually designed under the able guidance of Dr. Robin Tribhuwan, an eminent anthropologist, and my research supervisor, further reveals that the Katkaris brick kiln labourers and the Bhil sugarcane cutters and pushed into seasonal migration due to following push factors. These push factors are:

1. Poverty
2. Landless and/or marginal farmer's status
3. Economic, food and debt crisis
4. Heavy interest on loan
5. Unemployment
6. Temporary and poor housing
7. Unskilled Labour
8. Illiteracy
9. Social and Economic Insecurity
10. Absence of Economic Assets

The above mentioned factors push the Katkaris and Bhils to migrate seasonally and hook them into bonded labour. *Kharchi* (Weekly expenses) and *Uchal* (loan) are two powerful pull factors that attract them to the sugarcane factories and brick kilns. Brick kiln owners and mukadams are like banks for them.

Bonded Labour

The bonded labour system refers to the relationship between a creditor and a debtor who obtains loan owing to the economic compulsions confronting his day to day life and agrees to abide by the terms dictated by the creditor. The important term of the agreement is that the debtor agrees to mortgage his services of any or all members of his family, for a specified or unspecified period.

In the case of brick kilns and sugarcane cutters i.e. the Katkaris and Bhils have been observed to be made to mortgage their service of any and all members of the family till they repay the loan borrowed with interest from the brick kiln owners and sugarcane cutting Mukadams. It was observed that both the Katkaris and Bhils get hooked into bonded labour for two to six generations, till they repay the loans with interest. The Government and NGOs must seriously look into this issue in order to free them out of bonded labour.

Heavy Workload Targets and Less Adult Manpower in the Family

It was observed that heavy workload targets (daily, weekly, monthly) and lack of adult manpower in the family including poor socio-economic background forces the parents to push children in labour. The concept of child labour and its various forms have been discussed in the review of literature.

Thus, jobs like collecting sugarcane and tying them into bundles, carrying the bundle to the bullock cart or truck, loading and unloading is done by children between the age group 10-15 years. Children between the age 16-18 years are involved in cutting cane. Similarly the Katkari children between age 8-15 carry bricks help parents in loading and unloading. Those between the age group 16-18 get trained to handle almost all labour jobs related to manufacturing of bricks when they become adults, they manage to show for their nuclear families. Once the children are hooked into child labour they are deprived of their rights.

Child Rights

The concept of freedom, Neo-liberalism, human rights, democracy and the freedom to express oneself has brought about drastic change in Western societies in particular regarding the rights of a child. Issues of child exploitation, labour, child rights are taken very seriously in the West. In a country like India, although there are laws to safeguard the interests of children, the level of awareness regarding child rights is very low among poor, illiterate and ignorant people. Hence their children are deprived of following child rights.

1. *Right to family environment:* Adoption and other non-institutional services.
2. *Right to parental care:* Custody and Guardianship
3. *Right against economic exploitation:* Child Labour
4. Right to protection against sexual abuse and exploitation
5. Juvenile Justice
6. Right to Development:
   (i) Elementary Education – the right of every child
   (ii) Right to play and recreation
7. Right to Survival:
   (i) Right to Health
   (ii) Rights of unborn child and rights during early childhood
   (iii) Rights during early childhood
   (iv) Rights of the Child and working mothers
   (v) Children's Right to Shelter/housing

To sum up the Katkari brick kiln and Bhil sugarcane cutting labourers are pushed or forced into seasonal migration due to major ten push factors, which hook them into bonded labour. The daily, weekly and monthly targets of bonded labour, bestowed upon the creditor on the debtor and the lack of adult man power in the family forces the parents to push into child labour, further deprives the children of their rights.

The facts presented in data chapters have proved this model correct, by supporting the same with qualitative and quantitative data. It is argued that using this model, social scientists can study child labour and child rights issues of other unorganized labour sectors.

REVIEW OF LITERATURE

Introduction

The purpose of review of literature is three fold:

1. It places on record general and discipline specific literature on the research problem selected by the researcher.
2. It contributes in exploring research gaps in the existing knowledge.
3. It guides collection of empirical facts (data) and contributes in developing hypothesis and set of research questions.

The review of literature done by the researcher with regard to the present study is grouped into two categories namely: (a) General review of literature, (b) Sociological literature.

A. ***General Review of Literature:***

In this category, references of general writers, social thinkers and social scientists other than sociologists are made. The reflections of these scientists on the concept of migration, seasonal migration, bonded labour, child, child labour, child rights, awareness of child rights, informal sector, cultural issues of child rights and child labour and the issues of sugarcane cutters and brick kiln labourers is made. This section also discusses policy issues regarding child labour and child rights among tribal communities.

B. ***Theoretical Framework:***

In this section the theoretical framework and structural model related to research problem is discussed. Based on the analytical reflections on the research reported in above two categories hypothesis have been developed. Given this background, the first part of the general review of literature present the concept of child, child labour and child work.

A. General Review of Literature:

Tribes are "scheduled" under Article 342 of the Indian Constitution. These scheduled tribes are the tribal communities or groups within these communities that are listed in each State/Union territory separately under the Presidential Order "The Scheduled Castes and Scheduled Tribes List, Modification Order, 1956," (Census of India, 1991).

The Constitution of India incorporates several special provisions for the promotion of educational and economic interests of scheduled tribes are their protection from injustice and exploitation. The Tribal Sub-Plan strategy is the vehicle for this. This initiative was adopted at the start of the Fifth Five Year Plan, (1975-1979). The Ministry of Tribal Affairs was formed in October 1999 to take care of scheduled tribes. At around the same time, the Ministry of Social Justice and Empowerment was formed to assist Scheduled Castes (Tribhuwan Robin & Sherry Karen; 2004).

I. Profile of Tribals in India

According to Anthropological Survey of India, there are 750 tribal groups having a population of 843 lakhs (84 million), which amounts to 8.15 per cent to the total population of the country according to the 2001 census. The State of Maharashtra ranks second in the country after Madhya Pradesh as regards the size of tribal population is concerned. Out of the 750 tribal groups, the Government of India, Ministry of Tribal Affairs has classified 75 groups as PVTGs. Recently the Government of India, Ministry of Tribal Affairs has used another term for PVTGs and i.e. Particularly Vulnerable Tribal Groups (PVTGs). This change has been done considering the discriminatory term Primitive Tribal Groups, as it does not fit into the International Human Rights concept. In Maharashtra there are three PVTGs, namely the Katkaris, Kolams and Madias. The focus of the study is on Katkaris – The Brick Kiln Workers and another major tribe from North-western Maharashtra called Bhils – the sugar cane cutting tribe. Table 1.1 reveals the population of the tribals in the country.

Table 1.1: State-wise Total and Tribal Population of India (Figures in Thousand)

Sr.No.	State/Union Territory	Population		Percentage of Tribal Population
		Total	Tribal	
1	2	3		4
I.	**States**			
1.	Andhra Pradesh	762.10	50.24	6.59
2.	Arunachal Pradesh	10.98	7.05	• 64.21
3.	Assam	266.55	33.09	12.41
4.	Bihar	829.98	7.58	0.91
5.	Chhattisgarh	208.34	66.17	31.76
6.	Delhi	138.51	–	–
7.	Goa	13.48	0.01	0.07
8.	Gujarat	506.71	74.81	14.76
9.	Haryana	211.44	–	–
10.	Himachal Pradesh	60.78	2.45	4.03
11.	Jammu & Kashmir	101.43	11.06	10.90
12.	Jharkhand	269.46	70.87	26.30
13.	Karnataka	528.51	34.64	6.55
14.	Kerala	318.41	3.64	1.14

(Contd...)

1	2	3		4
15.	Madhya Pradesh	603.48	122.34	20.27
16.	Maharashtra	968.79	85.77	8.85
17.	Manipur	21.67	7.41	34.19
18.	Meghalaya	23.19	19.93	85.94
19.	Mizoram	8.89	8.39	94.38
20.	Nagaland	19.90	17.74	89.15
21.	Orissa	368.05	81.45	22.13
22.	Punjab	243.59	–	–
23.	Rajasthan	565.07	70.98	12.56
24.	Sikkim	5.41	1.11	20.52
25.	Tamilnadu	624.06	6.51	1.04
26.	Tripura	31.99	9.93	31.04
27.	Uttar Pradesh	1661.98	1.08	0.06
28.	Uttaranchal	84.89	2.56	3.01
29.	West Bengal	801.76	44.07	5.50
II.	**Union Territories**			
1.	Andaman & Nichobar	3.56	0.30	8.43
2.	Chandigarh	9.01	–	–
3.	Dadra & Nagar Haveli	2.20	1.37	62.27
4.	Diu and Daman	1.58	0.14	8.86
5.	Lakshadweep	0.61	0.57	93.44
6.	Pondicherry	9.74	–	–
	INDIA	10,286.10	843.26	8.20

Source: Census of India, 2001.

It is evident from the Table 1.1 that the tribal population of Maharashtra is second largest tribal population after the State of Madhya Pradesh.

II. Profile of Tribals in Maharashtra

Now we shall see what tribes are found in the State of Maharashtra, what are their names, what their population is and what is their decadal growth from 1981 census, as would be revealed by table 1.2 and table 1.3 respectively.

Table 1.2: Tribe-wise Total Population of the Maharashtra as per 1981, 1991, 2001 Census

Sr. No.	Name of Tribe	Total Population		
		1981	1991	2001
1.	Andh	231871	295380	372875
2.	Baiga	546	886	481
3.	Barda	10293	9100	320
4.	Bavacha, Bamcha	336	436	97
5.	Bhaina	1293	1696	235
6.	Bharia Bhumia, Bhuinhar, Bhumia, Pando	1022	2240	608
7.	Bhattra	124	1102	129
8.	Bhil, Bhil Garasia, Dholi Bhil,Dungri Bhil, Dungri Garasia, Mewasi Bhil, Rawal Bhil, Todi Bhil, Bhagalio, Bhilala Pawra, Vasava, Vasave	993074	1344554	1818792
9.	Bhunjia	1940	2807	2193
10.	Binjhwar	6216	7479	8156
11.	Birhul, Birhor	212	1003	40
12.	Omitted	179	549	
13.	Dhanka, Tadvi, Tetaria, Valvi	55880	62110	45741
14.	Dhanwar	69809	79030	20120
15.	Dhodia	10980	14866	9636
16.	Dubla, Talavia, Halpati	16019	21168	17017
17.	Gamit, Gamta, Gavit, Mavchi, Padvi	110828	122407	86776
18.	Gond, Rajgond, Arakh, Arrakh, Agario, Asur Bedi Maria, Boda Maria, Bhatok, Bhimma, Bhuta, Koilabhuta, Koilabhuti, Bhar, Bisonhorn Maria, Chota Maria, Dandami Maria, Dhuru, Dhurwa, Dhoba, Dhulia, Dora, Kaiki, Gatta, Gatti, Gaita, Gond Gowari Hill Mario, Kandaro Kalanga, Khatola, Koitar, Koya, Khirwo, Khirwara, Kucha Maria, Kucheki Maria, Madia, Maria, Mong, Mannewar, Moghya, Mogia, Monghya, Mudio, Muria, Nagarchi, Naikpod, Nagwanshi, Ojha, Faj, Sonjhari, Jhareka, Thotia, Thotya, Wade Maria, Vade Maria	1162735	1442986	1554894
19.	Halba, Halbi	242819	278378	297923
20.	Kamar	5940	7489	4209

(Contd…)

Sr. No.	Name of Tribe	Total Population		
		1981	1991	2001
21.	Kathodi, Katkari, Dhor Kathodi, Dhor Kathkari, Son Kathodi, Son Katkari	174602	202203	235022
22.	Kawar, Kanwar, Kaur, Cherwa, Rathia, Tanwar, Chattri	20321	25508	23365
23.	Khairwar	2344	2680	819
24.	Kharia	11411	12921	529
25.	Kokna, Kokni, Kukna	352932	463585	571916
26.	Kol	4187	5225	5691
27.	Kolam, Mannervarlu	118073	147843	173646
28.	Koli Dhor, Tokre Koli, Kolcha, Kolgha	77435	117091	170656
29.	Koli Mahadev, Dongar Koli	787448	999321	1227562
30.	Koli Malhar	177367	206741	233617
31.	Kondh, Khond, Kandh	407	1122	293
32.	Korku, Bopchi, Mouasi, Nihal, Nahul, Bondhi, Bondeya	115974	141202	211692
33.	Koya, Bhine Koya, Rajkoya	441	564	241
34.	Nagesia, Nagasia	126	436	217
35.	Naikda, Nayaka, Cholivala Nayaka, Kapadia Nayaka, Moto Nayaka, Nana Nayaka	35053	72029	27786
36.	Oraon, Dhangad	70984	96524	28921
37.	Pardhan, Pathari, Saroti	98685	120836	126134
38.	Pardhi; Advichinchor, Phans Pardhi, Phanse Pardhi, Langoli Pardhi, Bahelia, Bahellia, Chita Pardhi, Shikari, Takankar, Takia	95115	123813	159875
39.	Parja	806	1780	469
40.	Patelia	1044	2547	1191
41.	Pomla	219	539	62
42.	Rathawa	1009	1258	810
43.	Sawar, Sawara	302	357	254
44.	Thakur, Thakar, Ka Thakur, Ka Thakar, Ma Thakur, Ma Thakar	323191	400583	487696
45.	Omitted	209	568	–
46.	Varli	361271	461916	627197
47.	Vitolia, Kotwalia, Barodia	1012	1203	363
48.	Unclassified	–	12220	21010

Source: Census of India 1981, 1991 & 2001.

The decadal growth of tribals in Maharashtra is given in table 1.3.

Table 1.3: The Decadal Growth of Tribals in Maharashtra

Census Year	State's Total Population (lakh)	Tribal Population (lakh)	Percentage
1971	504.12	38.41	7.62
1981	627.84	57.72	9.19
1991	789.37	73.18	9.27
2001	968.79	85.77	8.85

Source: Census of India 1971 to 2001.

III. Socio-economic, educational and health status of tribals in Maharashtra

Studies by various social scientists and TRTI, Pune have unveiled the socio-economic, educational and health status of the tribals in Maharashtra. Given below are extracts of the above-mentioned studies.

- **Economic Status**: Nadeem Hasnain (1987: 19), in his book captioned, 'Tribal India Today' has classified the economic life of tribals in India as follows:

1. Food gathering and hunting tribes
2. Tribes engaged un hilly cultivation
3. Tribe engaged in cultivation on plain lands
4. Simple artesian tribes
5. Pastoral tribes
6. Tribes living as folk artists
7. Agricultural and non-agricultural labourers
8. Tribes engaged in private and government service or trade.

In Maharashtra all the above categories are found except pastoral tribes.

Majority of tribes however are small-scale cultivators who are engaged in cultivation for period of six months i.e. from May to October. From November to April they get into daily wage, agriculture labour, brick kiln work, sugar cane cutting, saltpan workers, PWD etc. jobs. According to TRTI, Pune Bench Mark Survey, 1996-97, on an average 90 per cent of the tribals living in the Tribal Sub-Plan (TSP) area is below the poverty line. Table No. 1.4 presents ITDP-wise BPL status of tribals in Maharashtra. Furthermore, table no. 1.5 presents BPL status as per a survey conducted by District Rural Development Agency, (DRDA), 1980. According to DRDA statistics the average BPL percentage of tribals in Maharashtra is 91.11 per cent. A comparative look at both the figures reveals that a very high percentage of tribals in Maharashtra are Below the Poverty Line.

Table 1.4: Total No. of Scheduled Tribe Families and those Below Poverty Line in the Tribal Sub-Plan Area of Maharashtra State

Sr. No.	I.T.D.P.	S.T. Families		Percentage of Families Below Poverty Line
		Total	Below Poverty Line	
1.	Thane (Dahanu)	66447	59595	89.69
2.	Thane (Jawhar)	46556	40939	87.93
3.	Thane (Shahapur)	22260	19743	88.69
4.	Raigad (Pen)	9929	9396	94.63
5.	Nashik (Kalwan)	40446	36717	90.78
6.	Nashik (Trimbak)	58019	52776	90.96
7.	Dhule (Taloda)	69622	66305	95.24
8.	Dhule (Nandurbar)	91588	83496	91.16
9.	Jalgaon (Yawal)	5935	5479	92.32
10.	Ahmednagar (Rajur)	13208	11486	86.96
11.	Pune (Ghodegaon)	14340	12042	83.97
12.	Nanded (Kinwat)	20288	17837	87.92
13.	Amravati (Akola)	9378	8692	92.69
14.	Amravati (Dharni)	27326	23977	87.74
15.	Nagpur (Ramtek)	15110	13718	90.79
16.	Gondia (Deori)	20090	18396	91.57
17.	Yavatmal (Pandharkawada)	36561	33562	91.79
18.	Chandrapur (Rajura)	28682	26287	91.65
19.	Chandrapur (Chimur)	11091	10165	91.65
20.	Gadchiroli (Ettapalli)	12445	11772	94.59
21.	Gadchiroli (Dhanora)	5413	4921	90.91
22.	Bhamragad	11846	10835	91.47
	State Total of Tribal Sub Plan Area	**634580**	**578136**	**91.11**

Source: Bench Mark Survey TRTI, 1996-97.

As evident from table number 1.4, Nandurbar, Raigad and Gadchiroli districts show highest BPL percentage.

Table number 1.5 presents district-wise BPL status of ST families in the state of Maharashtra as per DRDA survey conducted in 1980. In the DRDA survey (1980) it is seen that, the figures of four districts namely Sindhudurg, Kolhapur, Nanded and Chandrapur have not reported while the figures of some districts have given jointly/together e.g.statistics of Dhule & Nandurbar,

Aurangabad & Jalna districts have given together. It is evident from the table number 6 that maximum number i.e. 97.99 per cent BPL ST families were found in Satara district followed by Nagpur 82.52 per cent.

Table 1.5: District-wise Total Scheduled Tribe Families below Poverty Line as per D.R.D.A. Survey (1980)

Sr. No.	District	Total Rural	Scheduled Tribe Families	
			Below Poverty Line	Percentage
1.	Thane	1,33,593	83,648	62.61
2.	Raigad	36,907	26,743	72.46
3.	Ratnagiri	7,510	3,438	45.78
4.	Sindhudurg	*	*	–
5.	Nashik	114,071	79,629	69.80
6.	Dhule	1,44,183	1,04,019	72.14
7.	Nandurbar			
8.	Jalgaon	36,890	25,459	69.01
9.	Ahmednagar	34,869	21,584	61.90
10.	Pune	26,141	15,205	58.16
11.	Satara	2,396	2,348	97.99
12.	Sangli	2,499	1,852	74.11
13.	Solapur	6,832	3,419	50.04
14.	Kolhapur	4,507	*	–
15.	Aurangabad	13,324	7,003	52.56
16.	Jalna			
17.	Parbhani	13,702	3,453	25.20
18.	Hingoli			
19.	Nanded	2,252	*	–
20.	Beed	29,609	10,939	36.94
21.	Osmanabad	8,137	2,676	32.88
22.	Latur			
23.	Buldhana	12,071	5,035	41.71
24.	Akola	20,264	13,808	68.14
25.	Washim			
26.	Amravati	39,570	20,977	53.01
27.	Yavatmal	71,232	52,070	73.09
28.	Nagpur	25,241	20,830	82.52
29.	Wardha	37,434	17,424	46.54
30.	Bhandara	54,751	43,274	79.04
31.	Gondia			
32.	Gadchiroli	1,01,832	59,440	58.37
33.	Chandrapur	*	*	*
	Total for State	**9,79,817**	**6,24,521**	**63.73**

Source: D.R.D.A.Survey 1980, * Not reported.

Educational Status

It is well-known that Maharashtra is industrially and commercially a very advanced state in India. Large numbers of industries are being set-up in the backward regions in private and public sectors due to package schemes of incentives offered by Government. The industrialization and urbanization in Maharashtra is taking place very speedily with its effect on the rural population in all the speres of life. The percentage of urban population to total population was 38.89 in the year 1991. It may around 45 in the year 1995. There has been a large scale migration from rural to urban areas for employment and in this whirpool; the tribal population has been caught unaware. Their efforts to stick to their deep-rooted traditional value system, their customs, their religious practices have pulled them further down leaving an ever increasing gap between the tribals and non-tribals. In the initial stages of economic development (say up to 5th Plan), the tribal community has not joined the mainstream of society inreal sense and were, therefore, left behind in the process of development. This is also true in respect of educational status. Overall lieracy percentage in the State is about 64.87 per cent, while it is only 36.77 per cent among the Scheduled Tribes as per 1991 census. It is also pertinent to note that literacy rate among the males for the general population is 76.56 per cent and that of females is 52.32 per cent, whereas it is only 24.08 per cent for females and 49.08 per cent for males in the Scheduled Tribe communities. Thus there is a very wide gap so far as the literacy percentage among the tribals and non- tribals is concerned (Jain N.S. & Tribhuwan R.D, 1996:81-82).

In their book captioned, "Mirage of Health and Development", (1996:149), Dr. Jain and Dr. Tribhuwan, have mentioned the educational status of Bhils and Pawras of Lakkadkot Village of Shahada Block. According to this study, out of 512 Bhil respondents, 471 i.e.92 per cent were illiterate, 8 i.e.1.5 per cent studied up to only pre-primary school, 12 i.e 2.34 per cent studied up to primary school, 16 i.e. 3.3 per cent studied up to secondary school, 3 i.e 0.6 per cent studied up to higher secondary school while only 1 i.e. 0.19 per cent was graduate. High illiteracy, low level of income, and ignorance among Bhils has certainly become a barrier for educators in rendering health and educational services. In their report captioned, "Malnutrition Realed deaths of Tribal Children in Nandurbar District", Bhatia Arun and Tribhuwan Robin (2002:11), states that percentage of illiteracy in women was 94.4 per cent and in the husbands 82.5 per cent.

In their report captioned, "Dying Children", Bhatia Arun and Tribhuwan Robin (2002:17), have revealed the educational status of the Katkari studied. They stated that 92 per cent of mothers of deceased children were illiterate. Further, same report revealed that 76 per cent of the fathers of deceased children were illiterate.

In their book captioned, "Mirage of Health and Development" Jain N.S. and Tribhuwan Robin, (1996:257), have revealed that the data on educational status of Korku women pictured out that almost 82.6 per cent of the Korku women within the age range of 15-45 years were illiterates, while 11.8 per cent studied up to 4th grade, 2.48 per cent studied from 5th to 7th grade and 2.48 per cent from 8th to 10th grade and very unfortunately not a single soul out of 160 women interviewed was found to have studied above 10th grade. This is an indication of the level of illiteracy among Korku women.

It is however, interesting to note that in the year 1990, the study was conducted by UNICEF revealed that the illiteracy level of eligible women was 88.8 per cent in Dharni and 92.6 per cent in Achalpur blocks of Amaravati district and 64.0 per cent and 75 per cent in their husbands, respectively are illiterate and the large majority of the rest of the women and their husbands have had not more than a primary education.

Above statistics regarding the educational staus of both tribal men and women presents a gloomy picture of the tribals in Maharashtra. There is a lot that needs to be done to elevate the status of tribal men, women and children.

Health and Nutritional Status

Malnutrition

Studies by TRTI, 2000 revealed that 92 per cent of children below the age 5 years were malnourished while 70 per cent of women between the ages 15 to 45 years.

The table given below is taken from the report 'Dying Children" (2002:Vol. 2) by TRTI, Pune to understand the malnourishment status of tribal children. The study was conducted in Thane district. It is evident from the table given below that 92 per cent ofthe siblings of the deceased children were malnourished; of these 55 per cent were suffering from severe malnourishment.

Table 1.6: Degree of Malnourishment in 27 Siblings of the Deceased Children

Sr.No.	Gradations	No. of Children	Percentage
1.	Normal	2	8%
2.	Grade I- Mild malnutrition (body weight b/w 70% to 80% of the expected weight for age)	1	4%
3.	Grade II- Moderate malnutrition	9	33%
4.	Grade III – Severe malnutrition (Body wt. 50% to 60%)	7	26%
5.	Grade IV – Severe malnutrition (Body wt. below 50%)	8	29%
	Total	**27**	**100%**

The table given below reflects tribe-wise status of deceased children during the period of April to August 2002. It is evident from the given table that maximum number i.e. 15 (58%) of deceased children belongs to Katkari Tribe. Katkari is one of the Particularly Vulnerable Tribe (i.e. primitive tribe) of Maharashtra and even after 64 years of Independence Katkaris eat rats and bandicoots. Their poverty and unawareness makes them and their children more vulnerable and push them into vicious circle of bonded labour.

Table 1.7: Tribe-wise Status of Deceased Children in Khanevali PHC during the Period April to August 2002

Sr. No.	Tribe	Males	Females	Total
1.	Katkari	8	7	15 (58%)
2.	Malhar Koli	4	1	5 (19%)
3.	Warli	6	–	6 (23%)
	Total	**18 (68%)**	**8 (32%)**	**26 (100%)**

The table given below depicts the percentage of malnourished tribal children in the selected villages in Thane district. The study was conducted by TRTI, Pune during period of 1st September to 31st August 2002.

Table 1.8: Percentage of Malnourished Tribal Children in the Selected Villages in Thane District

Sr. No.	Village	Children under 5 Population in Settlement	Total No. of Children Measured	No. of under-nourished Children	Percentage of under-nourished Children
1.	Katkari pada of Ambiste Budruk	28	14	13	93%
2.	Warli pada of Palsai	33	17	17	100%
3.	Murabi pada of Vasuri Budruk	30	15	15	100%
4.	Neheroli	202	101	87	85%
5.	Sadkecha pada of Gandhre	54	27	14	93%
	Total	**347**	**164**	**148**	**90. 2%**

Report by TRTI: The truth about malnutrition deaths, Vol. 3, report no. 10 of 2002.

Malnutrition among the Bhils of Nandurbar

The nutritional status of the 136 siblings of the deceased children is given in the table below. It is evident from the table, 76.5 per cent of the siblings were malnourished. Of these 40 per cent was suffering from severe malnourishment. These conclusions are derived from actual weight for age measurements taken by TRTI, (Pune) staff during the survey (TRTI, Pune; 5/2002). The study was conducted in Nandurbar district.

Table 1.9: Degree of Malnourishment in 136 Siblings of the Deceased Children in Nandurbar District

Sr. No.	Gradations	No. of Children	Percentage
1.	Normal	32	23.5
2.	Grade I- Mild malnutrition (body weight b/w 70% to 80% of the expected weight for age)	24	17.6
3.	Grade II- Moderate malnutrition	38	28.0
4.	Grade III – Severe malnutrition (Body wt. 50% to 60%)	17	12.5
5.	Grade IV – Severe malnutrition (Body wt. below 50%)	25	18.4
	Total	**136**	**100%**

Source: TRTI, Pune, 2002.

Health and nutrition related other indicators were also covered in the same report. Some important indicators relevant for the study such as land holding size, food availability, diets during pregnancy, place of delivery etc. are given below.

Land Holding Size

Land holding status of the tribal families is given in the table below.It is evident from the table that 72 per cent of the families owned land less than 3 acres of which 40 per cent were landless or owned less than 1 acre. The rent for tenants was as high as 50 per cent of the produce.

Table 1.10: Land Holding Status of Tribal Families Studied

Sr. No.	Land Holding	Families	Percentage
1.	Landless	35	24.47
2.	Landless but cultivating as tenants	4	02.80
3.	0-1 acres	17	11.80
4.	1-3 acres	46	32.17
5.	3-5 acres	27	18.88
6.	5-10 acres	6	04.20
7.	10 and above	8	05.60
	Total	**143**	**100.00**

Source: TRTI, Pune, 6/5/2002.

Food Availability

The table given below indicates the number of months of food availability from their own land. It is evident from the table that out of 143 families, 123 (86%) were food deficit. 78% of the households had a food deficit from their own farms. These figures tell story of great poverty. Employment opportunities in these remote areas are limited especially for work that is assured or of a reasonable duration. The highly exploitative rent for tenanted land (50% of the produce) is an indication of the absence of employment opportunities.

Table 1.11: Months of Food Availability

Sr.No.	Months of Food Availability	No. of Families	Percentage
1.	0 to 2 months	4+39 (landless)	35
2.	2 to 4 months	29	24
3.	4 to 6 months	23	19
4.	6 to 8 months	19	15
5.	8 to 10 months	08	06
6.	More. than 10	01	01
	Total	**123**	**100**

Source: TRTI, Pune, 2002.

Nutritional Supplement from ICDS

Out of 143 tribal families, it was observed that 112 i.e. 78.33 per cent women received nutrition supplement from Anganwadi while 30 i.e. 20.98 per cent women did not receive any nutrition supplement from Anganwadi.

Special Nutritious Diet taken during Pregnancy

Out of 143 women, 123 (86.01) stated that they had not taken special diet during pregnancy. 19 (13.29%) of the women stated that had taken special nutritious food such as dry coconut, peanuts, fruit, and chicken etc. during pregnancy, while one woman did not respond.

T.T. Injections during Pregnancy

Out of 143 women, 114 i.e. 79.73 per cent of the women responded that they took T.T. injections during pregnancy while 28 i.e. 19.58 per cent stated that they did not take T.T. injections during pregnancy. One woman did not respond.

Place of Delivery

It was observed that out of 143 women, 142 i.e. 99.31 per cent of the women delivered at home.

Personnel who Conducted Delivery

In the same study, it was found that out of 143 women, 136 i.e. 95 per cent and 5 i.e.3.52 per cent of the women responded that their deliveries were conducted by traditional female (Huvakari) and male birth attendants respectively in their houses. Only one delivery was conducted by an ANM. This is because the traditional birth attendants observe the birth rituals.

Secondly, according to some tribal women, the traditional birth attendants are more accessible, arrive in time are available at all times of the night also and therefore more preferable.

Some of the main findings of the report "Malnutrition Related Deaths of Tribal Children in Nandurbar district" (2002), by TRTI, Pune are as follows:

1. Based on the nutritional status of the siblings of the deceased children it would be true to say that over 75 per cent of the deaths were malnutrition related.
2. In six villages where the official death figures given by the District Health Officer were tested it was found that 57 per cent of the deaths were unreported.
3. The fact that the Employment Guarantee Scheme is not answering the employment needs of the tribals is evident from the fact that they continue to migrate to Gujarat to work under harsh conditions.
4. Health cover has been poor. 45 per cent of the mothers of deceased children did not have a medical check during pregnancy.
5. 21 per cent of the mothers of deceased children did not receive any nutritional supplement during pregnancy under the ICDS even though the villages were covered by the scheme.
6. 20 per cent of the mothers of deceased children were not protected against tetanus. Similarly iron tablets did not reach 20 per cent of the women.
7. 99 per cent of the births were at home in spite of the Government scheme to motivate women to go to health centers. Motivation for institutional delivers has failed.
8. In 35 per cent of the cases the Primary Health Center staff did not visit the household after the death of the child.

Social Status

The table given below is taken from the report "Dying Children" (2002:Vol. 2) by TRTI, Pune to understand the status of ration-card holders. The study was conducted in Thane district.

Table 1.12:

Sr.No.	Status	No. of Families	Percentage
1.	No. of BPL Card holders	24	96%
2.	Non-BPL card holders	01	4%
	Total	**25**	**100%**

Reasons stated by tribals for not lifting ration from the fair price shop during March-August 2002.

Table 1.13:

Sr.No.	Reasons	No. of Families	Percentage
1.	Lack of cash during rainy season	24	96%
2.	Did not state anything	01	04%
	Total	**25**	**100%**

('Dying Children" (2002:Vol.2) by TRTI, Pune)

Table 1.14: Loan taken by the 25 Families

Sr.No.	Status	No. of Families	Percentage
1.	Families that took loan during 2002	17	68%
2.	Families did not take loan	8	32%
	Total	**25**	**100%**

("Dying Children" (2002: Vol. 2) by TRTI, Pune)

Note: This table Reveals that 68 per cent of the families had debt, mostly taken from brick kiln owners. This money is taken in the month of May., for food and other basic necessities, up till October. It is paid back to the brick kiln owner by working as labourers till the amount is recovered.

Table 1.15: Reasons for taking Loan

Sr.No.	Reasons	No. of Families	Percentage
1.	Food & essential basic needs	16	94%
2.	Son's sickness & food for the family	01	06%
	Total	**17**	**100%**

('Dying Children" (2002: Vol. 2) by TRTI, Pune)

Table 1.16: Land Holding Status of Tribal Families Studied

Sr. No.	Land Holding	No. of Families	Percentage
1.	Landless	21	84%
2.	Landless but cultivating as tenants	1	4%
3.	0-1 acres	0	0
4.	1-3 acres	0	0
5.	3-5 acres	3	12%
6.	5-10 acres	0	0
7.	10 and above	0	0
	Total	**25**	**100**

('Dying Children" (2002:Vol.2) by TRTI, Pune)

Table 1.17: Occupational Status of the Families Surveyed

Sr.No.	Occupation	No. of Families	Percentage
1.	Cultivators and labourers	04	16%
2.	Farm and brick kiln labourers	21	84%
	Total	**25**	**100%**

("Dying Children" (2002: Vol. 2) by TRTI, Pune)

Table 1.18: Possession of Live Stock

Sr. No.	Live Stock	No. of Families	Percentage
1.	Bulls	1	4%
2.	Cows	0	0
3.	Buffaloes	0	0
4.	Goats	0	0
5.	Sheep	0	0
6.	Poultry birds	6	24%
7.	No live stock at all	18	72%
	Total	**25**	**100**

('Dying Children" (2002:Vol.2) by TRTI, Pune)

Development Status of Sugarcane Cutting & Brick-making Migrant Labourers

From the above facts it is evident that the social, economic, educational, health, nutritional and political status of the general tribes and those involved in informal sector and more precisely in sugar cane cutting and brick making profession is totally different and projects a wide gap between both the groups. In Maharashtra predominantly found tribes working in these two sectors are the Bhils & Katkaris.

The issue of child rights and child labour among the Bhils (Sugarcane cutters) and among the Katkaris (brick kiln workers) is multi-faceted and is linked with several factors such as:

- Economic background of the migrants
- Educational background of the migrants
- Social background of the migrants
- Health & nutritional status of the migrants
- Migration types and patterns
- Factors that force/push them into seasonal migration
- Factors that force/push them into bonded labour
- Factors that push their children in labour enculturation process.
- Why their children take up jobs as child labourers?
- What rights are the children of sugar cane cutters (the Bhils) and brick kiln workers (the Katkaris) are deprived of?

- What is the level of awareness among the parents regarding child rights and child labour?
- What steps has Government and NGOs taken to tackle the issue of childlabour and child rights among the Bhils (Sugar cane cutters) and Katkaris (Brick kiln workers).

IV. Theoretical Framework

A. What is Migration?

The concept of migration is as old as human civilizations. Migration is a process through which people move from one place of residence to another. The change in residence results in redistribution of population, both at its origin and at the destination. People migrate on account of economic, social, political, marital, educational and religious reasons. An integral feature of demographic transformation is migration. The process of migration changes the size and structure of population. It affects both the places of origin and destination, of migrants. Migratory movements are considered as physical events shaped by environmental forces. Migratory movements are caused due to pressure on land because of rapid growth of population, decline in the rural industries and handicrafts, lack of employment and livelihood etc. Thus, migration is one of the dynamic constituents of population change and a vital component of development. (Tripathy S.N, 2005:24)

War, prosecution, climatic changes and economic forces have been principal movers of the people. Internal migration refers to the movements, which results in a change of usual place of residence. It may consist of the crossing of village or town boundary as a minimum condition for qualifying the movement as integral migration. (Tripathy S.N, 2005:1)

Some social scientists have analyzed migration in terms of psychological difference between movers and non-movers. Some have attempted to illustrate movements in terms of individual migrant's revealed 'reasons'. Some have highlighted on socio-economic and structural characteristics of different areas, and others have discussed on geographical or natural resource factors. Indeed, conceptualizing migration is a complex process, which includes four crucial elements – space, residence, and time and activity changes (Tripathy S.N. 2006; 2).

Migration may be classified on the basis of 'duration of stay'. Labourers may move 'permanently' or for a prolonged period. They may move for a short period. (Tripathy S.N. 2006; 2).

If the labourers move for a short duration with the intention to return to his place of usual residence, it is known as 'circular migrants' or 'turnover migrants' or short- term period. (Tripathy S.N. 2006;2).

An important group of circular migrants consist of 'seasonal migrants' those who combine activities in several places according to seasonal labour requirements and availability of seasonal work opportunities. (Tripathy S.N. 2006; 2).

B. General Terms or Concepts of Migration:

It is customary to study migration with respect to (1) Internal migration; and (2) International migration. Internal migration is the migration of persons *within* a country, while international migration refers to the movement of people from one country to another. In their book captioned' "Principles of Population Studies" (1978), Bhende Asha & Kanitkar Tara have discussed some important concepts or terms of migration which are given below:

- **Migration:** The United Nations Multilingual Demographic Dictionary defined migration as follows: "Migration is a form of geographical mobility or spatial mobility between one geographical unit and another, generally involving a change in residence from the place of origin or place of departure to the place of destination or place of arrival. Such migration is called permanent migration and should be distinguished from other forms of movement which do not involve a permanent change of residence."
- **Immigration and Emigration:** The terms immigration and emigration refer respectively to movement into or out of a particular territory, and are used only in connection with international migration. Thus migrants leaving India to settle down in the United States are immigrants for the United States and emigrants from India.
- **In-migration and Out migration:** In-migration refers to movement into a particular area, while out-migration refers to movement out of a particular area, both referring to movements within a country, that is, internal migration. Thus migrants who come from Tamil Nadu to Maharashtra are considered to be in-migrants for Maharashtra and out-migrants for Tamil Nadu. Each move is either immigration or an in-migration with respect to the place of origin or departure.
- **Migratory Movement:** This term is used for that section of population movements which is due to migration.
- **Place of Origin or Place of Departure and Place of Destination or Place of Arrival:** The place from which a move is made is the place of origin or departure. The place of arrival or the place of destination refers to the place art which a move terminates.
- **Gross and Net Migration:** The total of the arrivals of immigrants and in-migrants and departures of emigrants and out-migrants is known as gross migration or the volume of migration. Net migration is the difference between the total number of persons who arrive and the total number of persons who leave. This is also referred to as the balance of migration.
- **Migration Streams:** The phrase 'migration stream' refers to the total number of moves made during a given migration interval which have a common area of origin and a common area of destination. In practice, it refers to a body of migrants having a common area of origin and a common area of destination.

C. Definitions of Migration:

- **Everett Lee:** Permanent or semi-permanent change of residence. No restriction is placed upon the distance of the move or upon the voluntary or involuntary nature of the act and no distinction is made between external and internal migration. Thus, a move across the hall from one apartment to another is counted as just as much an act of migration as a move from Bombay, India to Cedar, Iowa.
- **Tripathy S.N. & Das C.:** Migration may be the phenomenon of the flow of the people over shorter or longer distances from one origin to a destination either for temporary or permanent settlement.
- Migration may be defined as a physical transition of an individual or a group from one society to another, this moves learning one social setting and entering a different one.
- **Winberg (1961):** Winberg defines migration as the change of place permanently or temporarily for an appreciable duration as in case of seasonal labourers.
- **Mangalam (1968):** According to Mangalam migration is relatively permanent moving away of a collectivity, called migrants, from one geographical region to another, related by decision making on the part of the migrants on the basis of hierarchically ordered set of valued ends and resulting changes in the interactional systems of the migrants.

D. Seasonal Migration:

The booming Indian economy has provided tremendous opportunities of growth for the top 20 per cent of its population, but those at the bottom have been further marginalized. This has given rise to many new challenges that need to be continuously grappled with. One such challenge is the rising trend of "distress seasonal migration"- tens of millions of families being forced to leave their homes and villages for several months every year, to head for locations near and far, in search of livelihood. In these migrations families are also forced to take their children along. All evidence indicates that the number of children below 14 years of age may already be of the order of 9 million (Panjiar Smita, 2007).

In her book captioned, "Locked Homes Empty Schools"(2007) Panjiar Smita has given some facts which are relevant to this study are as follows:

Distress Seasonal Migration: An Emerging Phenomenon

Distress Seasonal Migration has been attributed as much to uneven development (National Commission on Rural Labour – NCRL – 1991) as to caste and social structure. Large scale distress seasonal migrations were triggered off in the late 60s by persistent drought in rainfall-deficit regions of the country. This coincided with the creation of irrigation facilities and commercial agriculture in surplus areas, resulting in high labour demand during specific seasons. Urbanization and infrastructure development in recent decades have also proved catalytic, with employers constantly and persistently reaching out for the unending supply of cheap labour from remote, impoverished pockets.

Migrant populations overwhelmingly belong to Scheduled Caste (SC), Scheduled Tribe (ST) and Other Backward Class (OBC) categories. They comprise landless and land poor who possess the least amount of assets, skills or education. Studies reveal that the majority of the migrant labourers in states like Rajasthan, Karnataka, Gujarat, Andhra Pradesh, Tamil Nadu and Maharashtra are from the most marginalized sections of society (also see Srivastava, 2005).

Definition of a Migrant Worker

A migrant worker has been defined under Article 2 of the International Convention on the protection of the rights of all migrant workers and members of their families, as a worker who is to be engaged or has been engaged in a remunerated activity in a state of which he or she is not a national. Further, members of the family has been defined under Artcle 4 as persons married to migrant workers or having with them a relationship that, according to applicable law, produces effects equivalent to marriage, as well as their dependent children and other dependent persons who are recognized as members of the family by applicable bilateral or multilateral agreements between the States concerned.

In the instant case, the migrants, studied migrated within the same district. The question of inter-state migration therefore does not apply herein.

Sectors that Attract Migrant Labour

Many industrial and agro-industrial sectors, like brick making, salt manufacture, sugar-cane harvesting, stone quarrying, construction, fisheries, plantation, and rice mills and so on, run largely on migrant labour. A high incidence of migrant labour is also found in the agriculture sector. Industrial migrations are for long periods of six to eight months and take place once a year. Agricultural migrations are for shorter durations of a few weeks and take place several times a year for operations such as sowing, harvesting and transplantation. Almost all major states appear to be affected by migration, although to varying degrees. The agriculturally and industrially developed states are likely to be the net receiving states for migrant labour, while the less developed states the net sending ones. Likewise there is also substantial intra state migration taking place.

Categorizing Seasonal Migration

Migrations can be categorized according to various parameters:

- Nature of industry/work
  Partially organized/unorganized
  Agricultural/industrial/agro industrial

- Duration of Migration
  Short (4-8 weeks)/long (6-8 months)/round the year
- Distance of migration
  Intra district/inter district/interstate
- Destination of migration
  Intra rural
  Rural-urban peripheries
  Rural-urban centers
- Who migrates
  Male migration/family migration/child migration
- Purpose of migration
  For accumulation/for survival

Defining 'Distress Seasonal Migration'

It is important to distinguish migrations for accumulation from those for survival or those that occur because of distress. While the former are by choice, usually undertaken by able-bodied males of the family, involve basic negotiation abilit;, on the part of the migrants, and enable investment in asset creation, the latter fail to display any of the above characteristics. Three elements which appear to characterize distress seasonal migration are:

1. A lack of alternatives in sending areas which forces entire families, including children, to migrate in search of work, and pushes children into hazardous labour and the vicious migration cycle.
2. Work which is based on debt bondedness, generates little or no surplus for the labourer at the end of the season, and is merely for survival.
3. Work which involves large scale violation of labour laws and child rights.

The Causes of Migration

There are pull & push factors which causes distress migration.

A major push factors which triggers distress migration include:

1. The lack of livelihood options in rain fed areas, in various parts of the country, particularly after the monsoon (kharif) crop.
2. The consequent indebtedness and food insecurity forces large numbers to migrate in search of work.
3. The reasons vary from place to place, but stem from persistent drought, land and environmental degradation, salinity ingress in coastal areas, displacement due to large scale mining, mega dams, heavy industry etc.
4. Inter-regional disparity, variations in development policy also play a role.

Pull factors include:

1. High seasonal demand for manual labour in agriculturally advantaged areas, as well as labour intensive industries such as salt manufacture, brick making, sugarcane harvesting, stone-quarrying etc.
2. These sectors are characterized by predominance of manual processes, seasonality, and remoteness, work done out in the open and contract labour.

Types & Patterns of Migration

In her book captioned 'Locked Homes Empty Schools' Smita Panjiar, has mentioned patterns and types of migration.

Agriculture based migrations are of short duration - may takes place several times a year making 4-8 week trips for sowing, harvesting, transplantation. There are variations in pattern depending on the crop. Migrations are usually short distance and highly scattered.

Long Duration Migration – Industrial, agro-industrial and related migrations, such as brick-making salt manufacture, tile making, fisheries-based, sugarcane – harvesting, work at rice mills etc., have single cycle of 6 to 8 months per year.

Round the year Migration – migration periods for those living in extreme poverty may become longer; also employers often try to retain some labour round the year. Many migrant families are forced from one type of work to another to clear accumulated debt. The stone quarries in parts of Maharashtra and U.P have begun to operate round the year. They have installed technology to pump water out from the quarries during the monsoon. Thus, more and more families who migrate for stone quarrying are not returning to their villages, and settling down at the work sites. They can no longer be called 'Seasonal Migrants' as there is no seasonality in this work anymore.

Seasonal Migration: Some Theoretical Perspectives

There have been numerous studies on the migration of poor in India, but most of these are concerned with rural-urban migration, concentrating on the demographic and social characteristics of urban migrants or on case studies of individual migrants in the city slums. This urban focus has led to the relative neglect of the role of agriculture: not much attention has been devoted to intra-rural seasonal migration although there has been an increasing demand for seasonal labour in rural areas where Green Revolution has been implemented. In India, for example, increasing numbers of people migrate reasonably short distances to harvest crops, dig irrigation canals or engage themselves in other agricultural activities before returning to their villages. In her study Rensje Teerink has focused on labour migration (i.e. not on migration of more affluent classes of castes). It is necessary to define the concept of seasonal labour migration, circulation, return migration, wage-labour migration, sojourner movements etc. Breman has pointed out that it is only appropriate to use the term 'circulation' when there is a persistent, continuous return to the place of origin for a short while or a longer period (1990:48). The term 'return migration' seems more suitable when the period of time between settlement and departure is longer than a year. (As quoted in Rensje Teerink, 1996:214). In her study Teerink has opted for the term *'seasonal migration'* or 'circulation' as defined by Mitchell (1985:30): "..the process in which people periodically leave their permanent residence in search of employment at places too far away to enable them to commute daily, stay at these labour centers for extensive periods and then return to their homes", with 'extensive periods' here lasting up to eight months. Seasonal labour migration can be distinguished from regular migration by the fact that it does not alter the long term distribution of the people because all seasonal migrants will eventually return to their home areas (Chapman & Prothero:1975:39). The concept of 'seasonal migration' or 'circulation' is particularly useful when we deal with groups of people who are involved in a process of wage labour for which they are forced to leave their home areas on a regular basis, especially when entire household, consisting of men, women and children, are affected. As Breman has stressed in his recent study that, 'Circular mobility accompanies the labour strategy of an entire household and cannot be reduced only to the behaviour of an individual. The price demanded by circulation is the detachment, for a longer or a shorter time, of one or more working members of the household (Breman, 1990:51)'.

E. Migration in Maharashtra

Maharashtra being the most developed State in India is a hub of migration. It provides a dynamic environment for migration for both inter and intra state. Interstate migrations are mostly semi permanent or permanent in nature, whereas intrastate migrations are seasonal in nature. Seasonal employment provides livelihood to millions of poor in the state, especially in rural areas. People from socio-economically deprived categories and resource poor regions migrate to those with intensive agriculture or other labour opportunities. In the destination areas, migrants work in cultivation, mining, quarrying and construction for low wages. Migration therefore plays a very important part of the livelihood strategies of the rural poor. (Wadikar J. & Das M., 2004)

Seasonal migration is a norm in Maharashtra. It has long history of labour mobility and labour migration. There are basically two categories of seasonal migrants. The first category consists of regular seasonal migrants who travel for work during the non-agricultural season. The second category consists of small and medium farmers who migrate to support their livelihoods as a consequence of agro-ecological crisis in the areas they live in. Though the percentage of regular seasonal labour is usually more in the state due to vagaries of the monsoons, lack of adequate infrastructure in terms of irrigation is one of the main reasons for the number of migrants from the second category to be on the rise. Irrespective of these considerations, migrations acts as a compensating mechanism to reduce the disadvantageous position of the poor. (Wadikar J. & Das M., 2004)

The sugar factories in western Maharashtra, the brick kilns in Thane district, quarries in Ratnagiri and various construction sites form the centers of seasonal migrations. People from under-developed areas who are prone to calamities and lack employment opportunities outside the agricultural season, prefer migration. Usually, labourers migrate with their families. Women and children constitute a high proportion of the migrant population. The motive behind migrating with the family is obviously more employment. According to statistics, Maharashtra occupies the third place in India in the use of child labour. They contribute significantly to the income of households. Migration often involves longer working hours, poor living and working conditions and poor access to basic facilities like access to education, health, food contribution system, etc. (Wadikar J. & Das M., 2004).

F. The Migrant Labourers

It has been recognized that seasonal migration is an accepted option in the normal livelihood strategies of the rural poor. For the sugarcane cutters, migration started as a strategy to cope with the worsening situation of dry-land agriculture created by drought, crop failure and poor terms of trade. Sugarcane cutting is labour intensive activity requiring very high levels of physical stamina and energy. (Wadikar J. & Das M., 2004).

The sugarcane crushing season is operational from November to April/ May. During this six-month period, people from central Maharashtra and Marathwada region, migrate to the lush sugarcane belt. A large majority of labourers come from Beed, Jalgaon, Ahmednagar, Nashik, Jalna, Parbhani, Aurangabad and Latur districts, all in Marathwada region except Ahmednagar, Jalgaon and Nashik. Those families normally belong to the poorest strata of the society and are mostly landless or marginal farmers. Scarcity of resources and debt burden accompanied with dry spells of monsoon force people from these areas to migrate to nearby districts. (Wadikar J. & Das M., 2004).

A recent survey of the sending villages indicates that 20 per cent of migrating families belong to the Maratha community while the remaining 80 per cent include groups from the Other Backward Castes (OBC), Scheduled Castes (SC) and Scheduled Tribes (ST) covering the Vanjaris, Bhills, Dhangars, Bouddhas , Matangs, Gujjars and a few Muslims.(Dhamankar Mona;2005:2) These labourers come through contractors/agents, popularly known as *Mukadams* appointed by the factory management system. Contractors/Agents bring labourers in *tolis* or groups. Each *toli* consists of 30 to 100 labourers. The factory management makes advance payments to these agents, who in turn give advances to the labourers. The agents get a commission from the wages of the labourers. (Wadikar J. & Das M., 2004).

The advance amount is offset against their labour. If they are unable to pay off the advance money in a season, they have to go in for employment for another season. It is a vicious cycle. (Wadikar J. & Das M., 2004).

According to the Office of the Sugar Commissioner, the cyclical, seasonal migrations of sugarcane labourers started in 1960 when the first cooperative sugar factories were established. The system of contracting labor is the same for cooperative and private factories. Generally, adult couples migrate leaving older people behind to look after the land and cattle, if any. Older children (>14 yrs) though not part of the sugarcane cutting labor unit accompany their parents to the fields everyday while those between 6 to 14 yrs old are brought along to be looked after by the younger siblings. *At present, around 500,000 to 700,000 laborers migrate with approx.200, 000 children in the 6 to 12 age group.*

S.N. Tripathy conducted a study in Kalahandi, Bolangir and Malkangiri districts of Orissa, which are drought prone, tribal dominated and backward districts of the State. The research study was conducted to study 'dynamics of tribal migration'. An analysis of primary data collected from 300 tribal migrant and 150 non-migrant households brings into light the following findings:

1. 50 per cent of the migrant households and 60 per cent of non-migrant households are in the family size of 3-4 members. The family size of the non-migrant household is higher than the migrant households.
2. 66 per cent of the sample migrant households reported their marital status as "married".
3. It is revealed from the study that 65 per cent of the households were migrated through contractors.
4. A high percentage (55.97) of tribal has migrated to outside the state.
5. Tribal migrants in the age group of 20-40 (61.36%) constitute a sizeable portion of the total migrant workmen.
6. The different tribal groups who have migrated are Mundas (31.82%), Kandhs (27.98%), Santhals (14.35%) and Koyas (6.10%).
7. Agriculture is the main occupation of the migrant households at their place of origin.
8. There is extremely high rate of dropout among the children of the tribal migrant households.
9. Educationally the children of non-migrant household are better than the migrant households.
10. Moneylenders do provide the maximum percentage of loans to the migrant households.

11. More the 53 per cent of migrant households reported the annual remittance in the range of Rs. 1000 to 2000 only.
12. More than 45 per cent of migrant households' annual income has been in the range of Rs. 15000 to Rs. 20000. The level of income of the migrant household is better than the non-migrant households.
13. The standard of living migrant household is better than the non-migrant households.
14. Compared to the non-migrant households the "non-consumption" expenditure of the migrant households is better. Therefore, the migrant households enjoy comparatively higher living standard.
15. A significant percentage is diverted towards loan payment by the migrant households, which has adverse affect on their living standard and keep them in the vicious circle of poverty.
16. The important reasons of migration are poverty, search for livelihood and compelled by advance taken.
17. Poor sanitation, unhygienic environment long hours of work are the important problems reported by the migration workmen.
18. 62 per cent of migrant households have reported that they perform 8 to 11 + hours at work in a day.

In their book captioned, "Down and Out" (2000), Breman Jan & Das Arvind, has given some facts which are relevant to this study are as follows:

- An initial study, started in 1977, into their coming and mode of employment throughout the campaign, showed that the majority of the 50,000 men, women and children had been recruited from the neighbouring State of Maharashtra.
- Ten years later, a repeat survey showed that the army of workers had doubled in the meantime.
- At the end of 1980s, it could be stated with reasonable certainty that seasonal migrants mobilized for the sugarcane harvest in South Gujarat totaled 1,50,000. Today their numbers are even greater.
- It is a fact that some 20 years ago the inflow of migrant labour began to increase strongly. The workers are almost all Adivasi and Dalit (Tribal & Scheduled Caste) peasants from the eastern hills bordering Maharashtra.
- The need to earn more cash on the one hand and the increasing pressure of population - particularly due to the felling of forests which had provided many sorts of subsidiary income- on the other hand, have caused an increasing outflow of labour to the plains of south Gujarat. The mass – but nevertheless temporary and cyclical – migration starts immediately after the monsoon.
- In 'normal' years these migrant workers come in groups of 10 to 15 men and women around the time for harvesting various crops in order,

to satisfy their needs for money. They bring their own food for the duration of their stay.

The migrants go directly go their addresses where they have been before and old contacts send them on to possible new employers. They do not migrate for an indefinite time but for a few weeks only, until the grain brought with them is exhausted. The gang then returns home, to make the same journey again somewhat later in the season.

Arrangements made long beforehand and sometimes sealed with a cash advance, contribute to the fairly tight rhythm that characterizes seasonal migration.

G. Theory of Migration

Everett Lee's Conceptual Framework for Migration Analysis

In their book captioned Principles of Population Studies (1978), Bhende Asha and Kanitkar Tara had discussed the Everett Lee's conceptual framework for Migration. Everett Lee has conceptualized the factors associated with the decision to migrate and the process of migration into the following four categories: *(i)* Factors associated with the area of origin; *(ii)* Factors associated with the area of destination; *(iii)* Intervening Obstacles; *(iv)* Personal factors.

Lee elaborates all these four categories by pointing out that, in each area, there are numerous factors which act to drive away the people from the area, or to hold the people in the area or to attract the people to it. In this respect, there are significant differences between the factors associated with the area of origin and those associated with the area of destination. Migration may take place after both these are weighed. Usually, however, a person has better and more realistic knowledge about the place of origin, while his knowledge about the place of destination is somewhat superficial and inexact. Intervening obstacles also have to be overcome before migration finally takes place. These include distance and transportation. Technological advances, however, have lessoned their importance in modern times. Finally, the personal factors are of the utmost importance because, instead of the actual factors associated with the place of origin and/or destination, the individual's perception of these factors is found to influence the actual act of migration. Individual differences, too, play their part, as some persons are generally resistant to change of any kind, specially, to a change of residence, while others are eager for such a change. Lee is therefore; of the opinion that the decision to migrate is never completely rational, and hence it follows that it is always possible to come across exceptions to any type of generalization about migration.

Another point to take into consideration in this connection is that not all migrants migrate as a result of their own decision; for example, children have generally to go along with their parents, and wives accompany or follow their husbands. Such type of migration is known as sequential migration.

Lee has further attempted to formulate several hypotheses within his conceptual framework regarding the four types of factors associated with migration, which incorporate the push and pull factors both at the place of origin and the place of destination. These hypotheses cover the volume of migration, the development of streams and counter-streams of migration, the characteristics of the migrants, for explaining why some people migrate and others do not. The hypotheses may be listed as follows:

Volume of Migration:

1. The volume of migration within a given territory varies with the degree of areas included in that territory.
2. The volume of migration varies with the diversity of the people.
3. The volume of migration is related to the difficulty of surmounting the intervening variables.
4. The volume of migration varies with fluctuations in the economy.
5. Unless severe checks are imposed, both the volume and the rate of migration tend to increase with time.
6. The volume and the rate of migration vary with the state of progress in a country or area.

Streams and Counter-streams of Migration:

1. Migration tends to take place largely within well-defined streams.
2. For every major migration stream, a counter-streamalso develops.
3. The efficiency of the stream (ratio of stream to counter stream or the net redistribution of population affected by the opposite flow) is high if major factors in the development of a migration stream are minus factors at origin.
4. The efficiency of the stream and the counter-stream of migration tend to be low if the place of origin and the place of destination are similar.
5. The efficiency of migration streams will be high if the intervening obstacles are great.
6. The deficiency of the migration stream varies with economic conditions, being high in prosperous times and low in times of depression.

Characteristics of Migrants:

1. Migration is selective.
2. Migrants responding primarily to plus factors at destination tend to be positively selected.
3. Migrants responding primarily to minus factors at origin tend to be negatively selected; or where the minus factors are overwhelmingly for the entire population group they may no be selected by at all for migration.
4. When all migrants are considered to be together, selection for migration tends to be bimodal.

5. The degree of positive selection increases with the difficulties posed by the intervening obstacles.
6. The heightened propensity to migrate at certain stages of the life cycle is important in the selection of migrants.
7. The characteristics of migrants tend to be intermediate between the characteristics of the population of the place of origin and of the population of the place of destination.

Push and Pull Factors in Migration

This traditional approach to the motivation for migration takes, as a starting point, the differences between the characteristics of the two places, namely, the place of origin and the place of destination. Researchers have attempted to determine whether people migrated because the circumstances prevailing at the place of origin pushed them out or whether they were lured by the attractive conditions in the new place. among the various push factors operating at the place of origin may be included in the following: high natural rate of population growth creating population pressure on the existing resources: exhaustion of natural resources; droughts, floods and natural calamities, such as earthquakes and famines; and acute social, religious and political conflicts compelling people to migrate to other places for reasons of safety. The following may be included as the pull factors: establishment of new industries with the provision of new opportunities for gainful employment; facilities for higher education in cities; pleasant climatic conditions, etc.

It is obvious that the push-pull approach has been useful in listing the several factors which affect migratory movements and has several times offered convincing explanations of migratory phenomena. It is also apparent that, in most cases, migrations occurs not because of either push or pull factors alone but as a result of the combined effect of both (Bhende & Kanitkar, 1978).

Reventain's laws of migration restated by Everett Lee in 1956. To him, the forces exerting an influence on migrant perceptions into 'push' and 'pull' factors. The former are negative factors, which force migrants to leave origin areas, while the latter are 'positive' factors attracting migrants to destination areas. (Tripathy S.N. 2005:27)

As discussed in the conceptual model, researcher has identified certain key push factors namely poverty, landlessness, economic and food crisis, indebtedness, unemployment, temporary housing conditions, unskilled labour, illiteracy, victims of social and economic insecurity as well as three pull factors namely *Kharchi* i.e. weekly expenses, *Uchal* i.e. loan and labour guarantee that forced the Katkari brick kiln labourers and Bhil sugarcane cutters into seasonal migration. Their poor socio-economic conditions and status of financial insecurity further forces their children who migrate to the place of destination into domestic and commercial child labour. This further deprives their children of their rights. Thus, the children get deprived from all the rights and their young parents spend their early adulthood as victims of economic exploitation, bonded labour indebtedness, hardships etc. at the worksites.

The concept of seasonal migration is most usually associated with agriculture labour and daily wage labour. It often involves change in residence for a short or reasonably long period. Though migrant labourers are found everywhere in the world, India has probably more migrant workers than any other Asian countries. These are involved mainly in the harvesting of plantation crops such as tea, cotton, rice and sugarcane (Lahiri:1984). Seasonal Migration is not a new phenomenon and is observed throughout India (Kasar: 1992). In Maharashtra, there are some 1.5 lakhs migrants from poor peasants and labourers families in dry districts who work from six to eight months a year for cutting and hauling sugarcane in the irrigated belts (Omvedt: 1981).

Breman Jan, 1979, stated that the type of seasonal migration that takes place in and around sugar factories is mostly bound with capitalist development. He narrated the socio-economic life of workers including the role of mukadams, recruitment of workers, wages, working conditions, working hours and nature of exploitation etc. He found that the seasonal migration among the Bhils is spread over the areas of North Gujarat to Narmada. The labourers from Khandesh region of Maharashtra also migrate seasonally to the sugar factories in South Gujarat.

Jugale (1997), in his book entitled, "Employment Wages and Industrial Relations" explored two aspects namely: *(i)* most of the recruitments were made through contractors; *(ii)* No provision of holiday, leave facilities were made available to the seasonal workers.

Salve (1991), emphasized the economic and socio-cultural life of migrant cane cutters in Kolhapur district, in the state of Maharashtra. He further analyzed the conditions at work places and focused on every day problems extensively.

Kasar (1992), in his study brought out that the cooperative sugar industry has significant contribution in the gross annual income and income of migrant household indicating beneficial effects of seasonal migration on the economy of migrant farm labourers in Maharashtra.

Deshpande (2008), in her study captioned, "Health and Nutritional Status of seasonal Migrants" has studied three aspects namely physical, reproductive and mental healthcare practices.

In his study captioned, "Migration and Development : A Sociological Study of Migrant Sugarcane Cutters in Kolhapur district", Kendre Balaji (2009) studied problems and development issues of following castes: Maratha, Gujar, Kumbhar, Nhavi, Vanjari, Dhangar, Telangi, Hatkar, Lamani,

Chambhar, Bhil, Mang, Mahar, Kasab (Muslim). Kendre Balaji however, has not studied child labour and child rights issues of sugarcane cutters. Similarly Bajpai Asha (2003),(2006) too has not studied child rights and child labour issues of children of sugarcane cutters and Brick kiln workers. Bokil Milind (2006) highlighted the problems of Katkaris at the brick kilns, but he too did not touch the subject. Hence the present subject is original in its kind.

H. Bonded labour

The Concept: The 'bonded labour system' refers to the relationship between a creditor and a debtor who obtains loan owing to the economic compulsions confronting his day-to day life and agrees to abide by the terms dictated by the creditor. The important term of the agreement is that the debtor agrees to mortgage his services of any or all the members of his family, for a specified or unspecified period. The relationship built on an agreement is on such unequal terms that while for every labour or service, there must be fair remuneration equivalent to the price of labour in the market, under the bonded labour system; the service is rendered for the debt or in lieu of the interest accruing to the debt. The debtor either works without receiving any remuneration or if at all there is any remuneration it is much less than the minimum wage (notified under a Minimum Wages Act) or the prevailing rate of market wage.

The 1976 Bonded Labour (Abolition) Act defines 'bonded labour system' as the system of forced labour under which a debtor enters into an agreement with the creditor that he would render service to him either by himself or through any member of his family or any person dependent on him, for a specified or unspecified period, either without wages or for nominal wages, in consideration of loan or any other economic consideration obtained by him or any of his ascendants, or in pursuance of any social obligation, or in pursuance of any obligation devolving on him by succession.

The 'bonded labour' has been defined by the National Commission on Labour as 'labour, which remains in bondage for a specific period for the debt incurred'. The Commissioner for Scheduled Castes and Scheduled Tribes explained the term-bonded labour in its 24th Report as 'persons who are forced to work for the creditors for the loan incurred either without wage or on nominal wage'. (Sharma, 1990:52)

The 'bonded labour' is different from 'contract labour' employed in industries, mines, plantations and docks, etc. The contract labour includes workers who are not directly recruited by the establishment, whose names do not appear on pay roll, and who are not paid wages directly by the employer. In theory, the contract labourers in India are covered by the Factory Act, 1948, the Mines Act, 1952, the Plantations Labour Act, 1951, the Dock Workers Act, 1948 so as to give them benefits as are admissible to labour directly employed. However, the advantages of employing both bonded labour and contract labour are the same: *(i)* the labour is engaged at the lower cost; *(ii)* the employers have not to extend the fringe benefits to the workers; and *(iii)* the employers are not under any obligation of providing welfare and security measures to the workers as stipulated in various Acts.

I. Karl Marx on Labour and Capitalism

One cannot by pass the views on Karl Marx on labour and capitalism. Marx's most important book, "Capital (Vol -1)" was published in 1867 and the rest two volumes were completed by his associate Engles after the death of Marx. In Capital, Marx argued that man's labour power becomes a commodity. The wage labourer sells his labour to the owner of the land, factories and instruments of labour.

Marx also pointed out that the worker spends one part of the day covering the cost of maintaining himself and his family (wages), while the other part of the day he works without remuneration, creating for the capitalist, " surplus – value", the source of profit, the source of wealth of the capitalist class. The doctrine of "surplus value" is the central theme of Marx's economic theory. Marx again argued that the capital created by the labour of the worker, crusehes the worker, ruining small proprietors and creating an army of unemployed persons.

Marx's economic theory justifies the economic exploitation of the Katkari brick kiln labourers whose labour is exploited by the owner (capitalist) to gain surplus value (source of wealth). A Katkari joint family makes 1,00,000 bricks a month. The owner sells these bricks for 5 lakh rupees and pays the joint family a sum of Rs. 3000/- to 5000/- per month as "kharchi" (monthly expenses). The brick kiln owner extracts maximum labour. The workers (Katkaris) sell their labour power. In doing so the owner gets "surplus value" – the source of profit, the source of wealth.

As rightly argued by Marx, the capital created through the labour of the Katkaris, in this case, crushes them and creates unemployment. This research further reveals, that both the Katkaris and Bhil migrant labourers get hooked into indebtedness, bonded labour because of key push factors such as poverty, unemployment, illiteracy, lnadlessness, marginal farmer's statu, unskilled labour, economic and hunger crisis, poor housing and the Uchal (loan), Kharchi (expenses) and labour guarantee (pull factors).

Breman's work among the various occupational groups of South Gujarat, especially in the unorganized labour sector, throws light on the impact of global capitalism.

J. Labour and Global Capitalism

It was Breman Jan who brought with him the experience of both the deprivation suffered by the working class in Europe till the Second World War as well as the dynamics of the prosperous social democratic society and the welfare state created then. His contribution of the knowledge he had gathered during more than a decade of field work among the labourers of South Gujarat:

- The transformation of the Kaliparaj black skinned;
- Hali bonded into Halpatis;
- The changing forms of bondage;
- Attachement and other forms of employment;
- Altering forms of self perceptions among untouchables, from traditional untouchables through the Gandhian Harijan (Child of God) to Dalit (oppressed). Since then much has happened to labourers not only in the rural milieu but also in the urban setting.

From one, the wall that is supposed to divide urban and rural, formal and informal, organized and unorganized labour has been shown up to have nothing more than an illusion. This duality was questioned by Breman Jan and others and was demonstrated as being false; there is infact a continuam between these various forms of labour in social, economic as well as political context.

His book captioned, "Down and Out" with Das Arvind (2000), looks at the conditions of workers in the formal sector in and around Surat, in South Gujarat, which was the site of Breman's research reported in "Footloose Labour" (1996) and out breaks the world of Indian labour.

Presenting text and snapshots from the lives of labourers – in villages, on the move and at work sites – the book engages with the experience of laboring in different industries – textile, sugar, brick making and construction. He has thrown light on new theorectical insights such as distress seasonal migration, struggles and hardships of labourers for survival, gender, oldage and division of labour, labour and inequalities in an Indian village, labour and globalization, living, socio-economic and working conditions of migrant labourers both in rural and urban areas.

He is of the view that, as the tides of globalization and privatization sweep across the world, it sometimes appears as if the labourer has been ablitrated from public discourse. The processes of contractiualization and casulaization push workers out from the so called formal sector to largely non-unionised informal sector. Hence millions of labourers languish in squalor, poverty and misery.

The Katakari brick kiln labourers and Bhil sugarcane cutters – the target population of the present study is no exception to the rule. Thus far no Sociological study has been conducted on these groups, hence it has been undertaken.

K. Concept and definition of a child

The concept and definition of a child varies from one nation of another. In this section of chapter one an attempt has been made to throw light on the definition and the concepts of a child.

Definitions of a Child

Scientific progress in the fields of anthropology, biology, medicine, psychology and social research during the past hundred years has changed the attitude of society towards the child. He no longer is treated as an adult person only smaller in stature but as a human being with his own different rhythm of life and with his own laws of biological and mental growth. We are aware that the child is following drives, social forces and motivations which are basically different from those which govern adult behaviour."(Friedlander W.A., 1955:327)

According to Oxford Dictionary of Sociology, the term child can be used to mean either an offspring or someone who has not reached full economic and jural status as an adult in a society.

Age limits are formal reflections of society's judgment about the evolution of children's capacities and responsibilities. Age limits differ from activity to activity and from country to country. According to Census of India, "persons below the age of fourteen are children". (Bajpai Asha, 2003:2)

According to Article 1, of the United Nations Convention on the Rights of the child 1989, "a child means every human being below the age of 18years unless, under the law applicable to the child, majority is attained earlier." The Article thus grants the discretion to individual countries to determine by law whether childhood should cease at 12, 14, 16 or whatever age they find appropriate. In India the age at which a person ceases to be a child varies in different laws.

The age of the child is different according to the definitions given under various legislations. There is also an admixture of other terms such as juvenile; minor; adolescent and youth and hence, it becomes very difficult to define a child. This is because age criteria vary across different systems or different cultures. (Shinganapure Vijay; 2007:18)

Some of these legislations where definitions of child differ are as follows:

1. The Plantation Labour Act, 1951 in 1986 amendment defines a child is an adolescent who has completed 14 years and not 18 years of age.
2. The Merchant Shipping (Amendment) Act, 1984 defined adolescent, as a person who has completed 14 years but not 18 years and a child is a person who has not completed 14 years of age.
3. As per Children (Pledging of Labour) Act, 1933 a child is a person who is under the age of 15 years.
4. Minimum Wages Act, 1948, defined the child is a person who has not completed his 14 years of age as amended in 1986.
5. According to the Beedi and Cigar Workers Act, 1966, the age of children is fixed below 14 years as per 1986 amendment.
6. Shops and Establishment Act, 1966 - Different age is specified by the different States in this act, the prescribe minimum age of the child is

14 years in States of Andhra Pradesh, Haryana, Tamilnadu, Pondichery, Kerla, Punjab, Himachal Pradesh, Meghalaya, Delhi and Chandigarh while the prescribed minimum age is 12 years in the States of Bihar, Gujrat, Jammu & Kashmir, Karnataka, Madhya Pradesh, Goa, Diu & Daman. According to the Act mentioned the minimum age is 15 years only in the State of Maharashtra.

7. The Indian Factories Act 1948 defined a child, who has not completed his 15 years of age.
8. Child Labour (Prohibition & Regulation) Act, 1986 – defined child as a person who has not completed 14 years of age. The minimum age is reduced from 15 to 14 years and do not include the children working in agriculture and family establishment, except the children working on construction sites, this prohibits the employment of children in certain occupations (Shinganapure Vijay; 2007:19).

The various stages of childhood, which have been recognized, are the prenatal, the post-natal, infant, the pre-school and the school stage. According to the Committee for the Preparation of a Program for Children (1968) (GoI, Dept. of Social Welfare) there are five stages in the growth of the child: 1) conception to birth, 2) infancy (0-1 year), 3) pre-school from 1-3 years, 4) pre-school 3 to 6 years, and 5) primary school stage from 6 to 16 years. (Madan G.R., 1967:93)

L. Poverty

Poverty is one of the major factor which is responsible for the migration of Bhil Sugarcane cutters and Katkari Brick kiln labourers, therefore it is necessary to discuss the concept of Poverty at this juncture. Concepts given by various social Sociologists have been discussed here.

Poverty and richness are relative terms. The poverty line in any given society is determines by the customs and mode of living. The poverty line in India is not at the same point as in the USA or UK. As defined by Gillin and Gillin "Poverty is that condition in which a person, either because of inadequate income or unwise expenditures, does not maintain a scale of living high enough to provide for his physical and mental efficiency and to enable him and his natural dependents to function usefully according to the standards of the society of which he is a member." (Madan G.R, 2009).

Poverty is a situation that gives rise to a feeling of a discrepancy between what one has and what one "should have". What one should have is an internal construct; hence each person's felling and experience of poverty is individual and unique. But the feeling of 'powerlessness' and 'resourcelessness' is possessed by all poor people. Berstein Henry (1992) has identified the following dimensions of poverty:

- Lack of livelihood strategies
- Inaccessibility to resources (money, land, credit)

- Feeling of insecurity and frustrations
- Inability to maintain and develop social relations with others as a consequence of lack of resources.

Harrington (1958:83) defined poverty with reference to 'deprivation'. According to him, poverty is the deprivation of those minimal levels of food, health, housing, education, and recreation which are compatible with the contemporary technology, beliefs and values of a particular society. Rein (1968:16) identifies three elements in Poverty: subsistence, inequality and externality. Subsistence emphasizes the provisions of sufficient resources to maintain health and working capacity in the sense of survival, and capacity to maintain physical efficiency. Inequality compares the lot of individuals at the bottom layer of stratified income levels with that of the more priviledged people in the same society. Their deprivation is relative. Externality focuses on the social consequences of poverty for the rest of society, apart from the impact on the poor themselves (Ahuja Ram;2007:30).

Sociologically speaking, the poor are caught up in vicious circles. Being poor means poor neighborhood, which means being unable to send children to schools, which means not only the poor themselves but their children too will have low-paying jobs or no jobs at all, which means being doomed to remain poor forever. Also being poor means eating poor food, which means having poor health, which in turn means being handicapped or too weak to handle the heavy manual work, which also means accepting low paid work, which leads to remaining poor forever. Thus, each circle begins and ends with being poor. No wonder, Sociologists, like Thomas Gladwin (1967: 76-77) give more importance to 'inequality' or the social concept of poverty. (Ahuja Ram; 2007: 31).

K. Child Labour

Some Important Concepts related to Child Labour

It is necessary to look into some important concepts related to child labour. (As coated in Siddiqui M.I, 2003).

1. Work

"Work is the application of human energy to things; which application converts, maintains, or adds value to the workers, the thing worked on, and the system in which the work is performed" (Wallman, 1979).

The Census of India (1981:2) as cited in Shinganapure V (2007:110), defines "work as participation in any economically productive activity may be physical or mental in nature."

2. Child Work

A distinction should be made between child work and child labour. Some of the social scientists have made distinction between child work and child labour. "Work can be a gradual initiation into adulthood and a positive element in a child's development" (Fyfe, 1989). Activities of a child not at the cost of leisure, play and education and as a part of socialization as per the norms of the society, devoid of exploitation, mental or physical, tantamount to work.

Child does certain household activities in the initial phase of childhood, such as, fetching things for parents, minding younger siblings and assisting in household chores, all these are a part of socialization and hence child work. These activities are not directly or indirectly related to employment in economic sense. These are essential for child's physical and mental growth and also for socialization. The element of exploitation is not there. (Siddiqui M.I; 2003:10)

3. Child Labour

Child Labour practice is a worldwide phenomenon. Definition of child labour is not uniform all over the world. However, the working child, who is below the age of 14 and who is paid either in cash or kind, is normally considered as a child labour.

According to International Labour Organization, 1983, "child Labour includes children prematurely leading adult lives, working long hours for low wages, under conditions damaging to their health and to their physical and mental development, sometimes separated from their families, frequently deprived of meaningful education and training opportunities that could open up for them a better future."

According to Homer Falks, Chairman of the United Nations Child Labour Commission, "Any work by children that interferes with their full physical development and their opportunities for desirable minimum level of education or their needed recreation is child labour." (Labour Investigation Committee Main report, 1946)

UNICEF has made comprehensive efforts in formulating the whole concept of child labour, which are as follows:

- Starting full-time work at too early an age.
- Working for longer duration of time within or outside the family and unable to attend the school.
- Inadequate remuneration for working.
- Too many responsibilities at too early of an age as in the domestic situation where children below the age of ten years may have to look after their young siblings for a whole year, thereby preventing from school attendance.

According to Encyclopedia of Social Science, "when the business of wage earning or of participation in self or family support conflicts directly or indirectly with the business of growth and education, the result is child labour".

According to Fyfe A. (1989) as cited in Siddiqui (2003:10), "Child labour is work which impairs the health and development of children".

According to V.V. Giri, Former President of India, "The term child labour is commonly interpreted in two different ways – the first, as an economic practice and secondly, as social evil. In the first context, it signifies employment of children in gainful occupation with a view to adding income of children to that of the family. It is in second context that the term child labour is generally used. It is necessary to take into account the character of the job in which children are engaged, the hazards to which they are exposed and opportunities of development which they have been denied."

The Factory Act of 1948clearly states that, any person below the age of 15 years either under compulsion or voluntarily work in an organized or unorganized sector is termed as child labour.

According to Government of Andhra Pradesh, children who are not going to school are child labourers. (Yashmanthan, Issue I, April-June, 2005)

Thus, child labour is basically physical, mental and social abuse of childhood.

Characteristics of Child Labour

Child labour detracts from the other essential activities for children, such as, education, play and leisure, and hence involves an element of exploitation. It essentially entails deprivations of their rights to health or education or just to childhood (ILO, 1992). Child labour has the following characteristics:

- Working too young
- Working long hours
- Working under strain – physical, social or psychological
- Working conditions unhealthy
- Working for little pay
- Working with little stimulation
- Subject to intimidation (ILO, 1992)

Classification of Child Labour

Child Labour can be broadly classified into the following categories:

- Child labour covered by legislation,
- Child labour falling outside the legislative framework,
- Agriculture and allied activities, and
- Informal, unorganized, semi-urban, and urban sector (Public Hearing & second National Convention of Child Labourers: Reference Kit, CACL, March 1997) (As cited in Bajpai Asha, 2003).

4. Hazardous Work

The term 'hazardous work', in case of children means not only tangible threats to physical health and safety, an in the case of adults, but also implies impairment of their social, moral and psychological development.

Any activity of a child while in employment which affects physical development, cognitive development, and emotional development, social and moral development is hazardous work. There are two types of work hazards – physical work hazards and psychosocial work hazards. Physical work hazards are those "work" in which children engaged in a place where their lives in immediate "peril" (Bequele & Myers, 1995) Psychosocial work hazards are those which adversely affect psychologically and socially. It has been observed that a child worker may develop the following problems due to psychosocial factors:

1. Withdrawal
2. Regressive behaviour
3. Premature aging
4. Depression
5. Inferior Status identity
6. Resistance (Bequele & Myers, 1995)

5. Subcontracting

Decentralization of production units has led to the concept of subcontracting. A firm supplying a large quantity may assign specific quantity to each small production unit is known as subcontracting.

A firm subcontract work to the production units in villages, homes and other small workshops. In such cases child labour is used as these unit shave informal settings. Footwear, garment, embroidery, furniture and handicrafts industries, in the developing world, often subcontract work to villages, homes and small workshops (U.S. Dept. of labour, 1994). The most prevalent of subcontracting is home-based production, especially in Asia and Latin America. Child Labour is generally used in such subcontract work in the form of either family labour or labour on piece rate.

6. Bonded Labour

The 'bonded labour system' refers to the relationship between a creditor and a debtor who obtains loan owing to the economic compulsions confronting his day-to day life and agrees to abide by the terms dictated by the creditor. The important term of the agreement is that the debtor agrees to mortgage his services of any or all the members of his family, for a specified or unspecified period. The relationship built on an agreement is on such unequal terms that while for every labour or service, there must be fair remuneration equivalent to the price of labour in the market, under the bonded labour system; the service is rendered for the debt or in lieu of the interest accruing to the debt. The debtor either works without receiving any remuneration or if at all there is any remuneration it is much less than the minimum wage (notified under a Minimum Wages Act) or the prevailing rate of market wage.

The 1976 Bonded Labour (Abolition) Act defines 'bonded labour system' as the system of forced labour under which a debtor enters into an agreement with the creditor that he would render service to him either by himself or through any member of his family or any person dependent on him, for a specified or unspecified period, either without wages or for nominal wages, in consideration of loan or any other economic consideration obtained by him or any of his ascendants, or in pursuance of any social obligation, or in pursuance of any obligation devolving on him by succession.

The 'bonded labour' has been defined by the National Commission on Labour as 'labour, which remains in bondage for a specific period for the debt incurred'. The Commissioner for Scheduled Castes and Scheduled Tribes explained the term-bonded labour in its 24th Report as 'persons who are forced to work for the creditors for the loan incurred either without wage or on nominal wage'. (Sharma, 1990:52)

The UN recognizes 'debt-bondage' or bonded labour as a modern form of slavery (UN, 1956). "Debt bondage occurs when a person needing a 'loan' and having no security to offer, pledges his/her labour, or that of some one under his/her control, as a security for the loan." (US Dept. of Labour, 1994 as cited in Siddiqui M.I.,2008:12).

7. Contract Labour

The 'bonded labour' is different from 'contract labour' employed in industries, mines, plantations and docks, etc. The contract labour includes workers who are not directly recruited by the establishment, whose names do not appear on pay roll, and who are not paid wages directly by the employer. In theory, the contract labourers in India are covered by the Factory Act, 1948, the Mines Act, 1952, the Plantations Labour Act, 1951, the Dock Workers Act, 1948 so as to give them benefits as are admissible to labour directly employed. However, the advantages of employing both bonded labour and contract labour are the same: *(i)* the labour is engaged at the lower cost; *(ii)* the employers have not to extend the fringe benefits to the workers; and *(iii)* the employers are not under any obligation of providing welfare and security measures to the workers as stipulated in various Acts.

8. Forced Labour

It is another type of labour system observed in India and some other countries. If any laborer is forced or coerced to work against his/her wishes, with or without payment, is called forced labour. The societies characterized by their caste system have the problem of forced labour especially in India. (Siddiqui M.I. 2008:13)

9. Wage Labour

When a worker, be an adult or a child, is hired by the employer on some wage rate mutually agreed upon whether lower or higher the statutory minimum wage is wage labour. The mode of payment way varies from daily payment to weekly or monthly. Wage labour is generally on time basis, and not according to the mount of work to be done. The employment in household, construction and formal sector generally follows the system of wage labour. (Siddiqui M.I., 2008:13)

Child wage labour is essentially exploitative as children are invariably paid low wages than adults. Sometimes young children work as part of a family group n wage employment basis.(Rodgers & Standing, 1981). This practice is quite common among the agricultural sector of development countires. (Siddiqui M.I., 2008:13-14)

10. Formal Sector

Formal Sector is essentially an urban concept as industries and firms duly registered and licensed falling under the purview of Companies Act, Industries Act and other acts such as labour, environment, etc. are generally in the urban sector due to infrastructure facilities. (Siddiqui M.I., 2008:14)

11. Informal Sector

The informal sector is an urban phenomenon and has specific roles, which are linked to traditional and family organizations. Activities in the sector are an updated representation of the primitive accumulation process in the urban centers. Access to factors of production and technology is determined by social relations and heritage, and family and friendship more than by the market system and prices." (Aboagye & Gozo, 1986)

12. Worst Forms of Child Labour

ILO has given the concept of the worst forms of child labour for immediate abolition and elimination of the 87th session of the International Labour Conference. It says that "the worst forms of child labour" comprises:

1. all forms of slavery or practices similar to slavery; such as the sale and trafficking of children, forced or compulsory labour, debt bondage and serfdom;
2. the use, procuring or offering of a child for prostitution, for the production of pornography or for pornographic performances;
3. the use, procuring or offering a child for illicit activities, in particular for the production and trafficking of drugs as defined in the relevant international treaties;
4. work which, by its nature or the circumstances in which it is carried out, is likely to jeopardize the health, safety or morals of children (ILO, 1990).

Child labourers: The Facts

One out of six children in the world today is involved in child labour, doing work that is damaging to his or her mental, physical and emotional development.

These children work in a variety of industries, and in many parts of the world. The vast majorities are in the agricultural sector, where they may be exposed to dangerous chemicals and equipment. Others are street children, peddling or running errands to earn a living. Some are domestic workers, prostitutes, or factory workers. All are children who have no fair chance of a real childhood, an education, or a better life.

Children work because their survival and that of their families depend on it. Child labour persists even where it has been declared illegal, and is frequently surrounded by a wall of silence, indifference, and apathy.

But that wall is beginning to crumble. While the total elimination of child labour is a long-term goal in many countries, certain forms of child labour must be confronted immediately. An ILO study has shown for the first time that the economic benefits of eliminating child labour will be nearly seven times greater than the costs. This does not include the incalculable social and human benefits of eliminating the practice: nearly three-quarters of working children are engaged in what the world recognizes as the worst forms of child labour, including trafficking, armed conflict, slavery, sexual exploitation and hazardous work. The effective abolition of child labour is one of the most urgent challenges of our time.

Key Statistics of Child Labour by ILO:

- 246 million children are child labourers.
- 73 million working children are less than 10 years old.
- No country is immune: there are 2.5 million working children in the developed economies, and another 2.5 million in transition economies.
- Every year, 22000 children die in work-related accidents.
- The largest number of working children – 127 million – age 14 and under is in the Asia-Pacific region.
- Sub- Saharan Africa has the largest proportion of working children: nearly one- third of children age 14 and under (48 million children).
- Most children work in the informal sector, without legal or regulatory protection:
  - 70 per cent in agriculture, commercial hunting and fishing or forestry;
  - 8 per cent in manufacturing;
  - 8 per cent in wholesale and retail trade, restaurants and hotels;
  - 7 per cent in community, social and personal service, such as domestic work.
- 8.4 million Children are trapped in slavery, trafficking, debt bondage, prostitution, pornography and other illicit activities.
  - 1.2 million Of these children have been trafficked.

Some of the important causes and consequences of child labour are given by V. V. Giri National Labour Institute, New Delhi are as follow: (As quoted in survey report conducted by an NGO, Ganpatrao Nimbalkar Smruti Mukti Ashram, Latur)

Causes of Child Labour:

- Tradition of tolerating children working in the pretext of learning the family skill.
- Non availability of schools.
- Non accessibility to schools.
- Discrimination against children belonging to different economic and social background.
- Absence of universalisation of compulsory primary education.
- Unattractive method of imparting education.
- Lack of social responsibility towards schooling of children.
- Non-implementation of minimum wages.
- Illiteracy of parents.
- Ignorance of the parents about the adverse consequences of Child labour.
- Parents disenchantment towards education.
- Unemployment of the adults in the family.
- Infirmity of parents.
- Physical and/or mental disability of parents.
- Death of parents.
- Ineffective enforcement of child labour laws.
- Lack of political will.
- Unequal distribution of resources.
- Social inequality.
- Economic inequality.
- Social discrimination.
- Lack of social concern.
- Lack of determination.
- Among elected representatives of PRIs (Panchayati Raj Institutions) to end this practice.

Consequences of Child Labour:

- Stunted growth of future generation.
- Inability to harness human resources.
- Inability to contribute to development.
- Inability to benefit from development.
- Citizens with accumulated frustration.
- Citizens with accumulated anger.
- Adult unemployment.

- Depreciation in wages.
- Perpetuation of poverty.
- Persistence of child labour.
- Perpetuation of social inequality.
- Perpetuation of economic inequality.
- Increased abuse of children.
- Increased illiteracy.
- Ignorant populace.
- Citizens with inferiority complex.
- Malnourished citizens.
- Sick citizens.
- Political instability.
- Early morbidity of citizens.
- Physical deformity of citizens.
- Mental deformity.
- Perpetuation of ill treatment.
- Inter-generational phenomenon of child labour.
- Increased bottlenecks in the development process.
- Wasted human resources.
- Wasted human talents and skills.
- Scientists, artists and persons of eminence lost to child labour.

Causes of Child Labour: A Case Study

According to a survey conducted by an NGO, GNSMA (Ganpatrao Nimbalkar Smruti Mukti Ashram, Latur) on the situation of child labour in Nilanga & Latur talukas, for District Collector Office, Latur, causes of child labour are as below:

- Poverty, inequality, ignorance and oppression are the main causes if child labour.
- The economy in the area is based on subsistence dry land farming which is seasonal in nature. The agriculture is completely dependent on the vagaries of monsoon and the rainfall is scanty. The area lack irrigation. The secondary and tertiary sectors are undeveloped. Hence no diversification of occupations. Almost entire population is, therefore, dependent on agriculture and allied activities for income. Due to surplus labour and single kharip crop pattern, there are no work opportunities available locally for a vast majority of the population. The agricultural labourers have to scout around mainly in the nearest towns for work for 6-7 months in a year.
- To avoid starvation therefore, the families send children for work. The children get work easily, because it is easier and convenient for the employer to extra much more work in return of much to small wages.

The children are innocent and obedient. It is easy to control them and extract work. Thus, the economic compulsions deprive the children not only of education but a happy childhood.

- Social inequality, lack of knowledge and loss of faith in the education is another reason for wide spread incidence of child labour. It is a known fact that the caste based hierarchical social structure has deliberately kept the poor and the lowest in the hierarchy away from education. Even for personal or family level decision – making, the rural folks depend upon village influential such as village head or elderly who are essentially part of the rural elite. Such a person often influences these decisions to maintain their selfish interests. For instance, if a family wants to send a child for high school outside the village, the family head consults the village influential, who advises, "Why do you want to send the child to high school? Will that make him a Collector? No need to spend money on his education which will be waste because it is so difficult to get jobs, can't you see? Send him for work (at my place) from tomorrow.
- Obviously, poor illiterate families lack knowledge about the facilities programs and schemes that are available for the education of their children. Secondly, there has been so much increase in the number of educated unemployed that a poor illiterate man feels it to be better to send the child for work who will start earning money. He finds it pointless to spend money on the child's education who even after receiving education will roam around jobless and will refuse to work in farms.
- Children cannot form their unions to fight for their rights. That encourages the people who employ the child labour.

The same survey brought to the light the following facts about the child labourers:

1. It was generally observed that the proportion of Child labourers was very high among scheduled castes-tribes, nomadic tribes, other backward castes and Muslims as compared to non-Brahmins upper castes.
2. The child labourers belonged mainly to the families of bonded labourers, agriculture labourers, marginal farmers, artisans.
3. The child labourers were those children who either never went to school or those who were taken out of school even while at the primary level schooling.
4. There were no fixed hours of work for child labourers they normally worked for 12 to 14 hours and at times up to 16 hours.
5. The child labourers were engaged in occupations such as farm work own, cattle mending, baby-sitting, domestic work and construction work.

6. The child labourers were always abused both verbally and physically.
7. In case of some child labourers the parents send them to work forcibly.
8. The child labourers who were working continuously were deprived of personal and private life, social and cultural activities.
9. They did not have benefits such as weekly holiday or monthly holiday. If they remained absent due to illness or for other reason their wages for absent days are deducted from their remuneration or else they themselves must arrange a replacement.
10. In towns the child labourers are found mostly in hotels, motels, workshops or garages etc.

L. Child Rights

It is evident that legislation is one of the main weapons of empowerment of children. Legislation reflects the commitment of the State to promote an ideal and progressive value system. The notion of duty also applies to the State. The Constitution of India, the fundamental law of the country, came into effect on 26th January 1950. It provides protective umbrella for the rights of the children. These rights include:

- Right to equality (Article 14).
- Right to freedom including the freedom of speech and expressions [Art. 19 (1) (9)].
- Personal liberty, right to due process of law (Art. 21).
- Religious, cultural, educational rights (Art. 29).
- Right to Constitutional remedies (Art. 32).

1. Right To Parental Care: (Custody & Guardianship)

The legal relationship of parent and child is composed of rights and duties. Parents have parental rights by virtue of being natural guardians of their children.

During the British period, the courts developed the law of guardianship. The Guardians and Wards Act (GWA) was pass in 1980 and conferred on the district courts the power of appointing guardians of minor children belonging to any community.

A guardian is thus a person who has rights and duties with respect to the care and control of minor's person or property. Guardianship includes the right to make decisions about the minor's upbringing, disposal of his / her property etc. 'Care', the word used in defining guardian, indicates looking after in wider sense than 'custody' which is simply 'Physical keeping'. Custody is thus the right to the physical presence of the child. It includes the right to take day-to-decisions regarding the child's education, medical treatment, and general movement. Custody can only be of the person of the minor but not of its property.

The law of guardianship and custody of minors is governed by:

- The Guardians and Wards Act 1890
- The Hindu Minority and Guardianship Act 1956, and the unmodified Muslim law of custody and guardianship.
- The personal laws of Hindus, Parsis and Christians, which lay down the principles relating to the custody and guardianship of children during matrimonial proceedings.

The Guardian & Wards Act, 1890 (GWA)

It is a complete code defining the rights and remedies of guardians and wards.

- All matters relating to guardianship, their rights and obligation, the provisions of the Act regulate the removal and replacement of the guardian, and remedies available to the wards.
- This Act applies to all minor children of any caste and creed, though in appointing or declaring a person's guardian of the minor, the court will take into consideration the personal law of minor.
- The Guardians and wards Act deals with the guardian of the person and property of the minors.
- Once a certified guardian is appointed or declared, the powers of natural or testamentary guardian under the personal law stands suspended. Bu, if the personal law is not in conflict with any provision of the Act, the proposal law will apply.
- Under Section 20 of GWA, the relationship between a guardian and the ward is fiduciary relationship. This means guardians cannot profit from their guardianship and must act only with the ward's welfare in mind.
- There are two types of guardians: of the minor's property.
  1. A guardian of a minor person is expected to take custody of the minor and is obliged to provide financial support, healthcare, and education.
  2. Guardians of property have an obligation to deal with the minor's property as if it were his/her own and can act to protect or enhance the property. Guardians of the property appointed by the court cannot mortgage, transfer, or dispose of immovable property, or lease it without prior approval from the court.
- Section 7 (1) lays down the cardinal rule in the matter of guardianship and custody of children. In considering what will be for the welfare of the minor, the following factors have been mentioned all of which are contained in Sec. 17(2):
  - Age of the minor;
  - Sex of the minor;
  - Religion of the minor;
  - The character and capacity of proposed guardian;

- Nearness of kin to minor;
- Wishes, if any, of the deceased;
- Any existing or previous relations of the proposed guardian with the minor or his property; and
- If the minor is old enough to form an intelligent preference, the court may consider that preference

The Hindu Minority and Guardianship Act, 1956 (HMGA):

- Under this Act, the father is the natural guardian of the person and property of legitimate children and after him the guardianship vests in the mother (sec.6). The Supreme Court has now made the mother also the natural guardian.
- Under the Act mother is the natural guardian of her illegitimate children and after her death, the putative father is the natural guardian.
- Under the Act, both the parents have been given power of appointing testamentary guardians.
- A Hindu father cannot appoint a guardian of his minor illegitimate children, even when he is entitled to act as their natural guardian.
- The guardianship of a minor girl comes to an end on her marriage and it cannot be revised even if she becomes a widow during her minority. In that event, the guardianship would belong to the nearest 'sapinda' (near kinsmen) of her husband.
- Qualifications regarding natural guardians:
  - The provision to Section 6 lays down that the custody of a minor who has not completed the age of five years shall ordinarily be with the mother; and
  - Section 3(1) lays down that in the appointment or declaration of any person as guardian of a Hindu minor by a court, the welfare of the minor shall be the paramount consideration.

2. Right against Economic Exploitation – Child Labour

The Constitution of India has lay down that no child under the age of fourteen years shall be employed in any mine or engaged in any other hazardous employment (Article 24) and any contravention of this provision shall be an offence punishable in accordance with law. The directive principles of state policy in Article 39 (e) provide that the health and strength of workers, men and women, and the tender age of children are not abused and that citizens are not forced by economic necessity to enter avocations under suited to their age of strength. Article 39 (f) directs that the children are given opportunities and facilities to develop in a healthy manner and in conditions of freedom and dignity and that childhood and youth are protected against exploitation and moral and material abandonment. It has been made a duty of the State to raise the level of nutrition and the standard of living and to improve public health.

The Factories Act, 1881

- Minimum age (seven years);
- Successive employment (employment in two factories on the same day) prohibited;
- Duration of employment (working hours not to exceed nine hours a day and least four holidays to be given in a month);
- Factories employing one hundred or more persons were covered by this Act.

The Factories Act 1881 was revised in 1891with respect to the following matters:

- Minimum age – (increased to nine years)
- Hours of work – (maximum seven hours per day, with prohibition of work at night between 8pm and 5am)

The Mines Act, 1901

This Act prohibited employment of children under 12 years of age.

The Factories Act, 1911

This Act provides:

- Work between 7 pm and 5.30am prohibited;
- Work in certain dangerous processes, prohibited;
- Certificate of age and fitness required

The Factory (Amendment) Act, 1922

To implement the ILO Convention (No.5) 1919, the amendment provided for changes such as:

- Minimum age – (fifteen years in general);
- Working hours (maximum six hours, and also an interval of half an hour if children are employed for more than five-and a half hours);
- Establishment employing twenty or more persons with mechanical processes was covered under this Act with power vested in the local government to exclude the applications of provisions to premises employing ten or more persons.
- Prohibition of employment of children below eighteen and women in certain processes;
- Provision for medical certificate and also certificate of reexamination for continuing work.

The Indian Mines Act, 1923

This Act raised the minimum age for employment from twelve to thirteen years.

The Factories (Amendment) Act, 1926

This Act imposed certain penalties on the parents and guardians for allowing their children to work in two separate factories on the same day.

The Indian Ports (Amendment) Act, 1931

This Act laid down twelve years as the minimum age that could be prescribed for handling goods in ports. The report of the Royal Commission on Labour (1931) had an impact on legislation pertaining to child labour during the period between 1931 and 1949.

The Tea Districts' (Emigration Labour) Act, 1932

This Act was passed to check migration of labourers to districts in Assam. It provided that no under-age child is employed or allowed to migrate unless the child was accompanied by his or her parents or adults on whom the child was dependent.

Children (Pledging of Labour) Act, 1933

This Act prohibited pledging of children, i.e. taking of advances by parents and guardians in return for bonds, pledging the labour of their children – a system akin to the bonded labour system.

The Royal Commission noticed this practice of pledging of labour of children in areas such as Amritsar, Ahmedabad, Madrasetc. and in carpet and beedi factories. The children in these situations were found to be working under extremely unsatisfactory conditions.

The Factories (Amendment) Act, 1934

This Act had elaborate provisions for regulating the employment of children of various age-groups in the factories, such as:

- Employment of children between twelve and fifteen years was generally prohibited in certain areas.
- Employment of children under 12 and 15 years restricted to five hours a day in other areas;
- For employment of children between fifteen and seventeen years, certain restrictions were imposed.

The Mines (Amendment) Act, 1935

This also introduced divisions of children according to age groups and the position which emerged was as follows:

- Employment of children less than fifteen years in mines was prohibited.
- Underground employment was permitted only on production of certificate of physical fitness granted by a qualified medical practitioner for persons between fifteen and seventeen years.
- Working time restricted to a maximum of ten hours a day and fifty four hours a week for work above the ground and nine hours a day for work underground.

The Employment of Children Act, 1938

This Act was passed to implement the Convention adopted by the twenty-third session of ILO (1937) which inserted a special article on India:

- Children under the age of thirteen years shall not be employed or work in the transport of passengers, or goods, or mails, by rail, or in handling of goods at docks, quays, or wharves but excluding transport by hand. Children under the age of fifteen years shall not be employed or work in occupations to which this Article applies which are scheduled as dangerous or unhealthy by the competent authority.

This Act:

- Prohibited employment of children under fifteen years in occupations connected with transportation of goods, passengers, and, mails, or in the railways.
- Raised the minimum age of handling goods on docks from twelve to fourteen years.
- Provided for the requirement of a certificate of age.

The Factories Act, 1948

This Act raised minimum age for employment in factories to fourteen years.

Employment of Children (Amendment) Act, 1949

This Act raised the minimum age to fourteen years for employment in establishments governed by the Act.

Employment of Children (Amendment) Act, 1951

As a result of ILO Convention relating to night work of young persons, this Act prohibited the employment of children between fifteen and seventeen years at night in the railways and ports and also provided for requirement of maintaining a register for children under seventeen years.

The Plantation Labour Act, 1951

This Act prohibited the employment of children under twelve years in plantations.

The Mines Act 1952

This Act Prohibited the employment of children less than fifteen years in mines. The Act stipulates two conditions for underground work:

- Requirement to have completed sixteen years of age; and
- Requirement to obtain a certificate of physical fitness from a surgeon.

The Factories (Amendment) Act, 1954

This included prohibition of employment of persons under seventeen years at night ('night' was defined as a period of twelve consecutive hours which included hours between 10pm and 7am).

The Merchant Shipping Act, 1958

This prohibits children under fifteen to be engaged to work in any capacity in any ship except in certain specified cases.

The Motor Transport Workers Act, 1961

This Act prohibits the employment of children less than fifteen years in any motor transport undertaking.

The Apprentices Act, 1961

This Act prohibits the apprenticeship/training of a person less than fourteen years.

The Beedi and Cigar Workers (conditions of employment) Act, 1966

This Act Prohibits:

- The employment of children under fourteen years in any industrial premises manufacturing beedies and cigars.
- Persons between fourteen and eighteen years from working at night between 7pm and 6am

Employment of Children (Amendment) Act, 1978

This Act prohibited employment of a child below fifteen years in occupations in railway premises such as cinder picking or clearing of ash pit or building operations, in catering establishments and in any other work which is carried on in close proximity to or between the railway lines.

The Child Labour (Prohibition & Regulation) Act, 1986

The Child Labour (Prohibition & Regulation) Act 1986 (CLPRA), is an outcome of various recommendations made by a series of committees. (The national Commission on Labour 1969, the Committee on Child Labour 1976, and the Sanat Mehta Committee, 1984). Parliament enacted the Child Labour (Prohibition & Regulation) Act 1986 which came into force on 23rd December 1986. The Employment of Children Act 1938, which was the first enactment on child labour, was repealed by the Child Labour (regulation & Prohibition) Act, 1986.

Significant Provisions of the CLPRA

The preamble to the Act states that it is an act to prohibit the employment of any person who has not completed his fourteenth year of age in occupations and processes set forth in Part A and Part B of the Schedule of the Act. The Act thus classifies all establishments in any two categories.

1. Those in which employment of child labour is prohibited, and
2. Those in which the working conditions of child labour shall be regulated.

Penalties under the Act:

The penalties under this Act are relatively more stringent than the earlier Acts and violating the provisions relating to child labour in certain other Acts results in a penalty under this Act (CLPRA 1986, section 15).

- Whoever employs any child or permits any child to work in any hazardous employment shall be punishable with imprisonment for a term which shall not be less than three months but which mat extend to one year, or with fine which shall not be less than ten thousand rupees but which may extend to twenty thousand rupees, or with both for repeated offence. The punishment is imprisonment for a team which shall not be less than six months but which may extend to two years.

- For failing to give notice to the inspector as required by section 9 or failing to maintain a register as required by section 11, or making any false entry in the register, or failing to display an abstract of section 3, or failing to comply with any other provisions of this act or rules, the punishment is imprisonment which may extend to ten thousand rupees or both.

Positive features of the CLPRA:

- It increases and makes more stringent the penalties foe employing child labour in violation of the law for factories, mines, merchant shipping and motor transport [Section 15(1) & (2)].
- It defines 'family' and thereby makes it more explicit thus precluding the possibility of its abuse.
- It empowers the union government to bring into force provisions that regulate conditions of work of children in non hazardous employment and also empowers state government to make rules for further regulations. It provides the machinery i.e. the child labour technical advisory committee, for adding to the list of occupations and processes in which the employment of the child labour is prohibited. (This was not possible in the employment of children act 1938).
- It permits any person besides a police officer or inspector to file a complaint against anyone employing or permitting a child below fourteen in the prohibited occupation as processes.
- It makes the display of section 3 & 4 of CLPRA a mandatory requirement for the railway administration, the port authority and the occupier.

Although the Constitution of India has made several provisions to protect the interests of children who are victims of child labour there are several tribal children in the country who are not aware of these provisions are made for them. Further, the tribal migrants who are the part of unorganized labour are worst victims, child labour and domestic work.

3. Right to Protection against Sexual Abuse and Exploitation

Child sexual abuse and exploitation is not new, the extent of the problem is – children are sold, rented out, and sexually abused by adults everywhere. There is no uniformly accepted definition of 'Child abuse'. There have been a number of definitions of the phrase 'child sexual abuse'.

Child Sexual Abuse (CSA) has been defined as any kind of physical or mental violation of a child with sexual intent usually by a person who is in a position of trust or power vis-a vis the child. CSA is also defined as any sexual behavior directed at a person under sixteen, without informed consent.

The Standing Committee on Sexually Abused Children has defined Child Sexual Abuse as: 'Any child below the age of consent may be deemed to have been sexually abused when a sexually mature person has by design or by neglect of their usual societal or specific responsibilities in relation to the child engaged or permitted engagement of that child in activity of a sexual nature, which is intended to lead to the sexual gratification of the sexually mature person.

At present there is no comprehensive law on child sexual abuse. The Constitution of India contains provision for the protection of children. Under the Constitution, it is the duty of the State to secure that children of tender age are not abused and forced by economic necessity to enter vocations unsuited to their age and strength [Article 39 (e)] and to ensure that children are given opportunities and facilities to develop in a healthy manner and in conditions of freedom and dignity [Article 39(f)].

According to Article 23 of the Constitution, trafficking women for immoral purposes is prohibited.

In India, legal intervention is presently in the form of investigations which start with registration of offences under the earlier Juvenile Justice Act 1986 or the present Juvenile Justice (Care & Protection of Children) Act, 2000 or the Indian Penal Code or the Prevention of Immoral Traffic Act 1956(Amended in 1986).

The Juvenile Justice Act, 1986 (J J Act1986)

J J Act 1986 was enacted to provide for the care, protection, treatment, development and rehabilitation of neglected or delinquent children.

Under the Juvenile Justice Act 1986, a prostitute's child was automatically a neglected child. The magistrate had the power to segregate the prostitute from her child and place the child in a corrective institution. Besides, under the Act, while males above eighteen years were considered adults, the age was reduced to 16 years for females.

The Juvenile Welfare Boards generally were not equipped to deal with cases of child sexual abuse.

The Observation Homes could not provide special care and treatment for such victimized children.

Juvenile Justice (Care & Protection of Children) Act, 2000

Since the Juvenile Justice Act 1986 has been replaced by the Juvenile Justice (Care & Protection of Children) Act, 2000, such children are now being produced before the child Welfare Committees that have replaced the Juvenile Welfare Boards. In practice, at present, it appears that there has been a change only in the nomenclatures. The actual functioning of the earlier Boards and present committees remain almost the same.

Indian Penal Code:

There is, at present, neither a comprehensive law nor a policy to deal with child sexual abuse. The Indian Penal Code deals with the sexual abuse of children in the form of rape.

- Section 375 defines rape.

- Section 376 of Indian Penal Code provides for the punishment of rape which shall not be less than seven years but which may be for a term that may extend to ten years, unless the woman raped is his own wife and is not under twelve years of age, in which case, he shall be punished with imprisonment for a term which may extend to two years or with fine or both.
- The other provisions of IPC, which are invoked, are related to unnatural practices like section 377. This is generally invoked when boy children are sexually abused.
- Sections 366(A) and 366(B) relate to export and import of girls for prostitution. Under Sections 366-A and 366-B, the girl should be below eighteen years and she should be intentionally induced by the accused to go from any place or to any act that is likely to force her into prostitution.

The Prevention of Immoral Traffic Act, 1986 (PITA)

Under Section 8, children, both boys and girls, are given protection from sexual abuse. There are also provisions against brothel keepers and keeping minor girls. Discretionary powers have been given to magistrates for interim placement of children who are housed in institutions.

4. Juvenile Justice

The vast majority of the children are impoverished. This has given rise to children in especially difficult circumstances (CEDC) who are vulnerable, marginalized, destitute and neglected, and are quite frequently deprived of their basic rights to family care, protection, shelter, food, health and education. According to an estimate, there are around 340 million deprived children in India. Among the vulnerable groups of children, India has the largest population of street children in the world. At least 18 million children live or work on the streets of India (Bajpai Asha, 2003:277).

Delinquency – It is any act, course of conduct, or situation, which might be brought before the court and adjudicated whether in fact it comes to be treated there, or by some other resources or indeed remain untreated. The juvenile delinquent or a child in conflict with law, is thus a person who has been adjudicated as such by a court of proper jurisdiction though he may be no different, at any rate, up and until the time of court contact and adjudication, from masses of children who are not delinquents. Juvenile delinquency is an act or omission by a child or young fantasy, which is punishable by law under the legal system.

Studies indicate that juvenile delinquency is a result of the interaction of contextual, individual and situational factors. Some of these factors within a family are:

- Living with criminal parents;
- Harsh discipline;

- Physical abuse and neglect;
- Poor family management practices;
- Low level of parent involvement with the child;
- High levels of family conflict;
- Parental attitudes favorable to violence; and
- Separation from family.

After independence many of the States developed their separate Acts whereas the centrally governed States (Union territories) were covered under the Central Children Act 1960. Hence there was a need for a uniform legislation for the entire country.

The Juvenile Justice Act 1986

The Juvenile Justice Act 1986 replaced the Children's Acts, formerly in operation in the states and the Union Territories. It came into force in 1987 on a uniform basis for the whole country. The preamble of the Juvenile Justice Act 1986 states that the Act is to provide for the care, protection, treatment, development and rehabilitation of neglected and delinquent juveniles and adjudication of certain matters relating to disposition of delinquent juveniles.

Under the J J Act 1986, juvenile means a boy who has not attained the age of sixteen years or a girl who has not attained the age of eighteen years. The juveniles are further classified into neglected juveniles and delinquent juveniles. A neglected juvenile is a very wide term and includes a juvenile who is found begging or who lives in a brothel or with a prostitute, or who leads an immoral life, or a juvenile who is being abused or there is a possibility that in future he may be abused for immoral purposes. A delinquent juvenile is one who has committed an offence under any law of the land and comes in conflict with law. The Juvenile Welfare Board deals the neglected juvenile whereas the delinquent juveniles are brought before the juvenile court.

The Act has provided for the classification and separation of delinquents on the basis of their age, the kind of their delinquency, and the nature of their offences committed by them. The four types of institutions for under this Act are Observation Homes, Juvenile Homes, Special Homes, After-care Homes.

The Juvenile Justice (Care and Protection of Children) Act 2000

The preamble of this Act states that it is an Act to consolidate the law relating to juveniles in conflict with the law and children in need of care and protection, by providing for proper care , protection, and treatment, by catering to their development needs, and by adopting a child-friendly approach in the adjudication and disposition of matters in the best interest of children and for their ultimate rehabilitation through their various established institutions under this enactment.

In this Act, 'Juvenile' or 'child' means a person who has not completed eighteenth year of age whereas the 'juvenile in conflict with law' means a person who is alleged to have committed an offence. Thus there are two distinct categories of children under this Act: *(i)* 'juvenile' for children in conflict with law; and *(ii)* 'child' for children in need of care and protection.

Significant Changes Brought about by the Juvenile Justice Act 2000

The Juvenile Justice Act 2000 has brought in some significant changes in an attempt to make the system more child-friendly, these are as follows:

- The Act defines a child as a person who has not completed eighteen years of age. There is now no discrimination in ages between boys and girls and the age conforms to the CRC.
- Use of distinct terms such as 'juvenile' for children in conflict with law and 'child' for children in need of care and protection has been introduced.
- Juvenile Justice Board is to replace juvenile courts and Child Welfare Committees to replace the existing Juvenile Welfare Boards.
- The Juvenile Justice Act 2000 empowers the Board to give a child in adoption.
- The Juvenile Justice Act 2000 requires that the child's consent be taken into account before the adoption is completed.
- The new J J Act allows parents to adopt a child of the same sex irrespective of the number of living biological sons or daughters.
- Rehabilitation and social integration of a child is an important part of the Act.
- Non-institutional services are provided as alternatives to institutionalization.
- Non-governmental organizations have been involved in the Act.
- There is a provision for juveniles being placed under the change of special juvenile police unit.
- The Act provides for reception, classification, and pre-trial detention of juveniles.
- New dispositional alternatives such as group counseling and community service have been provided to the Juvenile Justice Boards.
- There are provisions for children's home or shelter home for children in need of care and protection.
- Provision for monitoring and evaluation of children's home and shelter homes by the Central and State governments have been incorporated.
- Restoration of child to the family is now considered as prime objective of any children's home or shelter home.

5. Right to Development

The Right to Development includes two rights namely – Elementary Education – the right of every child and right to play and recreation.

(i) Elementary Education – The Right of Every Child

Right to education of every child is clearly a human right. Education is important as it enables the child:

- To develop and realize her/his full potential as a human being.
- To develop the ability to think, question and judge independently.
- To develop a sense of self-respect, dignity, and self confidence.
- To develop and internalize a sense of moral values and critical judgment.
- To learn to love and respect fellow human beings and nature.
- To develop civic sense, citizenship, and values of participatory democracy.
- To enable decision making.

The first experiment of making primary education compulsory took place in 1893 when the ruler of state of Baroda, Maharaj Sayajirao Gaekwad, introduced compulsory education in the Amreli division of his state. In 1918 with the efforts of Vithalbhai Patel, Bombay passed a Primary Education Act permitting municipalities to introduce compulsory education in their areas. Within a few years, other provinces also passed laws aimed at compulsory education. By the early 1930s, the principle of compulsory education was written into state law.

After independence, the Constitution of India, in Article 45, made compulsory education a matter of national policy. The constitution, in Article 45, lays down as a directive principle that every child up to the age of 14 shall receive free and compulsory education. Article 29 of the Constitution provides the right to admission to educational institutes (receiving state aids) without discrimination on the basis of religion, race, caste and language.

In November 2001, the Loksabha passed Ninety-third Amendment Bill. The significant provisions of this Amendment are:

- The amendment makes education a fundamental right for children in the age group 6 to 14 years.
- The State shall endeavor to provide early childhood care and education for all children until they complete the age of six years.
- It shall be the fundamental duty of the parents and guardians to provide opportunities for education to their children or, as the case may be wards between the age of six and fourteen.

This amendment has made the right to free and compulsory education for the children a fundamental right. The State is now under the legal obligation to provide free and compulsory education to all children between 6 to 14 years of age.

(ii) Right to Play and Recreation

The Convention on the Rights of the Child guarantees the right to play and recreational activities to all children. The Convention on the Rights of the Child in Article 31 acknowledges the importance of play and recreation. The article recognizes the right of the child to engage in play and recreational activities appropriate for the age of the child.

Play is a fundamental to all aspects of child development and is a key component in preserving community and culture, in the broadest sense. Play is valuable in children's physical exercise and growth and in their development of motor skills. Children playing together present rich opportunities for social, moral and emotional development and hence for the development of their personality and their ability to handle stress and conflict. Therefore, specialists in children's play theory see play as fundamental to human development.

6. Right to Survival

The Right to Survival of a child includes:

- Access to health care services for children in emergency situation and for prevention of disease, through the existing health care network;
- Providing Shelter;
- Providing nutritional facilities for children in need of care and protection; and
- Providing an identity.

(i) Right to Health

In 1946, the World Health Organization (WHO) defined health in its Constitution as 'a state of complete physical, mental and social well being and not merely the absence of disease or infirmity'. The right to health is solidly embedded in international human rights law.

The Convention on the rights of the Child1989 addresses the issue of health in Articles 24 and 27. Article 24 says that the state parties recognize the right of the child to the enjoyment of the highest attainable standard of health and shall take appropriate measures to combat disease and malnutrition through the provision of adequate nutritious food, clean drinking water, and health care. Article 27 of the CRC says that in case of need, the State parties shall provide material assistance and support programmes, particularly with regard to nutrition, clothing and housing (Bajpai Asha, 2003;376). The concept of nutrition rights originated in the context of the Convention on the Rights of the Child (CRC) and was developed by the United Nations Children's Fund (UNICEF) which defined nutrition rights as the combination of access to food, health, and necessary care. These three components are necessary to guarantee adequate nutrition to children (Bajpai Asha, 2003;377).

The Constitution of India provides in Articles 39 (e) and (f) that the State shall, in particular, direct its policy towards securing the health of the children. Unfortunately, in the Constitution of India, health is not a fundamental right of citizens and, therefore, cannot be justifiable in courts. The provision of health care is contained in the directive principles and it is a duty of the State to raise the nutrition and the standard of living and to improve public health.

(ii) Rights of Unborn Child and Rights during Early Childhood

Femicide, which includes female infanticide, sex- selective abortion, sex selection of embryos and other methods of averting the natural formation of a female foetus (sperm selection), takes place every day in every corner of this country. According to the 1991 census the overall sex ratio of the country was 929 women per 1000 men. This sex ratio is becoming more skewed day by day.

There are provisions under the Indian Penal Code 1860 for foeticide and infanticide. Amniocentesis or sex-selective abortion is a crime under the Indian Penal Code (IPC). The IPC lays down stringent penalties if miscarriage is caused without the consent of the woman. The Prenatal Diagnostic Techniques (Regulation and Prevention of misuse) Act 1994 is aimed at banning selective abortions of females. The Medical Termination of Pregnancy Act 1971 permits termination of pregnancies before twenty weeks under certain circumstances.

The Medical Termination of Pregnancy Bill 2000 (MTP 2000): The MTP bill 2000, was approved by the Parliament of India to amend the MTP Act, 1971. Complications of unsafe and illegal abortions in India remain a major factor in high rates of maternal mortality. The MTP Act, 1971, legalized the termination of pregnancy on various socio-medical grounds. The amended Act is aimed at eliminating abortions by untrained persons and in unhygienic conditions, thus reducing maternal morbidity and mortality.

(iii) Rights during Early Childhood

Registration of Birth:This is another right of the child immediately after birth. Under Article 7 of the Convention on the rights of the Child, the child shall be registered immediately after birth and shall have a name and the right to acquire a nationality. The registration of Births and Deaths Act 1969 provides for the regulation of registration of births in India. It has been made the duty of the following persons to give the information to the registrar of births orally or in writings (Section 8):

- In respect of births in house, by the head of the household and in his/ her absence the oldest adult male member;
- In respect of the birth in a hospital, health centre, maternity or nursing home etc., the medical officer in-charge;
- In respect of births in a jail, the jailor in charge;
- In respect of birth in a hostel, boarding house, lodging house, or public place, the person in charge;
- In respect of any new born child deserted in a public place, the headman of the village or the officer in charge of the police station;
- In respect of the births in plantation (section9), the superintendent of the plantation.

Immunization

The series of immunization known as DPT can prevent diphtheria, pertussis (whooping cough), and tetanus, but these three diseases still kill 6,00,000 children and afflict million of others every year in developing countries. Immunization also consists of one dose of BCG, three doses of OPV, and one dose of measles vaccinations to be given to infants.

India launched its Expanded Immunization Programme (EPI) in 1978-79. This was changed to Universal Immunization Programme (UPI) with the support of the UNICEF, the World Health Organization (WHO) and the Indian Academy of Pediatrics (IAP) with the objective of increasing the coverage levels by districts, improving the quality of services, and achieving self sufficiency in vaccine production as well as indigenous manufacture of cold chain equipment. Fixed-day drives of Pulse Polio Immunization (PPI) cover a maximum of 127 million children on single day sessions twice a year.

Nutrition

The World Health Assembly, on 21 May 1981, adopted an International Code of Marketing of Breast Milk Substitutes for the proper nutrition and health of world's children. The aim of code is to contribute to the provision of safe and adequate nutrition for infants by the protection and promotion of breastfeeding and by ensuring the proper use of breast milk substitutes. India was a signatory to this International Code and the Government of India responded through the ministry of health by adopting the 'Indian National Code for Protection and Promotion of Breastfeeding' in 1983.

The Infant foods, Breast Milk Substitutes and Feeding Bottles Act 1992 (IMS Act 1992) sought to provide for the prohibition of advertisements, incentives, donation, and promotion of artificial milk-food substitutes and to promote, protect, and support breastfeeding (Bajpai Asha; 2003:403).

The Maternity Benefit Act 1961: The Maternity Benefit Act 1961 prohibits employment of women in any establishment for a period before and after childbirth, and provides for payment of maternity benefits to them. The Act provides that a woman (who has actually worked for a period of not less than eighty days immediately preceding the date of her expected delivery) shall be entitled to maternity benefit for a period not exceeding three months [section 5(3)]. This obviously restricts exclusive breastfeeding to a period ranging from six weeks at worst to ten weeks at best, since most women would prefer to take some part of the leave before childbirth.

Under Section 10 of the Maternity Benefit Act 1961 a woman is also entitled to an additional period of leave with wages up to a maximum of one month if she is suffering from illness arising out of pregnancy, delivery, premature birth, or miscarriage. This clause is intended to safeguard the mother's health but cannot be used to extend the period of breastfeeding.

Section 11 provides for two nursing breaks of fifteen minutes duration each in the course of the mother's working day. If the crèche is not attached to the workplace she can take not less than five or not more than fifteen minutes time for travel.

Day care and Crèche Facilities: The provision for crèche for children of working mothers is obligatory under certain labour laws in the organized sector. Laws with reference to crèches exist primarily in relation to the organized sector. The factories Act 1948, the Mines Act 1950, and the Plantations Act 1951 make it obligatory for the employer to provide crèches for children aged 0-6 years wherever more than a stipulated minimum of women are employed in factories, mines and plantations.

Laws in the Unorganized Sector: There are 120 million women in the unorganized sector needing childcare support, as a majority of young children are unsupervised or are cared by older siblings. In the unorganized sector, the Contract Labour Act 1970 and the Interstate Migrant Workers Act 1980, this is an upgraded version of the former, as well as the Bidi and Cigar Workers Act 1966 attempt to legislate for the provision of crèches.

These laws follow the same pattern in relation to crèches as in the case of factories, mines and plantations, laying down a minimum number of women to be employed for the rules to become operative, though this is extremely impractical in the case of industries such as construction and quarrying for which the former are intended against home-based workers in the latter case.

(iv) Children's Right to Shelter/Housing

Housing as a living impulse creates roots entailing security. Article 21 of the Constitution of India deals with the right to life and includes the right to housing and shelter. The right to life includes the right to live with human dignity and all that goes along with it, namely, the bare necessaries of life such as adequate nutrition, clothing and shelter over the head, and facilities for reading, writing and expressing oneself in diverse forms, freely moving about and mixing and commoningling with fellow human beings.

The government has given a low priority to provision for shelter as reflected in the declining direct public investment on housing in the successive five-year plans, from 16 per cent in the first to 1.5 per cent of the outlay in the seventh plan. Children are the worst affected because of lack of housing policy.

India is also a signatory to the Universal Declaration of Human Rights 1948 and the International Covenant on Economic, Social, and Cultural Rights 1966, which declare and establish housing as a universally recognized fundamental human right. In spite of these proclaimed stands, the Indian Government is yet to recognize the right to housing as a fundamental right.

(M) Content and Intent of CRC (Child rights Convention)

The United Nations child Rights convention (CRC) is considered to be the most powerful legal instrument for the recognition and protection of children's human rights (Brewster Dan 2: 160). It has 54 articles in all A convention is an agreement between countries to obey the same laws. When a government ratifies a convention, it means that it agrees to obey the law written in that convention. The basic provisions of the convention are in three categories namely:

- Protection (Protecting children from harm)
- Provision (Providing what children need to live and develop)
- Participation (engaging children in their world)

Some of the important provisions of CRC include the following (note that these are summary statements)

Article 1: Definition of a child

A child is recognized as a person under 18, unless national law recognize the age of majority earlier.

Article 5: Parental guidance and the child's evolving capacities.

The state must respect the rights and responsibilities of parents and the extended family to provide guidance for the child that is appropriate to his or her evolving capacities.

Article 6: Survival and development

Every child has the inherent right to life and the state has an obligation to ensure the child's survival and development.

Article 9: Separation from parents

The child has right to live with her or his own parents, unless this is deemed to be incompatible, with child's best interests.

Article 19: Protection from abuse and neglect.

The State shall protect the child from all forms of maltreatment by parents or other responsible for the care of the child and establish appropriate social programs for the prevention of abuse and the treatment of victims.

Article 24: Health and Health Services.

The child has a right to the highest standard of health and medical care attainable.

Article 27: Standard of Living

Every child has the right to a standard of adequate for his or her physical, mental, spiritual, moral and social development. Parents have the primary responsibility to ensure that the child has an adequate standard of living.

Article 28: Education

The child has a right to education and the state's duty is to ensure that education is free and compulsory

Article 31: Leisure, Recreation and cultural

The child has the right to leisure, play and participation in cultural and artistic activities.

Article 32: Child Labour

The child has right to be protected from work that threatens his or her own health, education or development. The state shall set minimum ages for employment and regulate working conditions.

Article 34: Sexual exploitation

The state shall protect children from sexual exploitation and abuse, including prostitution and involvement in pornography.

Article 35: Sale, Trafficking and Abduction

It is the state's obligation to make every effort to prevent the sale, trafficking and abduction of children.

Some of the other articles of CRC are:

Article 3: Best Interests of the child

All actions concerning the child shall take full account of his or her interests. The state shall provide the child with adequate care when parents or others charged with that responsibility fail to do so.

Article 12: The child's opinion

The child has right to express his or her opinion freely and to have that opinion taken into account in any matter or procedure affecting the child.

Article 13: Freedom of Expression

The child has the right to express his or her views, obtain information, make ideas or information known.

Article 14: Freedom of Thought, Conscience and religion

The state shall respect the child's freedom of thought, conscience and religion, subject to appropriate parental guidance.

Article 15: Freedom of Association.

Children have the right to meet with others and join or form associations.

Article 16: Protection of Privacy

Children have the right to protection from interference with privacy, family home and correspondence and from libel or slander.

Article 19: Protection from abuse and neglect.

The state shall protect the child from all forms of maltreatment by parents or others responsible for the care of the child.

All the 54 articles of CRC throw light on protection, provision and participation of children. India is part of the convention and therefore has the responsibility to look into every article of CRC and see that it is practically enforced in the form of laws, rules and regulations to safe guard and protect the interest of every child in India. The question that haunts the mind of a researcher is that what ever is planned at the international level, which includes CRS, how effective it is in India.

STATEMENT OF THE PROBLEM

All the 54 articles of the United Nations child rights convention bestow an important legal responsibility on the member states & nations that have signed to agree and obey the laws concerning the rights of every child in their respective nation. Even the achievement of Millennium Development Goals (MDG) is yet another responsibility best on the member nations. In fact there is a very close relationship between achieving MDG goals & child rights.

The research problem of this study revolves around the push factors such as extreme poverty, landless status, debt, food and economic crisis that hook sugar cane cutters & brick kiln labourers into bonded labour and lack of adult man power among the Katkari brick kilnand Bhil sugar cane cutting labourers, forces them to involve their children into labour. There by depriving the child of educational physical, mental, emotional & social development.

Before getting into the statistics on Bhil sugar cane cutters and Katkari brick kiln labourers. Let us take a quick glance at same relevant statistics of India & Maharashtra.

According to 2001 census, the total population of India is 1,028.61 million and Maharashtra's population is 96.88 million. The total Scheduled Caste population in India is 166.64 million (16.2%) while in Maharashtra it is 9.88 million (10.2%).

The total tribal population of India is 84.46 million (8.2%), while the total tribal population for Maharashtra is 8.58 million (8.9%). The sex ratio of India is 933 females per 1000 males, while for Maharashtra it is 922 females per 1000 males. The child sex ratio for India is 927 girls per 1000 boys, and for Maharashtra it is 913 girls per 1000 boys. Child sex ratio for tribals in Maharashtra according 2001 census is 965 girls per 1000 boys for the age range 0-6 years. The State Census 2001 states that the highest child sex ration is 990 girls per 1000 boys in Nandurbar district, while the lowest is 859 girls per 1000 boys in Kolhapur district.

The percentage of child population in Maharashtra as per 2001 Census for the age group (0-6) is 14.1 per cent It is highest in Nandurbar is 17.6 per cent and lowest in Mumbai in 10.2 per cent. The percentage of marginal workers among the scheduled tribes in Maharashtra is 23.1 per cent, where as the percentage of agricultural labourers is 26.3 per cent in Maharashtra. Further more the percentage of other workers in the state of Maharashtra as per 2001 census is 42.4 per cent, while it 37.3 per cent among the scheduled castes & 17.5 per cent among the scheduled tribes.

Seasonal migration among the Thakars of Ambala Village: A Case Study

1. Aim of the case study

   To unveil the poverty stricken back ground, indebt, economic and hunger crisis, bonded labour, child labour and child rights issues among the

Thakars of Ambala, sugar cane cutters, who migrates seasonally to Sangamner, Ahemednagar and other districts.

2. Back ground of the case

Ambala village, is geographically located in Kannad block of Aurangabad district, in the state of Maharashtra ,India. The village is pre-deminently in habited by the Thakars, who migrated from Thane and Nasik regions.Infact the Thakars of Ambala told us that their tribes men have migrated to Nandgaon in Nasik district, Chaligaon in Jalgaon and Khultabad and Soyegaon blocks in Aurangabad district.There are 38 Thakur sugarcane cutters' hamlets in Kannad, Soyegaon and Kannad blocks.Some of their major clans are: Shid, Agivle, Ughade, Gavande, Mengal, Madhe, Pathve, Khadke, Gangul, Pokale And Aghan.

There are 160 houses in Ambala village all belonging to the Thakars.The total population as revealed by the school teachers is around 2000.

- Salient features of the socio-economic back ground of the Thakars of Ambala village are:
    1. The entire village is inhabited by the Thakars.
    2. All the 160 families residing there are below poverty line.
    3. Over 95 per cent of the families are debtors, sugar cane culters and bonded labourers.
    4. Each family owes Rs. 20,000/- to 25,000/- debt, per year excluding interest taxed by the middle men (Mukadams).
    5. Economic, hunger and debt crisis forces them into bonded labour; hence they are pushed into seasonal migration.
    6. Bonded labour and lack of adult man power hooks their children in to child labour, both domestic and commercial.
    7. Poverty, seasonal migration and bonded labour of parents deprive their children of their rights.
    8. On an average, if two adults work for 20 days a month for 8 months, they get Rs. 42,000/- but most of the times lesser than this, as jobs are not available for the entire 8 months. From this amount they have to pay nearly 30,000/- debt with interest. The other remaining amount is spent on the family at the place of destination. The family is hardly left with any cash, when they go back to (Ambala) their place of origin.
    9. They are hence forced to borrow a loan of Rs.20,000/- to 30,000/- to survive at the place of their origin(Ambala).
    10. Mr.X, a male, Thakar, married, having four children, borrowed a loan of 40,000/- from a Mukardam, for a year. He was charged to 18,000/- interest for one year for the amount of Rs. 40,000/-. Besides this 58,000/- Mr. x had a balance of Rs.

10,000/- to be paid for last year. This meant Mr. x had a debt of Rs. 68,000/- in all. He and his wife worked for 8 months get Rs.40,000/- which went back to Mukardam. They still had to pay an interest for the remaining 28,000/- plus another 30,000/- they borrowed when they went back to Ambala. Mr.x, his wife and children are hooked into seasonal migration, due to poverty, economic, food and debt crisis. They have become bonded labourers, as a result of which their 3 children do not attend school. They are deprived of their rights. The children are left at the mercy of nature in the "khopis" small huts made up of bamboo mats.

Like Mr. X, nearly 95 per cent of the Thakar sugar cane culters and seasonal migrates from Ambala village face the same problem as Mr.x.The illiterate Thakars are not aware of how the middlemen and contractors charge heavy interest and manipulate records to see that they are confused and work as bonded labourers.

The school teacher told us that if a Thakar sugar cane cutter refuses to pay the money back to the contractors he is threatened. They scare him of sending him to jail, police station or sometimes threaten of murdering him. The villagers told us, they ask for young daughters if payment is not done.

3. Plight of children:

As a impact of seasonal migration, bonded labour, debt, hunger and economic crisis, their children suffer following problems:

1. They are forced to leave the school, to migrate with their parents.
2. They are forced to do house hold work, take care of the young ones, take care of the bulls, goats and chicken. Help the parents in picking up sugar cane, making bundles and transporting them to the bullock-carts, trucks or tractors. Those ones between 15 to 17 years of age work as labourers and get money for the family.
3. They become victims of snake bites, scorpion stings, bronchitis, fever, diarrhea, etc in the place of destination.
4. They become victims of malnutrition

   Gambhir R.D and Gujar Sumedh (2008) in their study captioned "Study of seasonal migration and its impact on the Nutritional status of children" reported that children of sugarcane migrant labourers were malnourished at the place of destination.
5. The children do not get attention and care of parents.
6. They are deprived of food, shelter and clothes.
7. They don't attend school. The Sakhar Shalas are of no use to them as they are located near sugar mills. The children are with their parents in the fields.

8. According to the school teacher of Ambala hamlet,90% of the students drop out from the school during October to May, due to seasonal migration
9. During the months of June to September the school is full,but the children cannot cope up with the syllabus nor studies.

4. Concluding remarks

Taking into account the socio-economic, educational, food crisis and indebt crisis back ground of the Thakar sugar cane culters,the bonded labourers and seasonal migrates,it can be concluded that seasonal migration among the Thakars is largely due to push factors such as:

- Poverty
- Illiteracy
- Food,debt,economic crisis.
- Unskilled labour.
- Marginal land holding/landless status.

This pushes the parents into bonded labour. Lack of adult manpower in the family bonded labour,and work targets,hook children into child labour and deprives them of their rights.

HYPOTHESIS

Based on the pilot study, actual fieldwork among the target population and review of literature following hypotheses were tested and proved.

1. Extreme poverty, unemployment, landlessness, economic, food and debt crisis, temporary and poor housing, heavy interests on loans, illiteracy, bonded labour, social and economic insecurity, lack of economic assets and unskilled labour status at the place of origin push the Katkari brick kiln labourers and Bhil sugarcane cutters to the kilns and sugarcane fields.
2. Assured *Kharchi* – the weekly expenses, *Uchal*- the loan and employment guarantee at the kilns and sugarcane fields pull the Katkaris and Bhils to the place of destination.
3. Push and the pull factors hook the parents into bonded labour.
4. Poor socio-economic background of the parents, heavy workload targets (i.e. daily, weekly and monthly) and less adult manpower in the family hook children into child labour and deprives them of their rights.
5. Awareness of child rights among the Katkari brick kiln labourers and Bhil sugarcane cutters is absent.

OBJECTIVES OF THE STUDY

1. To study the socio-economic and living conditions of sugar-cane cutting Bhil laborers and brick kiln Katkari workers of Nandurbar and Raigad Districts respectively.

2. To explore the process and patterns of seasonal migration and among the Bhils and Katkaris.
3. To assess the impact of socio-economic and environmental conditions of the brick kiln workers and sugar-cane cutters on the physical, mental, social, educational and economic growth of their children.
4. To study the impact of seasonal migration and bonded labor on the rights of their children.
5. To understand the factors that give rise to child labor among the brick-kiln and sugar-cane cutting laborers.
6. To document the level of awareness among Bhils & Katkari laborers regarding constitutional provisions, policies, laws and rights of their children.
7. To study the various Government Programs implemented for these communities and their children at the place of origin and destination.
8. To develop a conceptual model on the issue of child labour and rights among the unorganized tribal labourers.
9. To suggest an action plan for the development of children of brick-kiln and sugar cane cutting tribes and their children.

SIGNIFICANCE OF THE STUDY

Studies by social scientists and more particularly Economists and Social workers are available in abundance on informal sector and allied issues. Among the Sociologists other than Jan Breman's book captioned, "Footloose Labor" (1996), and "Down and Out: Laboring under Global Capitalism" (2000), there are hardly any Sociological studies on informal sector. One of the latest studies by Smita and Prashant Panjiar (2007), highlights the struggle and problems faced by the sugar-cane cutters and brick kiln workers due to migration. However, there are no studies on child rights and child labor among children of brick kiln workers and sugar cane cutters. Hence the findings reported in this study are significant.

This study will certainly give rise to new Sociological theoretical insights. The conceptual model evolved in this study has been proved with the help of statistical data as well as qualitative data presented in the form of case studies. With the help of present model social scientists will be able to study child labour and rights issues among migrant labourers working in other occupational categories of unorganized labour sector. Further, comparative studies on various occupational groups of migrant labourers among the Indian tribes, caste groups and nomadic communities can be carried out so as to test the model. The conceptual model is hence both theoretical as well as methodological contribution.

At the practical level the study will contribute in developing action plans and programmes for the welfare and appropriate policies for the development and empowerment of the brick kiln workers and sugar-cane cutters.

CHAPTER 2

Research Methodology

SOCIAL RELEVANCE OF INVESTIGATION

Man is considered to be a social animal. There is no human being in this world that can say that he does not belong to a society or any human group. Interpersonal relationships are what mark a society and as the societies go on developing; these inter-personal relationships among men also undergo changes. Where there is interaction of various individuals of different upbringings and varied lifestyles, there is bound to be problems encountered by everyone. Here, the role of the sociologists becomes very significant, as it is his prime responsibility to study the various challenges faced by the individual in the process of his socialization. The sociologist generally does not tend to prescribe a standard pattern of living for the humans, rather he studies about the reasons behind the great variety of differences that exists between individuals and between different ways of life and thus may portray man and his relationship with the society in an unbiased manner.

In earlier days, technological advancement was at a very rudimentary level. Many societies were isolated geographically, socially and culturally, leaving very little scope for advancement. However as men began utilizing the natural resources coupled with his skills, knowledge and manpower he began moving towards what we call civilization and modernization. Today, many societies have gradually given up a primitive lifestyle and adopted a modernized lifestyle. However, we observe that many societies that have advanced technologically still lag behind in the race of modernization because of the adherence to the age-old cultural values. Not that there is anything wrong in adhering to cultural values, but in process of the formation of any human society there comes a point in the life of the individual as well as the society where culture, once given birth to, tends to have an existence of own impact it supersedes the individual; thus according to sociology is termed as super organic nature of culture.

Today, human society can be studied scientifically, thus almost all-sociological research has a scientific edge to it. Social research has scientifically contributed to detailed and overall understanding of the human being and his relationship with the society that he is part of. But, however scientific our approach to the study of human societies, it is not an easy task to predict social behaviour and expect to find a standard pattern of behaviour to exist among the humans, because human nature is very illusive and ever changing. This aspect of the human nature often brings a lot of obstacles in the unbiased and clear understanding of human nature. Investigation in social context is a time, labour and money-consuming affair. However, these hurdles have never deterred the sociologists from continuing his quest for an in depth knowledge of the human nature.

According to P.V. Young, "Social Research may be defined as a scientific undertaking which, by means of logical and systematized techniques aims to:

1. Discover new facts or verify and test old facts;
2. Analyze their sequences, inter-relationships, and causal explanations which are derived within an appropriate theoretical frame of reference;
3. Develop new scientific tools, concepts and theories which would facilitate reliable and valid study of human behaviours."

The importance of social research has been summarized in the following points:

1. To have a clear understanding of the various sociological processes that either contributes towards or degenerate social progress/growth of any society.
2. To analyze the bearing of socio-cultural factors on the life of an individual and how the factors contribute to the overall development of the individual.
3. To view the bearing of norms and a formal system of government on the individuals and the group. To understand how social processes can either bring about disharmony or establish social control and also the adherence or deviance to them.
4. For social planning such that every human group or society moves towards modernization thus elevating the standard of living of the people.
5. To analyze the working of cultural norms on men and women and to see how these factors work differently for them such that we can gain an insight into the life of the weaker section of society – the woman.

6. To improvise the methods and tools that are utilized in social research such that, better and more scientific means can be adopted to study and gain a holistic understanding of man as a social being.
7. To realize the significance of research that is scientifically motivated and which will contribute for the further advancement of social sciences.
8. To gain an insight into the life and culture of different groups of communities thus help us to understand man in an unbiased manner, taking into account the different cultures and ways of life that enable us to understand and accept the different enculturation processes that each is subjected to.

OBJECTIVES OF SOCIAL RESEARCH

Redman and Mory define research as a "systematized effort to gain new knowledge." Some people consider research as a movement from known o unknown. Social research tries to rediscover every aspect of man's evolution as a social animal and every moment even adds new knowledge about the behaviour of man.

Research refers to the systematic method consisting of:

1. Enunciating the problem
2. Formulating a hypothesis
3. Collecting the fact or data
4. Analyzing the facts and
5. Reaching certain conclusions either in the form of solutions towards the concerned problem or generalization for certain theoretical formulations.

Social Research has gone a long way in studying the various socialization processes, the functioning of different social structures, to study the varied patterns of interrelationships in the society and how social systems need to be reorganized and restructured in dealing with them.

NEED FOR TRIBAL RESEARCH

The tribal population of India, according to the 2001 census was 84 million. This number is growing at a very fast pace. With the growth in their population, their problems are now becoming the forefront of government concern. In India some of the important features of the tribals are:

1. most of them live in isolated terrains;
2. the main resources of their livelihood are agriculture and gathering forest produce;
3. they do not cultivate for their profit;
4. they still rely on barter system;
5. they spend greater part of their earnings on social and religious ceremonies; and

6. a large number of them are illiterate and are victimized by unscrupulous forest contractors and moneylenders.

For many years the tribals were considered to be backward segment of society. Many still live in forests and hills without having more than a casual contact with the so-called civilized and modernized neighbors. Many anthropologists and sociologists are of the belief that it is not correct to impose alien values and beliefs on the tribals but to allow them to live in their own way without any interference from outside forces. Thus, for a long time pre-independence of India, the tribals were more or less ignored. However as time passed by and due to the increasing pressure of population and vested interests of the invaders many outsiders began settling in tribal regions. This brought about a lot of problems and as such gave rise to unrest, exploitation and feelings of deprivation, thus leading to agitations and movements among the tribals. This is the main reason why many tribal communities are still not susceptible to change and are suspicious of outsiders.

The constitution of India has laid down strong machinery for safeguarding the interests of the scheduled tribes and other backward communities, in the form of setting up a commission for Scheduled Castes and Scheduled Tribes. The state governments have separate departments to look after the welfare of these communities and have also been spending a sizeable amount on the welfare of tribals. A number of voluntary organizations also promote the welfare of tribals. Their welfare is also given special attention in the Five Year Plans. The tribals also are provided adequate representation in the legislative organs at different levels as well as reservation in services and educational institutions.

However, in spite of all these measures, governmental, non-governmental and individual, the tribals are still suffering from poverty, indebtedness, illiteracy, bondage, exploitation, disease and unemployment. This condition is worse among the Katkaris, Dhor Kolis and other landless tribal groups in Maharashtra.

Hence, a thorough social research that is scientifically maneuvered is very essential to probe into the socio-cultural, economic, religious, political, legal, occupational aspects that effect and shape the destiny of these deprived sections of society and more specially,migrant labourers, child labourers, bonded labourers who belong to the various tribal communities of India with special reference to Bhil and Katkari tribes of Maharashtra which are involved into sugarcane harvesting and brick making respectively .*The relevance of this sociological investigation lies in the fact that it is an in depth study of the child labour and rights of the Katkari brick kiln labourers and the Bhil sugarcane cutters in this context.*

More importantly, there are hardly any studies on the child labour and child rights among the Katkari brick kiln labourers and Bhil sugarcane cutters.

METHODOLOGICAL FRAMEWORK

Locale of the Study

The present study was conducted in 7 villages in the Shahada and Taloda blocks of Nandurbar district and & 14 villages in the Pen and Khalapur blocks of Raigad district in the state of Maharashtra.

The rationale behind selecting Raigad and Nandurbar districts was because maximum Bhils and Katkaris inhabit in these districts. Hence, the researcher selected these two districts. Out of the total 18,18,792 population of Bhils in Maharashtra 7,14,122 i.e. 39.26 per cent are found in Nandurbar. Similarly out of the total 2,35,022 population of Katkaris in Maharashtra 1,03,244 i.e. 43.92 per cent are found in Raigad (Census of India, 2001).

Target Population

The target population for the study was household heads who were brick kiln labourers and sugar cane cutters. The target population belongs to two tribal communities namely Katkaris and Bhils 200 respondents were selected. The rationale for selecting the Katkaris and Bhils for the present study is as below:

Why Katkaris?

Studies by Bhatia Arun and Tribhuwan Robin (2002) and Tribhuwan Robin and Patil Jayshree (2004) revealed that 68 per cent and 64 per cent of the Katakaris migrate to the brick kilns, as labourers. That these 68 per cent and 64 per cent borrow loan from the brick kiln owners and are hooked into bonded labour. Out of the 45 tribes in the State of Maharashtra maximum brick kiln workers are the Katkaris, followed by a few Dhor Kolis and other landless tribals. Studies by Gaikwad Nancy (1995) and Bokil Milind (2006) too reveal that Katkaris work as labourers at the brick kilns. Hence, the tribe was selected for the present study.

Why Bhils?

A study by Desai Mrinalini (2005) captioned Janarth Sakharshala – the Sending Villages Report revealed that some of the communities involved in sugar cane cutting profession in Maharashtra are shown in table 2.1.

It is clear from the table that only the Bhil work as sugarcane cutters. In his case study Tribhuwan Robin (2010), has made a mention of Thakars, Pawaras, Koknis and Mavchis including the Bhils. Kendre Balaji (2009) has also made a mention of Bhils working as sugarcane cutters. A study by Rensje Teerink, 1995, too states Bhils work as sugarcane cutters. Hence the Bhils were chosen for the present study.

Table 2.1: Caste/Community Profile

Sr. No.	Caste/Tribe	No. of Families	Percentage
1.	Vanjari	743	37.9
2.	Maratha	526	26.8
3.	Banjara	194	9.9
4.	Bhil	86	4.4
5.	Dhangar	79	4.0
6.	Mahar	79	4.0
7.	Matang	68	3.5
8.	Bouddha	47	2.4
9.	Muslim	28	1.4
10.	Gujar	21	1.1
11.	Others	89	4.6
	Total	**1960**	**100.0**

Sugarcane cutters are of three types:

1. **Tyre Centre:** Migrants who bring their bullocks and are provided technologically improved carts (with rubber tyres) to transport sugarcane; they live in large settlements closer to the factory. (Panjiar Smita, 2006:40)
2. **Gadi Centre:** Migrants who bring their own wooden bullock carts and animals and live further away from the factory. (Panjiar Smita, 2006:40)
3. **Doki centre:** Migrants who are mobile, they have no assets, they cut cane and load it into factory trucks, stay farthest away, work in groups of 15-20, and are shifted from site to site depending on cane availability and factory schedule. (Panjiar Smita, 2006:40).

The focus of the present study was on the child labour and rights issues of Bhil sugarcane cutters. The Doki centre, who camp in and around the sugarcane fields. There are hardly any studies by sociologists on this tribe and the topic too.

Similarly, although Katkaris work as agricultural labourers, small scale cultivators, daily wage labourers and brick kiln labourers. The present study focused on understanding the child labour and rights issues of the Katakris at the brick kiln sites. There are hardly any studies on this topic by sociologists.

Method of Data Collection

Both Primary and secondary sources were used to collect the data for the study.

- **Primary Data:** Primary data was collected from 29 Brick kilns and 9 Sugarcane cutters' camps by designing an interview schedule for the household heads. Besides this, an interview guide was also prepared for brick-kiln owner as well as middleman (mukadam). Observation method and photographs were used to validate the primary data. Case study method too was used to gather qualitative data.

- **Secondary Data:** Secondary data was collected from the books on castes, nomadic groups, unorganized sector, social security and social insecurity, labour problems, articles published in journals and newspapers etc. The researcher also referred unpublished Ph.D thesis, M.Phil and Master level dissertations related to the topic.

Research Tools

In recent years there is a trend among social scientists to use multiple research tools and different types of respondents so as to unveil a social phenomena form a holistic perspective. Yet another trend in social science research which gaining importance rapidly and that is use of quantitative and qualitative data.

The researcher has made use of both the trends i.e. use of multiple tools and techniques such as *interview schedule, interview guide, case study, ethnography and observation method, focused group discussions as well as photography*. Simultaneously different types of respondents were interviewed to gather relevant data. Quantitative data was gathered by using 200 interview schedules while the other research tools and techniques contributed in gaining qualitative data.

An *Interview Schedule* was designed to gather information relevant to the topic, from the respondents. A pilot study was conducted in order to design an interview schedule. 200 interview schedules were administered. 100 interview schedules were administered in Katkari Brick Kilns, while the other 100 were administered in sugarcane cutters' camps of Bhil tribe. The data gathered using an interview schedule was quantitative in nature. Heads of the household both at the brick kiln and sugarcane fields were interviewed to understand their socio-economic background. Besides this an *interview guide* was prepared to gather relevant data from the brick kiln owners and sugarcane contractors.

Ethnography: Before getting into understanding, why ethnography method was used by the researcher. It is necessary to understand what is ethnography? at this juncture.

Ethnography can be defined as the study of people in naturally occurring settings or 'fields' by methods of data collection which capture their ordinary activities, involving the researcher participating directly in the setting, if not also the activities, in order to collect data in a systematic manner but without meaning being imposed on them externally. Ethnography is not one particular method of data collection but a style of research that is distinguished by its objectives, which are to understand the social meanings and activities of people in a given 'field' or setting, and an approach, which involves close association with, and often participation in, this setting. To access social meanings, observe behaviour and work closely with informants and perhaps participate in the field with them, several methods of data collection tend to be used. 'Little' ethnography describes 'ethnography –understood-as fieldwork', to which this definition relates, while 'big' ethnography equates it with the whole qualitative method and describes 'ethnography-understood-as-qualitative-research'. (Brewer John, 2010:189)

Ethnography-understood-as-fieldwork comes in various types. 'Scientific Ethnography' involves the application of some features of scientific method to the above sort of study; 'humanistic ethnography' concentrates on the search for the meaning of social action and life from the perspective of the people concerned and is uninterested in the values and rhetoric of science; 'post-modern reflexive ethnography' adopts a critical approach to ethnography and seeks to ground its practice in postmodernism's ideas about the impossibility of definitive 'objective' study. Less extreme versions exist as a type of 'post post modern ethnography', which although it attacks *realism* us strongly committed to *realism's* ambition to disciplined, rigorous and systematic ethnographic practice. (Brewer John, 2010:189)

Haralambos & Holborn, (2000) define Ethnography is the study of a way of life. They state that it was first introduced into the social sciences by anthropologists who studied small-scale, pre-industrial societies. Bronislaw Malinowski's study of the Trobriand Islands (Malinowski, 1954) is an example of an ethnographic study. Anthropologist increasingly recognized the need to get as close as possible to the societies they were investigating. More recently, the same approach has been applied to the study of groups within industrial society.

Ethnographic can take various forms and is used by sociologist of different types. It is widely used by symbolic integrationists, and critical ethnography is a common type amongst critical social scientist. Ethnography can use different qualitative research methods, but the most common are in-depth interviews, participant observation, and the use of qualitative documents. It may also involve collecting some quantitative data. However, participant observation is often the most important single method used in ethnographic studies. (Haralambos & Holborn, 2000)

In this context, the researcher used Ethnography method in order to study briefly the cultural life of the Katkaris and Bhils- the target population. A brief ethnographic profile has been presented in chapters three and four.

Focused Group Interview: Besides using an interview schedules to obtain relevant data from the respondents, the researcher used case study, observation method and photography to generate richer data than those obtained from interview schedules. More importantly, Focused Group

Interviews were conducted by researcher, by involving the use of in-depth group interviews in which the respondents selected were brick kiln owners, brick kiln workers, social activists, social workers, mukadams i.e. middlemen, sugarcane cutters etc.

The rationale for conducting Focused Group Interviews of the above mentioned respondents was to generate relevant and richer data through social interaction with the respondents who were comfortable with the researcher and cooperated in generating the required data.

In all 8 Focused Group Interviews were conducted informally. Each Focused Group Interview was carried out by involving 5 to 10 respondents.

As rightly pointed out by Richard & Rabiee (2001), a Focused Group Interview is, according to Lederman (Thomas et.al.1995), a technique involving the use of in-depth group interviews in which participants are selected because they are purposive, although no necessarily representative sampling of a specific population. This group being focused on a given topic, participants in this type of research are therefore selected on the criteria that they would have something to say on the topic, are within the age-range, hive similar socio-characteristics and would be comfortable talking to the interviewer and each other.(Richrd & Rabiee, 2001).

One of the distinct features of focus group interview is its group dynamics, hence the type and range of data generated through the social interaction of the group are often deeper and richer than those obtained from one-to one interviews. (Thomas et.al,1995). The uniqueness of a focus group is its ability to generate data based on the synergy of the group interaction. (Green et al, 2003).

The optimum number of participants for a focus group may vary. Krueger & Casey (2006) suggest that between 6 to 8 participants as smaller group shows greater potential. However the number suggested as being manageable is between 6 to 10 participants; large enough to gain a variety of perspectives and small enough not to become disorderly or fragmented.

Qualitative data from the sugarcane cutters belonging to the Bhil tribe and Katkari brick kiln labourers was gathered through in-depth *informal interviews* of men, women and children. This data was presented in the form of 50 case studies. Thus, 25 case studies of Bhils and 25 case studies of Katkaris are presented in chapter three and four. The themes in the case studies revolved around the research problems related to seasonal migration, poverty, bonded labour, living conditions, indebtedness, exploitation, pull and push factors, and child labour and child rights issues of the target population. The rationale for using multiple research tools such as an interview schedule, interview guide, case studies, observation method and photography was to get an overall and holistic understanding of the life of katkari brick kiln labourers and Bhil sugarcane cutters, including the child rights and labour issues.

The researcher conducted a pilot study by visiting the brick kilns and sugarcane fields- their places of destination, as well as their native hamlets – their places of origin. 50 informants were informally interviewed to get an understanding of the research problem. Simultaneously, secondary literature was referred to analyze the problem. The researcher, under the guidance of Dr. Robin D. Tribhuwan developed a conceptual model which was tested later.

In order to understand health and nutritional problems of the brick makers and sugar cane cutters informal interviews with two medical doctors were conducted. Prof. Vandana Kakrani from the Department of Preventive and Social Medicne, B. J. Medical College was consulted to guide the researcher to analyze data on the nutritional status of children (0-14 yrs). Based on primary data, their Body-mass Index was plotted and nutritional grades of children were plotted using international standard tables.

Table 2.2 reveals village wise number of schedules administered, to gather data from the sugar cane cutters and brick kiln workers.

Table 2.2: Village-wise Number of Schedules Administered

Sr. No.	District	Block	No. of Villages Covered	No.of Brick kilns and Doki Centers Covered	No. of Schedules
1.	Raigad	Pen	06	16	48
		Khalapur	08	13	52
2.	Nandurbar	Shahada	03	05	50
		Taloda	04	04	50
	Total	**Blocks - 4**	**21**	**32**	**200**

Variables of the Study

For moving from abstract concepts to the practice of social research, one has to explore some additional terms. One such term is 'variable.' Variable is also known in social science research as an indicator.

A variable is a characteristic that takes on two or more values. It is something that varies. It is a characteristic that is common to a number of individuals, groups, events, objects, etc. The individual cases differ in the extent to which they possess the characteristic. (Ahuja Ram, 2001:60)

Although several qualitative and quantitative variables were considered for the present study, some of the major ones are as follows:

(a) **Quantitative Variables:** The quantitative variable is one whose values or categories consist of numbers and if differences between its categories can be expressed numerically. (E.g. Age, Income, Size are quantitative variables) (Ahuja Ram,2001:64).

Given below are the major quantitative variables of the study:

1. Age range
2. Marital status
3. Education
4. Types of family
5. Family size
6. Land holding
7. House types in native place
8. House types at the brick kiln
9. Live stock at place of origin
10. Live stock at place of destination
11. Annual income
12. Occupation at place of origin
13. Duration at place of origin
14. Duration of employment at place of origin
15. Food crisis at place of origin
16. Indebtedness
17. Loan range
18. Assets possessed
19. Number of children & adults
20. Educational status of children
21. Number of children involved in domestic labour
22. Diet of children
23. Number of children involved in brick kiln labour
24. Malnutrition among children
25. Age of starting domestic as well as commercial child labour
26. Recreation at the place of destination
27. Health problems at the place of destination
28. Drop outs
29. Awareness among parents regarding child rights

(b) **Qualitative Variables:** The qualitative variable is one which consists of discreet categories rather than numerical units. This variable has two or more categories that are distinguished from each other. (E.g. Class – upper, middle, lower) (Ahuja Ram, 2001:64)

Given below are the major qualitative variables in study:

- **Parents**
  1. Reasons for migration
  2. Push and Pull factors
  3. Reasons for bonded labour and indebtedness

4. Living conditions at destination
5. Facilities at destination
6. Reasons for Illiteracy
7. Social and economic security
8. Awareness about Tribal Development agencies and programmes
9. Awareness about child rights
10. Daily Routine of the parents

- **Children**
  1. Hazardous nature of child labour
  2. Reasons for child labour
  3. Types of child labour
  4. Domestic responsibilities
  5. Commercial labour responsibilities
  6. Reasons for drop outs
  7. Reasons for malnutrition among the children.
  8. Reasons for ill-health among the children
  9. Daily Routine of the children
  10. Recreational Facilities at destination

Sampling Procedures

Most difficult problem in social science research is the problem of sampling. Most statistical studies are based on samples. A statistical sample is a miniature picture of cross-section of the entire group or aggregate from which the sample is taken. The entire group from which a sample is chosen is known as 'population' or 'universe'. (Kumar:1985)

In this study two types of sampling methods have been used.

1. **Sampling by Regular Intervals:** In doing this the Tehasildars of Pen and Khalapur were approached to get the list of registered brick kilns. There were 64 registered brick kilns in Pen block and 52 registered brick kilns in Khalapur block. It was also observed that there were several unregistered illegal brick kilns. The researcher selected 25 per cent of kilns (i.e. 16 kilns from Pen block and 13 kilns from Khalapur block) which were registered with the Tehasildars of both the blocks. Thus, by selecting every fourth kiln from the list 25 per cent of the brick kilns were selected. A list of heads of the household was prepared from the selected Brick Kilns to administer 100 interview schedules and every fourth head from the list was interviewed using sampling by regular interval.

   Dr. Kumar (1985) elaborates on the concept of sampling by regular interval by stating, "to select the cases at regular intervals from a series, alphabetical list or any other arbitrary arrangement is termed as sampling by regular interval. For example in selecting a sample of 50 students, out of 500 students in a college, for this purpose every tenth case is selected from these 500 students thus the selected sample represent 10 per cent of the total universe. This type of sampling was appropriate for Katkari Brick Kiln labourers, and hence it was used.

2. **Snowball Sampling:** Detecting the Bhil sugarcane cutters out of the 16 to 17 different caste groups working in sugarcane fields was difficult a task. There is no data available with the sugar mills, Commissioner, Sakhar Sankul, Pune nor the 'Mukadams'. It was therefore necessary to enquire from the owner of the sugarcane field as well as the Bhil sugarcane cutters to detect the whereabouts of their tribesmen working in nearby fields. Snowball sampling is therefore appropriate method in these circumstances to detect and study the Bhil sugarcane cutters in the fields known to their own people in the absence of published data.

In his book captioned, "Social Research Methods", Bryman Alan,(2008:184-185) has made the concept of snowball sampling clear by stating that, 'with this approach to sampling, the researcher makes initial contact with a small group of people who are relevant to the research topic and then uses these to establish contacts with others. Bryman Alan used an approach like this to create a sample of British visitors to Disney theme parks (Bryman, 1999). Becker's comment on this method of creating a snowball is interesting: "the sample is, of course, in no sense "random"; it would not be possible to draw a random sample, since no one knows the nature of universe from which it would have to be drawn' (Becker 1963:46).

The problem with snowball sampling is that it is very unlikely that the sample will be representative of the population, though as Bryman have just suggested, the very notion of a population may be problematic in some circumstances. However, by and large, snowball sampling is used not within a quantitative research strategy, but within a qualitative one: both Becker's study and Bryman's study were carried out within a qualitative research framework. Concerns about external validity and the ability to generalize do not loom as large within a qualitative research strategy as they do in a quantitative research one. (Bryman Alan, 2008:185).

Analysis

Qualitative and quantitative both the methods were employed to analyze the data. Statistical indicators were entered in excel software to analyze quantitative data. Simple tables on various indicators such as caste, age, sex, marital status, education, family size, annual income, occupation, borrowing behaviour, type of house etc. were tabulated. Qualitative data was analyzed manually. Both quantitative data and qualitative data contributed in analysis and interpretation of facts gathered. Simple tables plotted through quantitative data were interpreted and presented in appropriate places.

Chapter Scheme

Data gathered, analyzed and interpreted through this study, has been presented in six chapters namely:

Chapter 1: Child Labour and Child Rights Issues Among Katkaris and Bhils: *The Brick Kiln and Sugarcane Cutting Labourers*

Chapter 2: Research Methodology

Chapter 3: Child Labour and Rights Issues Among the Katkari Brick Kiln Labourers

Chapter 4: Child Labour and Rights Issues Among the Bhil Sugarcane Cutters

Chapter 5: Child Welfare Programmes by Government and NGOs

Chapter 6: Summary of Findings, Conclusions and Recommendations

CHAPTER 3

Child Labour and Rights Issues Among the Katkari Brick Kiln Labourers

This chapter throws light on five major aspects of Katkari brick kiln labourers & their children. These aspects are:

- Brief ethnographic profile of the Katkaris.
- Occupational typologies among the Katkaris.
- Brick kiln scenario.
- Seasonal migration, child labour and child rights issues among the Katkari Brick Kiln Labourers: Case Studies.
- Socio-economic background of the Katkari brick kiln labourers.
- Analytical reflections.

Every aspect has been discussed in a logically sequential manner.

BRIEF ETHNOGRAPHIC PROFILE OF THE KATKARIS

The term 'Katkari' is said to be derived from Marathi word 'Kath' (Catechu- the thickened juice of Khair tree), 'Kari', refers to making 'Kath' or makers of catechu. Katkaris, including Dhor Kathodi were first notified as Scheduled Tribe against the name Kathodi or Katkari, under the constitution (Scheduled Tribes) order, 1950.There are two sub-groups of the community namely Dhor Kathodi (Katkari) and Son Kathodi. (Katkari) (Tribhuwan Robin, 2004; 62).

Population of Maharashtra: As per 2001 census population of Katakari tribe in Maharashtra is 2,35,022.

Geographical Distribution: Kathodi or Katkaris is one of the most backward tribes of Maharashtra. In fact, it has been categorized as one of the three primitive tribes of Maharashtra, the other two being Kolams and Madia. Katkaris and predominantly found in districts of Raigad, Thane, Pune, Nashik and Ratnagiri. (Tribhuwan Robin, 2004:62).

Their physical Features: The Katkaris as compared to their neighboring tribe the Thakurs, are dark in complexion. Medium height, broad nose and straight hair are their other physical traits.

Their Occupation: Most of the Katkaris are labourers. Besides earning through daily wage labour, they are known for hunting, fishing, collecting roots, fruits, corns etc. A very few Katkaris may have their own land. In her thesis, captioned "Patterns of occupation & Resource Utilisation" Patnaik Renuka (1996) has pointed out that the term "Katkaris" is linked with the original occupation of the tribe. Their original occupation was a making "Kath" or Katha (catechu) and "Kari" referring to makers hence "Kath Kari" – the makers of Kath. The tribe later on took up the occupation of making char coal, which too declined with the depletion of forests. The tribe is currently engaged in brick kiln work, for six months (i.e. from December to May) and agriculture and daily wage labour for six months. (i.e. from June to November). The tribe is also spelt as "Katkari" and/or Kathodi in Scheduled Tribe list of India and Maharashtra. Scholars such as Vyas N.N. (1982) in his book captioned, "Kathodi" – a tribe in transition; Masavi and Pandey (1996) in their paper captioned Kathodi ; Enthoven R.E. (1920); in his book "Tribes and Castes of Central Provinces of India" Vol. 3 have mentioned the term "Kathodi". This may be because the tribe was involved in skinning the dead cattle. The "Dhor Katkaris" a sub tribe of Katkaris are known by the name "Dhor" because they would drag dead cattle outside the village and/or feed on the meat of dead cattle thrown outside the village (Tribhuwan Robin and Cappel Marcus (1999).

Forms of Marriage: Marriage of cross cousins is prohibited. The Katkaris do not call a Brahman for performing the wedding ceremony, but the head of the community who is called 'Naik' presides over the ceremony. Monogamy is a common form of marriage, among Katkaris.

Type of Family: Both nuclear and joint family types are prevalent among the Kathkaris with patriarchy, patrilocal residency and patriliny as a norm.

Main Features of Katkari Panchayat:

- **Structure:** The traditional panchayat of the Katkaris consists of 3-5 members. They are selected by the villagers. The chief, of the panchas' is called the 'Naik'. He is assisted by Karbhari & pradhan (helpers). The office of the Naik is not hereditary. The meetings of the panchayats are called on during emergencies only. There is no fixed place or timing for having panchayat meetings (Tribhuwan Robin, 1995).
- **Disputes solved/tackled:** Adultery, divorce, quarrels, breaches of marriage and other taboos are some of the major complaints which are referred to these panchayats.

- **Forms of punishment:** One of the major forms of punishment is charging heavy fines in cash or kind to the culprit or party at fault. In case the fine is not paid he is taken to the local police station. Out-casting a person from the tribe has been fading away of late.
- **Other functions of the Panchayat:** The members of the traditional Katkari Panchayat are readily available to guide and support village and family activities. In fact the role of traditional panchayat members is very significant as far as co-ordination of village level and family level functions.
- **Selection of panchayat members:** The selection of Panchayat members is decided by the villagers based on their abilities and personal qualities & of course experience to lead & judge people's problems and finally solve them.
- **Settlement Patterns:** Katkaris dwell in small hamlets having a group of 15 to 100 houses. Katkari hamlets are usually known as "Wadis" or "Padas". The common pattern of their settlement is row house structures or separate houses in a line facing the other row or house. Their houses are aloof from the caste group settlement.
- **Traditional House Types:** Traditional houses of Katkaris are squarish in shape. The walls are made up of sticks, smeared with clay & cow dung. The roofs of traditional houses of Katkaris are made up of rice straw. The area of the house varies from 100 to 300 sq. feet.

OCCUPATIONAL TYPOLOGIES AMONG THE KATKARIS

Studies by Bokil Milind (2006); Tomar Y.P.S & Tribhuwan Robin (2004); Tribhuwan Robin (2004); Dhar, P.(2004); Patnaik Renuka (1996); Tribhuwan Robin(2000); Gaikwad Nancy (1995); Heredia Rudolf (1994); Kappel Marcus &Tribhuwan Robin (1999); Census of India, Notes on Scheduled Tribes of Maharashtra (1961); Enthoven R.E. (1920); Russel & Heeralal (1975) reveals that Katkaris were involved in following occupational typologies in past & present.

(a) **Catechu Makers:** Kath- meaning catechu & Kari- meaning, makers of catechu. In fact their name has been derived from the act of making catechu. As time passed by they gave up this profession.

(b) **Charcoal Makers:** Patnaik Renuka (1996) has stated that the tribe was involved in making charcoal.

(c) **Marginal Farmers:** Most Katkaris, in fact over 80 per cent are landless. Those who have land are marginal farmers. Over 90 per cent of the land possessed is non-irrigated. These marginal farmers grow vegetables, chilies, tomatoes and millets on the non-irrigated land they possess, for 3 to 4 months.

(d) **Agricultural labourers:** There are two types of agricultural labourers among the Katkaris. Those who work throughout the year & those who work from July to October. The ones working from July to October i.e. agricultural labourers are over 90 per cent.

(e) **Daily Wage Labourers:** Here again, one gets to see two types of daily wage labourers i.e. those who work throughout the year and those work from October to May.

(f) **Brick Kiln Labourers – The Seasonal Migrants:** A majority of Katkaris in Maharashtra work as Brick kiln labourers. They migrate to the brick kiln sites from October to June, live there in temporary houses, earn their living and are back to their native villages with some financial loan from the brick kiln owners. They repay the loan in the next season. From July to September they work on daily basis as agricultural labourers for the non-tribal farmers or progressive tribes such as the Kokna, Koli Mahadev, Warlis, Koli Malhar, Thakurs, etc.

It would be appropriate to mention at this juncture, that all the above mentioned categories perform at least two to three types of occupations throughout the year. These are brick kiln and agriculture labourers, including collection of Minor Forest Produce; agriculture and daily wage labour; cultivation, agriculture & daily wage labour.

BRICK KILN SCENARIO

This section of the chapter presents a brief journey of the Katkari brick kiln labourers from their native villages to the kilns and back home.

(a) Migration season

The study revealed that the Katkaris migrate seasonally to the brick kiln sites from October to June for a period of 8 months. For some it is from October to April or May. The Katkaris are generally at the kilns for a period of 6 to 8 months.

(b) Transportation

Depending on the distance of the native village and number of families migrating to the destined kiln, they are transported by a tractor or truck. The brick kiln owners pay the transportation charges. Some walk it to the kilns.

(c) Who are the brick kiln owners?

It was observed that the brick kiln owners belong to Maratha, Kunbi, Agri, and Muslim communities.

(d) Duration of work at the kilns?

As mentioned earlier, the Katkari families are at the kiln site for a period of 6-8 months, i.e. in winter and summer season.

(e) Facilities at the kilns

Civic amenities and facilities at the brick kilns are below standard and unfit for human habitation. Given below is the description of the same.

- **Toilets:** The Katkaris go in open air to defecate on defecation grounds.

- **Bathrooms:** Temporary bathrooms are made up of saris or plastic sheets covered from three sides for women especially. Men take bath in the open or go to a nearby stream, river or lake.
- **Drinking water:** Most Katkaris fetch drinking water from open streams, wells or rarely from taps in the neighboring village. Drinking water used by them is certainly unsafe and impure.
- **Cooking facility:** Almost all the Katkaris studied were found to cook food on the hearth. They fetch fuel wood from the fields and forests.
- **Housing:** It was observed that the Katkaris live in the four types of temporary houses at the kilns.
  - *(i)* **Karvi stick walled houses-** Houses made up of Karvi sticks, smeared with clay and cow-dung, with a thatched roof.
  - *(ii)* **Brick walled houses-** Houses made up of arranged bricks, with a thatched roof or roof with a plastic sheet.
  - *(iii)* **Tin walled houses-** We rarely get to see houses with tin wall and tin roof. Some kilns do have them.
  - *(iv)* **Plastic walled houses-** Yet another category of house type is seen at the kiln. These houses have plastic walls and plastic roof.

The doors are small and low. The area of the house is 60 to 100 sq. feet. Extreme heat and cold are typical characteristics of the Katkaris huts at the kilns. One gets to see pets such as dogs and cats in most huts. The Katkaris say that they prevent snakes and scorpions from getting in the huts.

- **Electricity:** Electricity facility was seen at most kilns. It is supplied legally by the owners.
- **Other facilities:** Facilities such as recreation, schools, I.C.D.S. units, first aid boxes, clinics, etc are not there at any brick kiln.
- The brick kiln owners make arrangements to fix tube lights outside, so that the labourers can work in the late nights as well. However, it was observed that there were no bulbs or tube lights in the huts of the labourers.

(f) Nature of work at the kilns

The brick kiln labourers are expected to do following jobs at the kilns.

(i) Loading and unloading clay, rice husk, char coal, bricks etc.

(ii) Mixing clay in water.

(iii) Making bricks, by using moulds.

(iv) Drying them and arranging them.

(v) Transporting the unbaked bricks to the furnace etc.

(g) Work targets

On an average every Katkari family is expected to make 7000 to 8000 bricks a week. Thus, they have to compulsorily achieve a target of 30,000 to 50,000 bricks per month depending on the family size.

(h) Payment system

Every family gets Rs. 400 to 500 per week as weekly expense called "*kharchi*". Thus, a monthly amount of Rs. 1600/- to 2000/- is compulsorily received by every family as Kharchi. Most of the money is spent on food, medicine and drinks.

Besides this, separate accounts are maintained by the brick kiln owner to check how many bricks are produced per family per month. If a family makes 20,000 bricks per month for Rs. 2000/- is deducted from the loan taken previous year. A Katkari family thus, on paper gets Rs. 16,000/- for eight months. If the loan amount is 16,000/-. They do not get cash for the hard labour for eight months. They are only able to repay the loan. However, while going back to their native village, they take a loan of Rs. 16,000/- to 20,000/- to get hooked as bonded labourers. Secondly, the *kharchi* amount given to them, while at the kilns, too gets deducted from the loan amount. The Katkaris are hardly left with any cash for their labour for eight months.

(i) Number of hours of work

On an average every Katkari family works for 10-14 hours at the kiln. The women folk have to cook as well wash vessels and clothes. It was observed that children, especially the girl child takes up household responsibilities of cleaning vessels, washing clothes, cleaning the house, etc. at an early age of 7 to 8 years, so as to support the working mother.

(j) Kharchi & Uchal concept

As mentioned earlier "Kharchi" refers to the weekly expenses and "Uchal" refers to loan taken from the owner, the previous year. While going back home in the month of June, the owner calculates total Kharchi given for eight months, medical expenses paid by him, and the amount due for the brick making target achieved for 8 months.

Thus, if a family has taken a loan of Rs. 30,000/- the previous year, the owner deducts Rs. 16,000/- kharchi, form the same, Rs. 2,000/- for drinks and medicine, Rs. 2,000/- taken for festival celebration & deducts another Rs. 10,000/- from the Rs. 20,000/- he owes them for labour work for eight months. The family has only Rs.10,000/-. This amount is spent on buying clothes, vessels, ration, soap, oil, kerosene, etc. Thus, they do not have any cash with them, and are forced to take loan of Rs. 30,000/- again. When they are in their native place they do not get kharchi. They have to renovate their house, buy plastic sheets, etc., which requires money. They are thus, hooked in the vicious cycle of bonded labour forever.

(k) Reasons for migration

Group discussion and focused group interviews with the Katkari brick kiln labourers revealed some of the major reasons for migration from their place of origin to the brick kilns. These are:

(i) Unemployment back home
(ii) Illiteracy
(iii) Landless status
(iv) Indebtedness & poverty
(v) Unskilled labour
(vi) Poor housing
(vii) Lack of economic assets
(viii) Economic & hunger crisis in the native place
(ix) Bonded labour
(x) Hope of survival at the kilns because of kharchi & loans

Case studies given in this chapter throw light on the above aspects in detail.

(l) Forms of child labour at the kilns

Since both the parents are into making bricks for 8-14 hours the children are neglected. They are forced to take up household responsibilities at an early age. They drop out early from school. In fact most of them do not go to school. At the age of 7-8 they start helping the parents at the kilns. We classify child labour into two categories, namely:

(i) Domestic labour
(ii) Commercial labour

The domestic labour includes children helping their parents by carrying bricks, mixing clay, etc. as well as managing household work. Commercial labour refers to children earning money by working at the kilns from the tender age of 14 to 17.

Why children are forced into child labour?

Some of the key factors that push the children into labour are:

(i) **Seasonal migration:** Since parents migrate, children are forced to migrate.

(ii) **Poverty, Unemployment, Bonded Labour:** Poverty, unemployment, bonded labour, etc. factors push their parents to the kilns. "Kharchi" & "Uchal" pull their parents to kilns.

(iii) **Full time involvement of parents:** Parents have to work for 10-14 hours a day. The children are therefore neglected. They have to manage household work, take care of the young ones, as well as themselves.

(iv) **Weekly Targets:** Every family has to make 7000 to 8000 bricks a week. This forces the children to help to take up labour work.

(v) **Lack of Adult Manpower:** Lack of adult manpower in the nuclear families, forces children to get into child labour.

(vi) **Work to survive:** Both the parents & children have to work to survive. No work -no ***kharchi***- no ***uchal***, no money- no food, no survival.

(vii) **Work to specialize the art of making brick:** Both children and parents are aware that after the age of 15, a Katkari child should specialize or master the art of making bricks. After 15 to 18, the child learns to become a responsible adult and is ready to get married and start another nuclear family. The children therefore work to master the art of brick making.

SEASONAL MIGRATION, CHILD LABOUR AND CHILD RIGHTS ISSUES AMONG THE KATKARI BRICK KILN LABOURERS : CASE STUDIES

Quantitative data in social science research answers questions such as how many, how much and other quantitative details, it does not answer Why, people behave the way they do. Qualitative data helps a researcher to understand solutions for the question Why? In this study, the researcher has made use of both qualitative and quantitative data to understand the research problem from a holistic angle. Given below are 25 case studies that throw light on the aspect of seasonal migration, child labour and child rights issues among the Katkari Brick kiln labourers.

CASE STUDY 1

(a) Aim of the case study

To understand the practice of child marriages among the Katkari Brick Kiln Labourers.

(b) Background

Ms. AN, a female, aged 14, illiterate, hails from Ramwadi Katkari hamlet of Kotimbe village, in Karjat block of Raigad district, in the State of Maharashtra. Ms. AN has been working as a domestic and commercial family child labourer, since she was 7 years old. After accompanying her parents as a child labourer depriving herself of her rights to education, nutrition, parental care etc. her parents decided that she should be married in February, 2011.

(c) Course of events

Ms. AN's parents decided that their daughter should get married in February 2011. The decision came about after AN's parents consulted a few elderly people in Ramwadi. Ms. AN will be married to Mr. K from Ramwadi itself. Mr. K too works as a brick kiln labourer in Karjat. Mr. K too assisted his parents for five years as a commercial labourer getting Rs. 30/- per day for loading bricks in the truck. Mr. K is 16 years old and worked at the brick kiln since he was 11 years old.

(d) Analysis

After having an informal interviews with parents of both Ms. AN and Mr. K, it was revealed that the brick kiln Katkari labourers get their children married at an early age. The age at marriage for girls is between 12 to 15 years and for boys 15-18. It was also observed that these children not only handle domestic work, but also help their parents in completing the brick making targets per month.

CASE STUDY 2

(a) Aim of the case study

1. To unveil the annual income of a katkari brick kiln labour family
2. To justify the co-relation between income, exploitation and bonded labour.

(b) Background

Gulab Pandurang Waghmare, a Katkari married female, a brick kiln labourer, a resident of Hemdi village, pen block of Raigad district, in the state of Maharashtra. Gulab, her husband and a ten year old son work at Ransai brick kiln about 4 kms away from their native village Hemdi.

On enquiring what were the sources of her family's income Gulab replied:

1. ***From October to May:*** The family works at the brick kiln for eight months. The family gets Rs. 1600/- per month i.e. Rs. 400/- per week as "kharchi" (weekly expenses). Thus for eight months the family gets Rs. 13,600/-.
2. ***From June to August:*** For 4 months in rainy season, Gulab & her husband work as agricultural labourers and daily wage labourers. Jobs are available only for month & a half. The family is able to earn about 2000/- cash for 4 months. This includes the sale of fire wood as well.
3. ***Total annual income for making bricks:*** Gulab told that the brick kiln owner pays them Rs. 200/- for making 1000 bricks. On an average the family makes 5000 bricks per week, i.e. 20000 brick per month. On an average Gulab's family earns Rs. 4000/- per month, i.e. Rs. 32,000/- for eight months.
4. ***Over all annual income:*** Gulab's family thus earns Rs. 32,000 for eight months & Rs. 2000/- for the remaining 4 months. Thus on an average Gulab's family on paper earns Rs. 34,000/- per year.
5. ***Actual income in hand:*** From the total Rs. 34,000/- earned on paper Rs. 13,600/- plus another Rs. 1,400/- i.e. Rs. 15,000/- gets deducted. Gulab's family also takes Rs. 10,000/- "Uchal" (loan), while going back to their native village, during times of crisis. Thus, out of

Rs. 34,000/- if Rs. 25,000/- is deducted the family left with Rs. 9,000/-. The remaining Rs. 9,000/- is spent on items such as clothes for Gulab, her husband, her son and her in-laws. Other expenses such as purchase of medicines, liquor, utensils, sweets, vegetables, soap, oil etc. get deducted from Rs.9000/-. Gulab's family is hence left with no cash in hand, by end of September, this economic crisis & foods crisis pushes the family back into bonded labour into the clutches of brick kiln owners. Brick kiln owners are like financers or banks which attract the katkari brick kiln labourers. These banks are pull factors that bring the katkari back to brick kiln.

(c) Analysis

Although Gulab's family earns Rs. 34,000/- per annum on paper, they actually receive Rs. 9,000/- per year in hand. This hard cash of Rs. 9,000/- too vanishes on expenses such as clothes, medicines, travel, soap, oil, liquor ration, blankets, bed sheets etc.

The family is high & dry by the end of September; hence they get hooked into bonded labour.

The data presented in the case study above certainly justifies why Gulab's family is:

- Poor;
- Landless;
- Into bonded labour;
- A victim of economic & hunger crisis;
- Socially & financially in secured;
- Unskilled;
- Educationally lagging behind;
- Forced to push their only son Darshan into child labour, depriving him of his rights;
- Asset less;
- Socially & politically impoverish.

(d) Concluding remarks

The criteria for earning Rs. 34,000/- on paper & actually receiving Rs. 9,000/- in hand, does not fit into the Governments norms of BPL criteria. In this case, the family earns Rs. 9,000/- after the brick kiln owner deducts loan & expense amount. Gulab's family therefore, may be classified as below the poverty line family as it gets Rs. 9,000/- per annum.

This aspect of exploiting labour service from the labourers for maximum financial gains is seen among the brick kiln owners.

CASE STUDY 3

(a) Aim of the case study

To explore the age at which katkari male children get into domestic work and brick kiln labour services to support the parents to meet their weekly brick making target.

(b) Background

Darshan Pandurang Waghmare aged 10, a male child living with his parents at Ransai brick kiln. He studied upto 3rd grade in the year 2008-2009. He was forced to leave the school and help his parents who work for 12 to 14 hours at the brick kiln.

House hold activities

At the age of nine Darshan started taking up following house hold activities:

1. Fetching water from the river.
2. Fetching grocery
3. Washing & drying clothes
4. Cleaning the house
5. Collecting firewood

Activities at brick kiln

Since the age of 10, Darshan has been involved in the following activities at the brick kiln to support his parents:

- Mixing clay in water
- Carrying unbaked bricks to the furnace
- Arranging unbaked bricks
- Carrying baked bricks to tractor or truck

(c) Analysis

Darshan's mother, Gulab stated that, Katkari male children start helping at home between the age of 7 to 9. Their children start helping the parents when they are between 10-12 years, at the brick kilns. Thus house hold work & child labour at the brick kilns to achieve family target becomes the prime priority for katkari male children thereby depriving them of their rights.

CASE STUDY 4

(a) Aim of the case study

To explore the age at which Katkari female children get into domestic work and brick kiln labour services to support the parents to meet their weekly brick making target.

(b) Background

Manisha Govinda Valhekar, a female aged 11 years, a member of katkari tribe, residing at Ransai brick kiln, in pen block of Raigad district in the state of Maharashtra. Manisha is an illiterate. She was deprived of her child rights as her parents happened to be bonded labourers at the brick kiln. Her mother Shanta as well as Manisha stated that girls of her age are into following house hold work & brick kiln work.

House hold activities

At the age of Eleven, Manisha started taking up following house hold activities.

- Cooking food & making tea.
- Fetching fire wood, grocery, minor forest produce etc.
- Washing and drying clothes.
- Cleaning the house.
- Fetching drinking water.
- Taking care of children between the age of 1 to 5 years in the family.
- Bathing children etc.

Activities at the brick kiln

Some of the activities in which Manish is involved at the brick kiln are:

- Mixing clay in water
- Making bricks, using moulds
- Carrying unbaked bricks to the furnace
- Arranging in baked bricks
- Carrying bake bricks to the tractor or truck.
- Carrying clay in a container.

(c) Analysis

Female katkari children at the brick kilns take up house hold work right from the age of 7. These girls start helping the parents in the house hold work when they are between the age of 7 to 9 years. From the age of 9 they start working at the brick kilns to help their parents achieve weekly & monthly targets.

Thus house hold work & child labour at brick kilns to achieve family targets becomes the prime priority for katkari female children thereby depriving them of their rights.

CASE STUDY 5

(a) Aim of the case study

To examine the quality of drinking water available to Katkari brick kiln labourers and their children.

(b) Background

Ms. Sangita , aged 7, a female katkari child, residing at Ambeghar brick kiln, of Pen block, in Raigad district in the state of Maharashtra, was spotted by the researcher near a stream close to the brick kiln. Ms. Sangita, was with a metal pot. She had a small glass, with the help of which she was taking water from a dug ditch and putting water in the pot.

On enquiring as to why she was taking the water, Sangita replied, that water was for drinking. Do you boil this water?, asked the researcher, Sangita smiled and said 'No, We drink this water'. Is it clean? 'Yes, it is clean,' said Sangita. How many metal pots are required for the family? Sangita said '2 to 3'. Whose responsibility is it to fetch drinking water? Sangita said, "it is my job".

Why don't you get tap water or well water, asked the researcher? Sangita said, 'both the sources are far off and the local villagers do not allow us to fill water from these sources.

(c) Analysis

Many Katkari children like Sangita are unlucky to become victims of circumstances such as this, wherein they have to drink unclean, unsafe and impure water from streams and rivers. They are certainly deprived of their right to drink safe water.

CASE STUDY 6

(a) Aim of the case study

To study the recreational activities of the Katkari children at brick kilns.

(b) Background

Ganesh aged 9, a male katkari child residing at Gagode brick kiln has dropped out from school, when he was in 1st grade. He was forced to join his parents, who work at the brick kiln. Ganesh was interviewed to find out what recreational activities he is into when he is free from domestic as well brick kiln work. Ganesh narrated following recreational activities.

(c) Recreational Activities

- Playing with clay at the brick kiln.
- Playing with household pets such as dogs and cats.
- Playing in the stream.
- Playing with the bicycle tyre.
- Learning to use a catapult.
- Playing stone marbles.
- Collecting berries.
- Climbing on mango trees or other small trees.
- Jumping on the clay heaps at the brick kilns.
- Making clay bulls and toys.

On enquiring has he seen football, cricket ball, a bat or hockey?' Ganesh said, he has seen a cricket bat and ball. Do you have them? He said, 'No, sometimes I play cricket using a wooden stick and a brick piece serves as a ball.' Three bricks serve as stumps.'

(d) Analysis

Poverty, bonded labour, illiteracy and ignorance of parents deprives several children like Ganesh of their right to recreation. They waste their time and talent growing up as children of the have not's at the brick kilns.

Sports such as cricket, foot ball, basket ball, hockey and other recreation activities availed by middle class and rich children in the cities and towns is a dream to the unfortunate – poor Katkari children.

CASE STUDY 7

(a) Aim of the case study

1. To study the birthing practices among the Katkaris at the brick kilns.
2. To understand the facilities and conditions for a new mother and child, at the brick kiln.

(b) Background

Ms. X, aged 18, was married to a Katkari boy aged 18 at the time of marriage. Ms. X, was 16 years of age at the time of marriage. Her mother Anandi works at Ransai brick kiln. Ms. X was married to a boy from Mangrul village. On the 15th of January, 2011, Ms. X came to Anandi's house at Ransai brick kiln for delivery.

Ms. X delivered a daughter on the 24th of January, 2011, in the small hut which is 4x6 sq.feet. The temporary house made up of sticks with thatched roof was the only place for delivering Ms. X's daughter. Ms. X decided to choose the small hut without any facilities for birthing, because she had her mother, the Traditional Birth Attendant, her mother's three sisters to give her moral support and take care of her.

Her delivery was conducted by a Katkari Midwife (Dai) using the customary rituals and techniques. The ritual of 'Pachvi Pujan' was performed on fifth day to appease the goddess of fertility – mother earth.

(c) Conditions and Facilities of Maternal and Child Health Care

There were no special health or nutritional care facilities for Ms. X, and the new born. She had the same food consumed by the other family members. There were less bed sheets and clothes for the new mother and child. The six days old baby was wrapped in pieces of old saris. The new born did not have clothes or woolen cap, or nickers etc. it was winter season i.e. January, 2011. The new mother too managed with a old blanket and a quilt (Godhadi). Her husband bought for her a cheap woolen scarf to cover her ears.

The dusty environment, the stagnate water around the hut, the mosquitoes, flies, cold air in the night, hot sun in the afternoon was the kind of situation in which the new mother and child lived. Such an environment is not fit for a new mother and a child. The new mother slept on the floor on a bed sheet and a quilt, without a mattress.

(d) Analysis

There are several young girls like Ms. X, who get married at an early age and when they are pregnant, they deliver their first born at the brick kilns for they have no choice.

Here again it is observed that, utter poverty, landless conditions, bonded labour push the Katkaris to the brick kilns to live in conditions, wherein their children and grand children are born, without any medical aid or under supervision of a medical expert or gynecologist.

CASE STUDY 8

(a) Aims of the case study

1. To study the male – female composition of Katkari brick kiln labourers.
2. To explore the sex composition of children of a brick kiln.
3. To assess the educational status of Katkari children staying at the brick kiln.
4. To unveil the number of children working as helpers at the brick kiln.

(b) Background

Gagode village has three brick kilns, the researcher selected the brick kiln owned by Shri. Mahadik, to unravel the above mentioned aims. The details of Katkari labourers and their children are as follows:

(i) ***Number of huts at the brick kiln***

It was observed that there were seven huts, made up of karvi sticks that formed the walls and roofs made up of rice straw and/ or plastic sheets.

(ii) ***Number of families***

There are seven Katkari families that live at the brick kiln of Gagode village in Pen block of Raigad district in the State of Maharashtra.

(iii) ***Male-Female composition***

The total population of Katkaris at the brick kiln studied is 32, with 15 adults (7 males and 8 females) and 17 children (8 males and 9 females).

(iv) ***Sex composition of children***

Out of the total 17 children, 8 are males and 9 are females.

(v) ***Age range of children***

The age range of brick kiln at Gagode is as follows:

Sr. No.	Age- Range	Males	Females	Total
1.	0-1 years	01	01	02
2.	1-5 years	03	07	10
3.	5-7 years	04	01	05
4.	7-14 years	00	00	00
	Total	**08**	**09**	**17**

(vi) ***Educational status of children***

Out of the 17 children, it was observed that only 6 studied up to primary, while 11 were illiterate. Out of the 6 who studied up to primary, 3 dropped out from school. Only 2 Katkari children went to an Anganwadi for mid-day meals. One boy was in 1st grade in a Zilla Parishad school.

(vii) ***Educational status of parents/adults***

Out of the total 15 adults, 7 were males and 8 were females. Out of the 7 males, 5 were illiterate and 2 studied up to 4th grade. Out of the 8 females all were illiterate.

(viii) ***Children helping at the brick kilns***

Out of the 17 children, four were between the age range 7 to 12 years, i.e. 2 males and 2 females. These four children helped their parents at the brick kilns to mix clay with water, transport bricks, making bricks etc.

(c) Analysis

Gagode brick kiln had only seven families of Katkaris having a population of 32 people. Out of the total 32 people, 15 are adults, and 17 are children. Out of the 15 adults only 2 were literate, the rest 13 were illiterate. All female adults are illiterate.

Out of the 17 children, 11 are illiterate, while 6 studied up to primary. Out of the 6 who studied up to primary, three were drop out, while 2 went to Anganwadi and one attended grade I.

Out of the total 17 children, 4 were found helping the parents at the brick kilns. Their age range was from 7 to 12 years of age. The rate of illiteracy among children is quite high. The moment they become 7 to 8 years of age, they start working as child labourers.

CASE STUDY 9

(a) Aim of the case study

To study the indebtedness among labourers of brick kilns with reference to the Katkaris.

(b) Background

Mr. PP owns a brick kiln in the village called Gagode. There are six Katkari families working at the Kiln. These labourers are brought to the work site in a tractor by the brick kiln owner, in the month of October-November after Diwali. The labourers work till June 7 to 10 every year. This case study throws light on the aspect of indebtedness among the Katkari labourers working as bonded labourers at the brick kilns.

(c) Wage payment pattern and "Kharchi"

Each family gets Rs. 400/- to 500/- per week for household expenses, depending on the number of active adult labourers. Thus their "kharchi" (expenses) per month is from Rs. 1600/- to 2000/- per family.

On an average every family makes 20,000 bricks per month, which fetches them another Rs. 2000/-. If they work for six months, this income shoots up to Rs. 12,000/-. From this Rs. 12,000/- six months' 'kharchi' and medical expenses gets deducted. The Katkari labourers are left with hardly any cash, when they go back to their native villages.

(d) The concept of "Uchal"

'Uchal' literally means to 'pick-up'. When the Katkari brick kiln labourers are left with no cash, they take loans to be repaid through labour. Every family takes Rs. 10,000/- to 20,000/- depending on their need.

(e) 'Uchal'at Gagode Brick Kiln

Given below are details of loan borrowed by the Katkari families from their owner in the year 2009 -2010.

i. Mr. M.W – Rs. 15,000/-
ii. Mr. R.P – Rs. 14,000/-
iii. Mr. V.P – Rs. 14,000/-
iv. Mr. L.W – Rs. 12,000/-
v. Mr. S.P – Rs. 10,000/-
vi. Mr. D.P – Rs. 12,000/-

All the above mentioned six families are back to the same brick kiln owner to repay the loan amount borrowed in the year 2009-2010. When enquired how much money will they borrow, while going back home in 2010-2011, they replied the amount will be more or less same. One of the labourers said, he may take six thousand more to treat his ailing father, who is in the native village.

(f) Analysis

Indebtedness, bonded labour, and the 'Kharchi' factor for six months' survival of the family are key factors that push them to the kilns. The 'Uchal' factor pulls them to the kilns.

CASE STUDY 10

(a) Aim of the case study

To study the daily routine of a Katkari labourer family at the brick kiln.

(b) Background

Ravi Jagan Pawar, aged 23, a male Katkari brick kiln labourer is married to Kusum, aged 20. They have a 4 year old daughter called, Urmila. The family has been into brick kiln labour, since last 5 years. Their daily routine at the brick kiln is as below:

(c) Daily Routine

Ravi and his wife wake up at 5.00 am, complete their morning duties of going to the defecation ground, brushing, bathing, up to 6.00 am. Both of them have tea by 6.00am and start working from 6.00am onwards till 11.00am. Kusum, Ravi's wife, comes home to cook rice and dal or 'Bhakar' and some curry. She is joined by her husband and her daughter for food. After an hour's break, they are back to work.

At 4.00 pm, another break of 15 to 20 minutes is taken to relax, have tea, and drink water. From 4.15 pm to 7.00pm they work to achieve a daily target of making 700 to 800 bricks.

Kusum and Ravi go home at 7.00pm Kusum cooks food, while Ravi goes out to drink liquor. They have dinner by 8.00 to 8.30 pm and are off to sleep.

Ravi said, that in the month of February, March, April and May, when it is hot, the brick kiln labourers work after dinner. The owner makes arrangement for fixing tube lights or bulbs at the kiln.

(d) Analysis

On an average a Katkari labourer works at a brick kiln for 12 hours to complete, the weekly target of the family. By the time it is evening, the adults are tired. Both adult males and females drink to relieve tiredness. Hard work, hard life and hard drinks are part and parcel of the Katkari labourers working at the brick kiln.

CASE STUDY 11

(a) Aim of the case study

To unravel the status and awareness of child rights to shelter/housing among the Katkari parents.

(b) Background

Nirmala Vishnu Pawar, a Katkari girl aged 2 & ½ years, residing in a brick kiln at Gagode village, Pen block of Raigad district, in the State of Maharashtra. Nirmala is the only daughter of Vishnu and Sarita Pawar. She stays at home, while her parents work. Her world revolves around the kiln and the small hut made up of stick walls and thatched roof.

There is a stone crusher about 100 meters away from her house. The dust released from the crusher directly comes into the houses of the Katkari labourers. Children like Nirmala inhale the dust with small dust particles. These particles also fall on the food consumed by the children. Besides this, the dust and the brick kiln smoke too are hazardous to the health of Katkari children. On enquiring whether she is aware of right to shelter /housing, no was her natural answer.

(c) Analysis

Dusty and smoky environment at the brick kilns, the temporary huts with damp floors without ventilations in extreme cold and hot conditions are no good for the health of children. The risk of snakes and scorpion entering the huts is yet another aspect of living conditions.

Poor housing and conditions at the brick kilns are not fit for children. They are forced to live in such conditions and poor housing. Nirmala's family members as well as other Katkari families are not aware of the children's right to shelter/housing.

CASE STUDY 12

(a) Aim of the case study

To unveil the trend of economic exploitation through child labour at the brick kilns.

(b) Background

Krishna, an illiterate, Katkari boy, aged 12 years, residing at the brick kiln in Gagode. Krishna has never gone to school. He ahs been deprived of education because of the semi- nomadic nature of his parents.

(c) Course of events

As a child, Krishna grew up at the brick kiln sites, till he was seven years old. He started helping in household work since the age of seven. At the same time, he started observing his parents work at the brick kiln.

At the age of nine, Krishna started helping his parents at the brick kiln. He learned the art of making bricks, using the mould for a year. At the age of 11 Krishna started getting Rs. 50/- per day for transporting bricks. Krishna is 12 years old. He is getting Rs. 100/- per day to transport unbaked bricks to the furnace, load and unload clay. Krishna works for ten hours for few days in a month, just to get Rs. 100/- per day.

(d) Analysis

Krishna never went to school; he was certainly deprived of his right to education, recreation, economic development etc. There are several children like Krishna, who are deprived of their rights.

CASE STUDY 13

(a) Aim of the study

To study the socio-economic status of a KatkariVillage to understand the occupational status of the village, to study the number of families that migrate seasonally at brick kilns for daily wage labour.

(b) Background of the study

Katkariwadi is a hamlet of Nangurle village, in Karjat block of Raigad District, in the State of Maharashtra. Tribhuwan Robin and Patil Jayshree (2006) conducted a survey of this hamlet. The survey was sponsored by the Women's International Club, Pune.

(c) Occupational and socio-economic profile

- The survey conducted revealed that, there are 14 houses in the hamlet.
- The total population of the hamlet is 80.
- The houses of the Katkaris are small and made up of stick walls with thatched roofs. The condition of the houses is poor and unfit for habitation. Out of 14families studied, it was observed that 9 migrate to brick kilns to work as migrant brick kiln labourers.
- On an average 100 per cent of the families were Below Povery Line.
- 13 of them were landless.
- 13 i.e. 93 per cent of the Katkaris studied were illiterate.

(d) Analysis

Out of the 45 tribes in the State of Maharashtra, Katkaris are the most backward people. Poverty, landlessness, unemployment, indebtedness and bonded labour force them to migrate to brick kilns with their children for a period of 6 to 8 months. During rainy season they are back to work as agriculture and daily wage labourers.

CASE STUDY 14

(a) Aim of the study

To unveil the impact of child labour on schooling.

(b) Background

Sunil Ram Waghmare, a male child, aged 13 years, a resident of a brick kiln is Khalapur block of Raigad district in the state of Maharashtra. He is currently in 5th grade in a Zila Parishad school.

(c) Course of events

Sunil was admitted in the Zilla Parishad School in the year 2004-2005, in 1st grade. He managed to go to school until he came 13 years old. Since he started attending the 5th grade class, his parents bestowed following responsibilities on him:

- Household responsibilities
- Commercial brick making and transporting responsibilities.

Being the eldest son in the family, the parents forced him to help them achieve their targets of making bricks. Sunil's younger brother Roshan, who is 8 years old was given the responsibility of taking care the youngest brother Rahul.

(d) Analysis

Since the responsibility of working at the brick kiln was bestowed on Sunil, his interest in going to school started diminishing. His parents were more interested in making him a courageous brick kiln laborer than getting him educated.

CASE STUDY 15

(a) Aim of the study

To study the co-relationship of brick kiln location and residential village of a Katkari family with that of a school enrolment of their children in the village school.

(b) Background

Sharda Waghmare is a Katkari girl aged 7 years, studying in 2nd grade, in the Zilla Parishad School, of Hal Budruk village of Khalapur Block, Raigad district in the state of Maharashtra. Sharda's parents live at a brick kiln site in the same village. Her parents along with 3 children live at the brick kiln site.

(c) Course of the study

Sharda was admitted in the village Zilla Parishad School in the year 2007-2008 in the 1st grade. She continued her schooling as well as helped her parents in brick kiln work. Sharda enjoyed going to school because she gained knowledge. She also received mid-day meal and availed the benefits given by the education department.

Sharda's parents were interviewed to explore their perception about educating their other two children. They replied by stating that their brick kiln is in the same village where they live. Hence, they can send their children to the village school. At the same time, when they need their children's help at the brick kiln, they can work at the site.

(d) Analysis

Katkari parents who work as laborers at the brick kilns of their native village tend to send their children to the Zilla Parishad School, so as to avail the educational, health, nutritional and other schemes implemented by the Government Departments.

CASE STUDY 16

(a) Aim of the study

To study the co-relationship between education of parents and enrolment of their children in the school.

(b) Background

Datta Vasant Pawar, a male Katkari laborer, aged 35 years is married with 3 children. Datta has studied up to 12th grade and his wife studied up to 10th grade. Though Datta was economically poor, he was educated and was progressive.

His educational background certainly inspired him to see that his children were enrolled in school. His eldest daughter aged 14, studies in 8th grade, his second son aged 10 years was in 5th grade and his last son aged 8 years is in 3rd grade.

(c) Course of events

Datta's children did help their parents in household and brick kiln work. But more importantly they went regularly to school.

(d) Analysis

Educational background of Katkari laborers does play a significant role in sending their children to schools. Such parents are conscious about the significance of education of their children in their career.

CASE STUDY 17

(a) Aim of the study

To study the impact of parent's illiteracy on the enrolment of their children in schools.

(b) Background

Mr. and Mrs. XY, a Katkari couple, married with two children, work at a brick kiln in Uchede village, of Pen block in Raigad district of Maharashtra State. Both Mr. and Mrs. XY are illiterate and their parents too were illiterate. Their eldest son is 12 years old and their daughter is 7 years old. Both their children are illiterate. The eldest son work helps the parents in making bricks and by the time he is 15 years of age he will start getting Rs. 100/- per day for the family. The girl who is 7 years is in the process of learning household jobs as well as brick kiln minor jobs, mixing clay, learning to make bricks using blocks, etc.

(c) Course of events

Mr. and Mrs. XY is a young couple, married early and have 2 children. Since their marriage, they have been working as bonded laborers for 13 years. Since both of them have gone through tough times and have realized that only the brick kiln owners are their saviors. They have come to believe that education will not get the food.

(d) Analysis

Illiterate background of Mr. and Mrs. XY, bonded labor status and their parents has made them believe that their children should not go to school. Hence they have not bothered to send their children to school.

CASE STUDY 18

(a) Aim of the study

To assess the facilities of the Government at the brick kiln.

(b) Background

Ransai is a village in Pen block of Raigad district in the State of Maharashtra. There are 3 brick kilns in Ransai. All the 3 kilns have around 26 Katkari families, living in there. Visits to all the 3 kilns revealed that all the 3 kilns did not have the following Government facilities.

- Anganwadi (ICDS unit)
- Zilla Parishad School
- Ration shop
- Bore well/hand pump
- Electricity
- Clinic/Sub-Center

(c) Analysis

Observation of all the 3 kilns revealed that there are no government schemes implemented at the brick kiln site studied. Some Katkari women stated that the ANM's and Anganwadi workers from the neighboring villages do come for immunization of children and women.

CASE STUDY 19

(a) Aim of the Study

To study the annual income of brick kiln labourers.

(b) Background

Jhambhulwadi is a village in Karjat block of Raigad district. The village has two brick kilns. One of the kilns has 9 katkari families. An informal discussion with all the heads of these families revealed that despite of giving Rs. 30,000/- per family every year on paper for the labor services, each family in hand gets Rs. 9,000 – 10,000/- in cash. The Rs. 20,000/- which is deducted from the main corpus fund of Rs. 30,000/ leave the family with Rs. 9,000 to 10,000 only.

(c) Course of events

Vitthal Mukne, a male Katkari aged 35, married with two children is a seasonal migrant to the brick kiln. He along with his family and eight other families from Jambhulwadi migrate to nearby kilns every year. Vitthal narrated the annual income of an average Katkari brick kiln migrant along with other respondents.

(d) Analysis

All the nine Katkari families get cash of Rs. 9,000/- to Rs. 10,000/- per year. These families thus can be categorized as BPL (Below Poverty Line).

CASE STUDY 20

(a) Aim of the study

To study malnutrition among the Katkari children living at brick kilns.

(b) Background

Sitaram Namdev Waghmare, a male Katkari aged 25 years is married to Manisha, aged 23 years and works at a brick kiln in Ransai village of Pen block, Raigad district in the State of Maharashtra. Sitaram got married at the age of 18 years and the age of marriage of his wife was 16 years.

The couple has two children named Drupad, a girl aged 6 years and Sameer, a boy aged 4 years. The daughter goes to 1st grade in the Zilla Parishad School. The boy goes to the village ICDS unit.

(c) Course of the study

During the year 2009-2010, when the researcher visited the Ransai brick kiln, the ages of Drupad and Sameer were 6 years and 4 years respectively. Drupad's height was 3'5" while Sameer's was 2.10 feet. Drupad's weight was 13 kg and Sameer's was 12.5 kg.

(d) Analysis

Data on the age and weight of Drupad and Sameer was compared with the standard four grades protein-energy malnutrition chart as per the classification of IndianAcademy of Pediatrics. It was observed that Sameer aged 4 was classified under grade 1.

Similarly Drupad, aged 6 weighing 13 kg too was in malnutrition grade 1. The researcher also noted down the ages and weights of 3 non-school going Katkari children. Their details are as below:

Age and Weight of Katkari Children

Sr. No.	Name	Sex	Age	Actual Weight	Expected Weight	Grade
1.	Miss DX	F	5	7kg	10.1 kg	II
2.	Miss BX	F	3	10kg	15.6 kg	II
3.	Master SS	M	1	6.5 kg	20.0 kg	II

From the data presented above, it is observed that both school going and non-school going children are malnourished. However, the malnutrition grades of the non-school going children were higher than the ones who attended school. This may be due to the mid-day meal received by the school and Anganwadi children, the care taken by the teachers and the monitoring and supervision of children in the school and Anganwadi by their teachers.

Those children, who did not go to school were deprived of the diet and mid-day meal given by the Anganwadi and the school every day. They had to eat what was available in the house. To conclude, prevalence of malnutrition among Katkari children is very high.

CASE STUDY 21

(a) Aim of the study

To explore the push and pull factors that drives the Katkari families to the brick kilns.

(b) Background

Gagode, a village in Pen block has eight brick kilns. The researcher conducted five focused group interviews for a period of 3 days at 5 brick kilns out of the 8 brick kilns. Each group consisted of 5 to 8 men and 3 to 5 women. The respondents were motivated to answer the reasons for coming to the brick kilns despite the hardships. The research explained them to outline important factors that pushed them to kilns and those that attracted them to the kilns.

Push Factors:An analysis of the five group interviews revealed the following facts.

(a) ***Unemployment:*** They said that there was no "majuri" or "rojgar" back home. Hence they were pushed here.

(b) ***Poverty:*** They were poor. Hence there was no other option other than coming to the kilns.

(c) ***Illiteracy:*** They were not so educated that they would get other jobs.

(d) ***Unskilled labourers:*** They were not skilled enough to get jobs in the companies.

(e) Food and economic crisis – It was difficult to earn in the native place. They did not get to eat food. At the brick kiln, all their weekly expenses were assured.

(f) ***Landless Status:*** If they owned land like the Thakurs, Mahadev, Kolis and Koknas, they would not have worked as brick kiln laborers.

(g) ***Indebtedness:*** Every Katkari family is indebted to the owner. Indebtedness forces them to come here.

(h) ***Bonded labour:*** Since they are indebted heavily, they are bound to the owner. This aspect also forces and pushes them t the kilns.

Pull Factors: All the respondents agreed that three aspects at the brick kilns gave them hope for survival. They are:

(a) ***Kharchi:*** The weekly expenses of Rs. 400 to Rs. 500 given by the owner for food and other daily needs for 6 to 8 months regularly.

(b) *Uchal:* Loan of Rs. 10,000/- to Rs. 25,000/- while going back to the village or any time of the year, without interest.

(c) *Employment Guarantee:* The owners of brick kilns endure employment guarantee.

(c) Analysis

The brick kiln owners are the saviors of the Katkaris. They provide them labour, because the Government does not rescue them out of their miseries. Kharchi and Uchal are the only means of survival. The brick kiln owners are like ATM machines and financial institutes, which do not ask for documents or records from the Katkaris for giving loans.

CASE STUDY 22

(a) Aim of the study

To study the awareness of child rights and bhonga shalas among the Katkari brick kiln laborers.

(b) Background

Jambhulwadi is a village in Karjat block of Raigad district in the state of Maharashtra. The village is exclusively inhabited by the Katkaris. It is geographically situated on the Karjat- Kashale road. From Jambhulwadi up to Karjat there are 15 brick kilns. The researcher visited 10 kilns out of the 15 to study the awareness of the Katkaris about child rights and bhonga shalas. Group discussions were organized in the evenings and some times in the mornings of 5 to 10 males and females.

(c) Awareness about child rights

It was observed that all the respondents interviewed at 10 different brick kiln sites were unaware of the following child rights:

(a) Right to family environment, adoption and other non-institutional services.

(b) Right to parental care, custody and guardianship.

(c) Right against economic exploitation and child labour.

(d) Right to development.
- Right to free and compulsory education.
- Right to play and recreation.

(e) Right to survival.

(f) Right to health.

(g) Right to early childhood.
- Birth registration.
- Immunization.
- Vaccination.
- Nutrition.

(h) Right of child and working mother.

– Day and crèche facility.

(i) A child's right to shelter/housing.

In fact all of them said that they are hearing about this concept for the first time that you arethe first person talking to us about child rights. Since they are busy with work from early mornings to late evenings, no one comes to talk to them. Their owners too do not allow anyone to talk to them.

(d) Awareness about Bhonga Shala

Similarly, their awareness regarding Bhonga Shalas was nil. They had never heard of such schools prior to this meeting.

(e) Analysis

The Katkari brick kiln workers are engrossed so much with their work that they hardly get time to know what is going around them. They are hardly aware of their rights, the development schemes, etc. Achieving brick targets is the main vision they have while they are at the kilns. It was observed that all of them are aware of educational institutes such as the Anganwadi (ICDS), Ashram Schools, Zila Parishad Schools and health institutes such as the sub-centre, primary health center and the gram panchayat.

CASE STUDY 23

(a) Aim of the study

To study the child care practices among the Katkari brick kiln labourers.

(b) Background

Mr. and Mrs.AB, a Katkari young couple works as laborers in a kiln of Jambhulwadi village. The native village of the couple is Ramwadi hamlet of Kotimbe village, in Karjat block of Raigad district in the state of Maharashtra.

Mr. and Mrs.AB have 3 children namely:

1. Ramesh, male, aged 6 years.
2. Suresh, male, aged 4 years.
3. Babita, female, aged 2 years.

Mr. and Mrs.AB start working at the brick kiln at 7:30 am in the morning. The couple and children do not have any thing for breakfast except for a cup of black tea.

(c) Child care at the Kiln

Ramesh, Suresh and Babita too do not have breakfast, except half a cup of black tea with lot of sugar. While the parents are at work the 3 children are in the hut either sleeping or playing. They brush their teeth with salt charcoal powder or ash. They also wash their faces. Their mother is back in the hut by 10 am, while the husband is still at work.

She prepares rice, dal and dry fish curry. By the time her food is ready it is 11am. Her husband and children then have their lunch. By this time, the children who do not attend school are extremely hungry and pounce on the food. At 12 noon, the couple is back at work. The 3 children spend their time in playing around the kiln with other children. It is the duty of Ramesh, the eldest son to take care of his younger brother and younger sister who is 2 years old. At 4 pm, the family is back at home for break. The mother prepares black tea for the family. At 4.30pm the couple is back to work. At 6 pm the mother is back home, while her husband is at the kiln. By 7.30pm the dinner is ready. The mother serves dinner to the children. The father comes back home, washes and goes to the nearby village for a drink. When he is back home by 8pm, he has dinner with his wife and is off to sleep.

This is the daily routine of the family. The children are bathed by the mother twice a week in the afternoon. She takes them to the nearby stream and bathes them. For the rest of the week they do not take a bath. The children are automatically neglected, because the parents have to work to complete their targets.

(d) Analysis

The work target of making 5000 to 7000 bricks a week forces the parents to be at the kiln. No target, no Kharchi. No Kharchi, no food. No work, no Uchal. These factors keep playing a role on the psyche of these distressed seasonal migrants. The children are ultimately neglected of parental care and love.

Only in case of emergency sickness of the children, their mother takes leave. She is with the child the whole day. The brick kiln owner does pay the medical bills, but deducts the amount from their total earnings. Ice-cream, chocolates, biscuits, cookies, cakes, etc are a dream for the children of the Katkari brick kiln labourers.

CASE STUDY 24

(a) Aim of the study

To study the number of clothes an average Katkari brick kiln laborer's child has.

(b) Background

Mrs. FX, aged 20, a married Katkari woman, has a girl child aged 2. Mrs. FX was interviewed by the researcher to find out how many clothes her child has. Mrs. FX told, when her daughter was born, she used to be wrapped in pieces of sari. A bed sheet was used to keep her warm. For one year, the girl did not have a undergarments. Pieces of sari were wrapped around the loins. Three cotton sleeveless frocks were brought from the market till the baby became one year old.

(c) The present scenario

Mrs. FX's girl child is 2 years old. The girl has 2 pairs of frocks and 2 undergarments only. During summer, she does not wear anything except undergarments. The two frocks brought from weekly market costed Rs. 80/- and undergarment of Rs. 20/-. The girl does not have slippers, socks nor shoes.

(d) Analysis

Most children of Katkari brick kiln labourers do not have enough clothes. They therefore suffer from cold, cough, pneumonia, bronchitis, skin diseases. Here again, it is necessary to note that Jackets, sweaters, shoes, slippers, jeans, shorts, cap etc. are a dream to the Katkari children.

CASE STUDY 25

(a) Aim of the study

To study the social, economic and educational status of two Katkari hamlets.

(b) Background

The present case study is based on the research work of Tomar, Y.P.S. and Tribhuwan, Robin (2004) on the Katkaris of two hamlets namely Khairaswadi of Khaparpada and Shitalwadi of Ambivali villages in Pen block of Raigad district in the State of Maharashtra. The basic objective was to unravel the socio-economic and educational status of the Katkaris of the above mentioned two hamlets.

(c) Socio-economic status

A few quantitative variables were taken by the authors. These are as follows:

(i) ***Land holding:*** the study revealed that 85 per cent of the Katkaris of both the hamlets were landless. Well, this is a micro-level situation. The Bench Mark survey conducted by TRTI (2001) states that 83 per cent of Katkaris in TSP Maharashtra are landless.

(ii) ***Poor housing:*** the Bench Mark survey revealed that 82 per cent of the houses of Katkaris in TSP Maharashtra lived in huts with stick walls and thatched or tiled roofs. Te statistics of both the hamlets studied by Tomar and Tribhuwan revealed that only 20 per cent of the Katkaris lived in huts. The reason being an NGO from Bombay which built brick walled and tiled roof houses for Katkaris of Khairaswadi and the Government provide houses to Katkaris of Shitalwadi.

(iii) ***Below the Poverty Line (BPL) Status:*** the micro-level status revealed that 100 per cent of the Katkaris of Khairaswadi and Shitalwadi were below the poverty line, whereas the BMS statistics of TRTI (2001) reveal that 97 per cent of Katkaris in Maharashtra are below the poverty line.

(iv) ***Illiteracy:*** 91.30 per cent of the Katkaris in Khairaswadi and Shitalwadi were illiterate. The BMS data shows that 84 per cent of Katkaris in Maharastra are illiterate.

(d) Analysis

The four basic indicators explained above reveals the crux of the poor socio-economic and educational status of the tribe. Lack of economic aspects and poor socio-economic background has made the Katkaris victims of bonded labour, child labor, hunger crisis, etc.

SOCIO-ECONOMIC BACKGROUND OF KATKARI BRICK-KILN LABOURERS

In order to understand the socio-economic & educational background of the Katkari brick kiln labourers the researcher designed an interview schedule for 100 brick kiln labourers belonging to Katkari Scheduled Tribe. Thus, 100 interview schedules were administered. The main aim was to understand social, economic and educational background, reasons or push factors as well pull factors supported by statistical data that drive them to brick kilns.

The earlier section of this chapter has provided description and interpretations of qualitative data related to the conceptual model conceived through this study in the form of 25 case studies. All the case studies scientifically prove the conceptual model right. To support the model scientifically, an interview schedule was developed to gather quantitative data from 200 respondents out of which 100 were Katkari brick kiln labourers. The quantitative variables reported in the research methodology chapter with regards to the socio-economic and the educational status of the Katkari respondents, the push and pull factors that cause seasonal migration; the factors that push the unfortunate and helpless children of the respondents, into child labour, thereby depriving them of their rights, have been reported in this section of Chapter Three. The analysis and interpretation of both qualitative as well as quantitative data support the model as well as the hypothesis scientifically and positively right.

Block-wise Number of Respondents

The researcher selected 100 Katkari Brick Kiln Labourers as respondents for the study from two blocks of Raigad District, namely Pen and Khalapur. Table 3.1 presents details of the same.

Table 3.1: Block-wise Number of Respondents

Sr.No.	Block	Number	Percentage
1.	Pen	48	48
2.	Khalapur	52	52
	Total	**100**	**100**

Sex-wise Number of Respondents

Out of the 100 respondents 84 were males and 16 were females. Table 3.2 gives details.

Table 3.2: Sex-wise Number of Respondents

Sr. No.	Sex	Number	Percentage
1.	Male	84	84
2.	Female	16	16
	Total	**100**	**100**

Village-wise Number of Respondents

Table 3.3 shows that the Katkari respondents interviewed were from 12 different villages of Pen and Khalapur blocks of Raigad District.

Table 3.3: Village-wise Number of Katkari Respondents

Sr.No.	Status	Number	Percentage
1.	Ambeghar	6	6
2.	Kamarli	6	6
3.	Gagode	18	18
4.	Vashi naka	4	4
5.	Uchede	6	6
6.	Kandlepada	13	13
7.	Ransai	7	7
8.	Kharvai	10	10
9.	Hal Budruk	7	7
10	Navghar	10	10
11.	Beed mangrun	4	4
12.	Jamrung	9	9
	Total	**100**	**100%**

Marital Status of Respondents

As evident from table 3.4, 97 per cent of the respondents interviewed were married, 1 per cent was unmarried, 1 per cent widow and 1 per cent widower.

Table 3.4: Marital Status of Respondents

Sr. No.	Status	Number	Percentage
1.	Married	97	97
2.	Single	01	01
3.	Widow	01	01
4.	Widower	01	01
5.	Separated	0	0
6.	Divorcee	0	0
7.	Deserted	0	0
8.	Others	0	0
	Total	**100**	**100%**

Age of Respondents

It was observed that 94 per cent of the Katkari Brick-kiln labourers studied belonged to the age group 18 to 45 years. This means that these labourers spend their peak time of adulthood in working as bonded labourers. Table 3.5 gives break –up of age-range and percentage of these labourers.

Table 3.5: Age of the Respondents

Sr. No.	Age Range	Number	Percentage
1.	Below 18	01	01
2.	18-25	27	27
3.	25-30	20	20
4.	30-35	17	17
5.	35-40	12	12
6.	40-45	18	18
7.	45-50	03	03
8.	50-55	01	01
9.	55-60	01	01
10.	Above 60	00	00
	Total	**100**	**100%**

Educational Status of Respondents

As evident from table 3.6, 87 per cent respondents studied were illiterate, 7 per cent studied up to primary and 12 per cent up to secondary school. It was however surprising to note that not a single respondent studied up to higher secondary, graduation, post-graduation and other higher studies. This data supports the model conceived in this study. Thus, lack of education according to the study is seen as a major push factor that is responsible for seasonal migration of Katkaris.

Table 3.6: Educational Status of Respondents

Sr. No.	Education	Number	Percentage
1.	Illiterate	81	81
2.	Primary (1-4)	07	07
3.	Secondary (5-10)	12	12
4.	Higher Secondary (11-12)	0	0
5.	Undergraduate	0	0
6.	Graduate	0	0
7.	Post-Graduate	0	0
8.	Diploma	0	0
9.	Others	0	0
	Total	**100**	**100**

Main Occupation

As revealed in table 3.7, 70 per cent of the respondents stated that their main occupation was brick making while 11 stated it was cultivation, 13 per cent were agriculture labour and 6 per cent were daily wage labour.

Table 3.7: Main Occupation

Sr. No.	Occupation	Number	Percentage
1.	Brick making	70	70
2.	Small scale cultivators	11	11
3.	Agriculture Labour	13	13
4.	Daily Wage Labour	06	06
	Total	**100**	**100**

Family Size

The study revealed that 63 per cent of the respondents had family size of 4 members; 32 per cent was of 5 to 6 members while 5 per cent of 7 to 8 members.

Table 3.8: Family Size

Sr. No.	Family Size	Number	Percentage
1.	Upto 4	63	63
2.	5-6	32	32
3.	7-8	05	05
4.	Above 8	0	0
	Total	**100**	**100**

Total Population Covered

Total population of 416 Katkaris comprising of 110 adult males (26%); 109 adult females (26%); 95 male children (23%)and 102 female children (25%) was covered for the study. Table 3.9 present details.

Table 3.9: Total Population Covered

Sr. No.	Family Size	Number	Percentage
1.	Adult males	110	26
2.	Adult females	109	26
3.	Male children	095	23
4.	Female children	102	25
	Total	**416**	**100**

Status of Migration to Brick-kilns

As revealed in table 3.10, 100 per cent respondents studied, migrated to the brick kilns as labourers.

Table 3.10: Status of Migration to Brick Kilns

Sr. No.	Status	Number	Percentage
1.	Migrate	100	100
2.	Do not migrate	00	00
	Total	**100**	**100**

Mode of Transportation

It was observed that 40 per cent of the respondents migrated to the brick kilns by using a truck sent by the owner, 14 per cent by tempo, 27 per cent walked to brick kilns, 6 per cent by bus, 3 per cent by train and 10 per cent by other modes of transportation. Table 3.11 present details.

Table 3.11: Mode of Transportation

Sr. No.	Mode of Transportation	Number	Percentage
1.	Tractor	00	00
2.	Truck	40	40
3.	Bullock Cart	01	01
4.	Bus	06	06
5.	Train	03	03
6.	Tempo	14	14
7.	Walk	27	27
8.	Other (eg.Auto etc.)	09	09
	Total	**100**	**100**

Payment of Transportation

When asked, who bears travel expenses to migrate to the brick kilns. It was observed that the brick kiln owners pay for 64 per cent, 9 per cent pay themselves, when they travel by bus or train. However 27 per cent of the respondents walk to the brick kiln with their family members hence the question of payment does not apply here. Table 3.12 explains it all.

Table 3.12: Bearing of Travel Expenses

Sr.No.	Travel Expenses Paid by	Number	Percentage
1.	Self	09	09
2.	Factory	0	0
3.	Mukadam/Middlemen	0	0
4.	Brick Owner	64	64
5.	Walk	27	27
	Total	**100**	**100**

Status of Employment at the Place of Origin

Here again, as seen in the table 3.13, 100 per cent of the respondents migrated to the brick kilns because of unemployment in the place of origin. Thus, unemployment according to the study is seen as a major push factor that is responsible for seasonal migration of Katkaris.

Table 3.13: Status of Employment at the Place of Origin

Sr. No.	Status	Number	Percentage
1.	Unemployed	100	100
2.	Employed	00	00
	Total	**100**	**100**

Type of Labourers

It was observed that 100 per cent Katkari labourers studied were unskilled. Table 3.14 gives details. Thus, unskilled labour, according to the study is seen as a major push factor that is responsible for seasonal migration of Katkaris.

Table 3.14: Type of Labourers

Sr. No.	Type of Labourers	Number	Percentage
1.	Unskilled	100	100
2.	Skilled	00	00
	Total	**100**	**100**

Land Holding

As clearly shown in the table number 3.15, 67 per cent studied are landless while 33 per cent had land. Details of the same are given in the table 3.15.

Table 15: Landholding Status of Respondents

Sr. No.	Status	Number	Percentage
1.	Landholders	33	33
2.	Landless	67	67
	Total	**100**	**100**

Type of Cultivable Land

Out of 33 Katkaris brick kiln labourers who owned land, 31 i.e. 94 per cent owned non-irrigated land while only 2 i.e. 6 per cent. This table certainly justifies that cultivation was the main occupation of the some respondents while brick kiln labour was subsidiary occupation for them.

Table 3.16: Type of Land

Sr. No.	Status	Number	Percentage
1.	Non-irrigated	31	94
2.	Irrigated	02	06
	Total	**33**	**100**

Acre-wise Land Owned

Table 3.17 shows that 58 per cent owned 1 to 3 acres of land, 27 per cent up to 3 to 6 acres, 12 per cent up to 6 to 9 acres and only 1 per cent owned land above 9 acres. It was also observed through focused group interviews that most of them do not cultivate rice on their land as there is no irrigation facility, and the quality of land is not for rice cultivation.

Table 3.17: Acre-wise Land Holding

Sr. No.	Area of Land in Acres	Number	Total
1.	1-3 Acres	19	58%
2.	3-6 Acres	09	27%
3.	6-9Acres	04	12%
4.	Above 9 Acres	01	3%
	Total	**33**	**100%**

Status of Housing at the Place of Origin

As per table 3.18, 91 per cent of the respondents stated that they have their own house in the place of origin, while 9 per cent said that they did not possess own house. Table 3.19, reveals that 91 per cent of the houses were with stick walls and thatched roof 6 per cent were with stick walls and tiles while 3 per cent were with tiled roof and brick walls. Table 3.20 reveals that 42 per cent of house owners had houses of an area less than 100 sq.ft.; 19 per cent between 100 to 200 sq.fft.; 31 per cent owned 201 to 300 sq.ft. while 8 per cent owned between 301 to 500 sq.ft.

Table 3.18: Possession of Own House at the Place of Origin

Sr. No.	Status	Number	Total
1.	Possess	91	91
2.	Do not possess	09	09
	Total	**100**	**100**

Table 3.19: Type of House at the Place of Origin

Sr. No.	Type of House	Number	Total
1.	Stick walls & thatched roof	91	91
2.	Stick walls with tiled roof	06	06
3.	Brick walls with tiled roof	03	03
	Total	**100**	**100**

Table 3.20: Area of House at the Place of Origin

Sr. No.	Area of Land in Acres	Number	Total
1.	Less than 100 Sq.ft	42	42
2.	100 to 200 sq.ft.	19	19
3.	200 to 300 sq.ft.	31	31
4.	300 to 500 sq.ft.	08	08
5.	Above 500sq.ft.	00	00
	Total	**100**	**100**

Status of Housing at the Place of Destination

As per table 3.21, 100 per cent of the respondents stated that they do not have their own house at the place of destination. Table 3.22, reveals that maximum i.e. 35 per cent houses made up of raw bricks and thatched or tin roof, 22 per cent of the houses were with stick walls and thatched roof 11 per cent were with brick walls tiled or tin sheet roof while 30 per cent of the houses were grass huts and only 2 per cent were with other type of houses. Table 3.23 reveals that 55 per cent of houses were of an area between 51 to 100 sq.ft ; 30 per cent them of an area less than 50 sq.ft.; 11 per cent between 100 to 150 sq.ft.; 2 per cent between 151 to 200 sq.ft while 1 per cent between 201 to 250 sq.ft and only 1 per cent of an area above 300 sq.ft.

Table 3.21: Possession of Own House at the Place of Destination

Sr. No.	Status	Number	Total
1.	Do not possess	100	100
2.	Possess	00	00
	Total	**100**	**100**

Table 3.22: Type of House at the Place of Destination

Sr. No.	Status	Number	Percentage
1.	Raw Bricks thatched/tin roof	35	35
2.	Thatched roof with stick walls	22	22
3.	Brick walls with tiled/tin roof	11	11
4.	Grass hut	30	30
5.	Others	02	02
	Total	**100**	**100**

Table 3.23: Area of House at the Place of Destination

Sr. No.	Status	Number	Percentage
1.	Less than 50 sq.ft	30	30
2.	51 to 100 sq.ft	55	55
3.	101 to 150 sq.ft	11	11
4.	151 to 200 sq.ft	02	02
5.	201 to 250 sq.ft	01	01
6.	251 to 300 sq.ft.	00	00
7.	Above 300 sq.ft	01	01
	Total	**100**	**100**

It is clear from tables 3.18, 3.19 and 3.20 that the houses owned by the Katkaris in the place of origin are poorly constructed, small in nature and do not have economic value as compared to the houses of economically well off tribes and caste groups. Poor housing conditions of the Katkaris at the place of origin have been identified as one of the major push factors of seasonal migration in this study. Similarly, it was observed that the housing conditions in place of destination are still worse as compared to the conditions of the houses at the place of origin. Tables 3.21, 3.22, and 3.23 highlight the conditions of the houses at the place of destination.

Position of Hearth

It is clear from the table 3.24 that maximum i.e. 73 per cent of the respondents were having their hearths inside the house, while 25 per cent of them were having the hearths outside their houses and 2 per cent were having hearths both inside and outside the house. Hearths situated in small houses gives rise to smoke in the houses, which further leads to breathing problems, as carbon-di-oxide is directly inhaled especially by women and children. The main reason for having hearths inside the house as revealed by the respondents was that during winter season live coal in the hearth creates warmth. Secondly, cooking in the house also is an act of preventing evil eye while the food is being cooked.

Table 3.24: Position of Hearth

Sr. No.	Status	Number	Percentage
1.	Inside the house	73	73
2.	outside the house	25	25
3.	Both	02	02
	Total	**100**	**100**

Sleeping Place

It is observed that 83 per cent of the respondents sleep inside the house though the area of house is less, to protect themselves from snake bites & scorpion stings. Another reason is to protect them from severe cold. 12 per cent of them sleep either inside or outside while 5 per cent of them prefer to sleep outside the house. However, during the months of April and May i.e during summer season they sleep outside, with dogs and cats around them.

Table 3.25: Sleeping Place

Sr.No.	Status	Number	Percentage
1.	Inside the house	83	83
2.	outside the house	05	05
3.	Both	12	12
	Total	**100**	**100**

Availability of Electricity

Out of 100 respondents, 52 stated that there is no source of electricity in their houses at the place of destination while only 12 i.e.12 per cent said that there is availability of the electricity. 36 per cent of them stated that there is a common source of electricity that is a single tube-light or bulb among two or three houses provided by the brick kiln owner.

Table 3.26: Availability of Electricity

Sr. No.	Status	Number	Percentage
1.	Available	12	12
2.	Not Available	52	52
3.	Common Source	36	36
	Total	**100**	**100**

Facility of Drainage

Table 3.27 shows that 100 per cent of the respondents stated that there is no facility of drainage system at the brick kilns as well as at the place of origin.

Table 3.27: Facility of Drainage

Sr. No.	Status	Number	Percentage
1.	Available	00	00
2.	Not Available	100	100
	Total	**100**	**100**

Facility of Bathrooms and Toilets

The most basic and important facilities are availability of bathrooms and toilets. It is evident from the tables 3.28 and 3.29 that 100 per cent of the respondents stated that there is no facility of bathroom and toilets respectively.

Table 3.28: Facility of Bathrooms

Sr. No.	Status	Number	Percentage
1.	Available	00	00
2.	Not Available	100	100
	Total	**100**	**100**

Table 3.29: Facility of Toilets

Sr. No.	Status	Number	Percentage
1.	Available	00	00
2.	Not Available	100	100
	Total	**100**	**100**

Source of Drinking Water

As per the table 3.30, 48 per cent of the respondents were getting drinking water from bore-well, 23 per cent were getting it from tap while 21 per cent of them were fetching it from the village wells and 8 per cent of them were fetching it from small pothole near the stream. The water fetched from the dug potholes near stream is impure and unclean; hence children as well as the brick kiln labourers often suffer from digestive disorders. They are deprived of the right to drink pure and clean water.

Table 3.30: Source of Drinking Water

Sr. No.	Source	Number	Percentage
1.	Well	21	21
2.	Tap	23	23
3.	Stream	0	00
4.	Bore Well	48	48
6.	Water tanker	0	0
7.	Pond	0	0
8.	Hand Pump	0	0
9.	River	0	0
10.	Others	0	0
11.	Pothole near a stream	8	08
	Total	**100**	**100**

Annual Income

One of the most important indicators in this study is annual income of the family. As per the table 3.31, 82 per cent of the families are below poverty line and only 10 per cent are above poverty line and their annual income range is minimum Rs. 20,001/- to maximum Rs. 80,000/-. Here again, it is very important to note that remaining 8 per cent of the families were having income ranging from Rs. -1000/- to Rs. -20,000/- this means these 8 per cent of the respondents still have to repay loan, which they will pay in the next season by working on the same brick kiln.

Table 3.31: Annual Income of the Family

Sr. No.	Source	Number	Percentage
1.	Up to Rs. 20,000/-	82	82
2.	Rs. 20,000 to 40,000/-	08	08
3.	Rs. 40,000 to 60,000/-	01	01
4.	Rs. 60,000 to 80,000/-	01	01
6.	Above Rs. 80,000/-	00	00
7.	Rs. -1,000 to -5,000/-	04	04
8.	Rs. -5,000 to -10,000/-	03	03
9.	Rs.-10,000 to -20,000/-	01	01
	Total	**100**	**100**

Bonded Labourer

It was observed that 86 per cent of the respondents were hooked into the bonded labour. The inability to clear the debt forced the couple, their brother or any other family members to come and work for the forthcoming years. Table 3.32 reveals it all.

Table 3.32: Bonded Labourer

Sr. No.	Status	Number	Percentage
1.	Bonded Labourers	86	86
2.	Non-bonded labourers	14	14
	Total	**100**	**100**

Borrowing Loan while Returning Home

As aptly shown in tables 3.33 and 3.34, 86 per cent of the Katkari brick kiln labourers take loan while returning home. They take Rs. 12,000/- to 25,000/- depending upon their need. The amount rises, if there is a wedding or some ritual in the family.

Table 3.33: Frequency of Borrowing Loan while Returning Home

Sr. No.	Status	Number	Percentage
1.	Borrow	86	86
2.	Do not borrow	14	14
	Total	**100**	**100**

Source of Borrowing Loan

Majority of the Katkari brick kiln labourers interviewed i.e. 84 per cent borrowed loan from the brick kiln owners, while 2 per cent from other sources such as farm owner at the place of origin. It can be concluded that the kiln owners are banks, ATM machines and credit cards for the Katkari labourers. They are the main source of money, food and survival. Our respondents said that they are better off at the brick kilns than back home, because they get food and money regularly from the owner for 6 to 8 months.

Table 3.34: Source of Borrowing Loan

Sr. No.	Status	Number	Percentage
1.	Contractor	0	00
2.	Mukadam	0	00
3.	Brick kiln owner	84	84
4.	Other	02	02
5.	N A	14	14
	Total	**100**	**100**

Possession of Livestock

37 per cent of the respondents studied did not possess live stock, while 63 per cent did not possess. Those who possessed live stock, stated they had chickens, goats, sheep, cow and bulls. Table 3.35 presents details.

Table 3.35: Possession of Livestock

Sr. No.	Status	Number	Percentage
1.	Possess	37	37
2.	Do not possess	63	63
	Total	**100**	**100**

Collection of Minor Forest Produce

As revealed in table 3.36 100 per cent of the respondents collected Minor Forest Produce, such as fire wood, fruits, gum, grass, leaves, Mahua flowers, Karvi sticks etc. from the forest. Table 3.36 gives details.

Table 3.36: Collect Minor Forest Produce

Sr. No.	Status	Number	Percentage
1.	Collect	100	100
2.	Do not Collect	00	00
	Total	**100**	**100**

Sale of Minor Forest Produce (MFP)

As revealed in table 3.37, only 21 per cent of the respondent sold minor forest produce when asked what they sell. The respondents replied fire wood is sold, both at the place of origin and destination. They sell fire wood to non-tribals and get Rs. 15 to 25 per bundle or head load. This money is used for daily expense

Table 3.37: Sale/Barter of MFP

Sr. No.	Status	Number	Percentage
1.	Sale	21	21
2.	Do not sale (for domestic use)	79	79
	Total	**100**	**100**

Hunting

Although hunting is ill-legal, the Katkaris do hunt birds, wild boars, hare, field mice, bandicoots etc. Hunting is usually carried out in winter and summer.

Snakebite and Scorpion Sting Cases

As seen in table 3.38, 13 per cent of the families of respondents experienced scorpion sting and snake bite problems while working at the brick kilns and staying in temporary houses. Majority of the Katkari brick kiln labourers keep cats and dogs in their houses at work place, so as to prevent snake bites and scorpion stings. The cats and dogs guard the families from snakes and scorpions while they are in the home or asleep.

Table 3.38: Cases of Snake or Scorpion Bite at Workplace

Sr. No.	Status	Number	Percentage
1.	Yes	13	13
2.	No	87	87
	Total	**100**	**100**

Social, Food, Health and Economic Security

All most all the respondents interviewed unanimously said there is no social and economic security at the place of origin. Their owner, the feudal lords, their saviors provide them social, economic, food and health security at the place of destination.

Number of Working Hours

Since the survival of the Katkari brick kiln labourers depend a lot on the number of bricks produced by them daily, weekly and monthly to achieve the target given by the owner. They are forced to work for 10 to 12 hours a day and even more. As rightly depicted in table 3.39 it is seen 23 per cent work between 8 to 10hours; 71 per cent work between 10 to 12 hours while 6 per cent work between 12 to 14 hours a day, for small financial earnings.

Table 3.39: Number of Working Hours

Sr. No.	Working Hours	Number	Percentage
1.	8 -10 hrs	23	23
2.	10 -12hrs	71	71
3.	12-14 hrs	06	06
4.	above 14 hrs	0	0
	Total	**100**	**100**

Possession of Documents

As compared to Bhils, the Katkaris do not possess important documents such as ration card (40%); election card (61%); land documents (18%); scheduled tribe certificate (7%); house property papers (55%) etc. This certainly reveals that the degree of awareness among the Katkaris regarding the significance of important documents is less than Bhils. This perhaps due to high illiteracy (81%) rate as compared to Bhils. Table 4.40, however reveals an important fact, that only 8 per cent of the Katkaris studied possessed bank pass book. This indicate that majority of them do not have money to save as they are hooked into debt and bonded labour. These respondents were educated and possessed irrigated agriculture land from 3 to 9 to acres and above.

Table 3.40: Possession of Documents

Sr. No.	Documents	Number	Percentage
1.	Ration Card	40	40
2.	Election card	61	61
3.	Identity card	03	03
4.	Birth certificate	13	13
5.	Marriage certificate	01	01
6.	Death Certificate	02	02
7.	Bank'sPass Book	08	08
8.	School leaving certificate	10	10
9.	Land documents	18	18
10.	House property papers	55	55
11.	Caste/Tribe certificate	07	07
12.	Any other	00	00
13.	No documents	05	05

Absence of Economic and Financially Valuable Assets

The data revealed in table 3.41 shows that 33 per cent of the respondents studied owned agricultural land. The same table shows that 91 per cent of the them owned houses at the place of origin. However after probing in detail it was observed that 2 to 3 families owned agricultural land as a result of which the yield reaped was meager and insufficient, hence agricultural land as an immovable asset possessed by the respondents was not really economically usefully productive. Further, the land possessed by them was non-irrigated. It was also observed that the economic value of this land was far less in the tribal area. Thus, as per the conceptual model evolved absence of economic assets or absence of financially valuable assets becomes a key push factor in distress seasonal migration among the Katkari Brick kiln labourers.

Table 3.41: Possession of Immovable Assets

Sr. No.	Immovable Assets	Number	Percentage
1.	Agricultural land	33 (out of 100 respondents)	33
2.	House	91 (out of 100 respondents)	91

As evident from table 3.42 it was observed that majority of the respondents did not have valuable movable assets such as gold, silver, hard cash, cupboard, TV , tape recorder, radio, utensils, mobile phones, mobikes, beds, cots, etc. except live stock. Few of them who possess movable items like TV set, Bed, kerosene stove etc. they never carry it to the place of destination but keep in their own house at the place of origin.

Table 3.42: Possession of Movable Assets

Sr. No.	Movable Assets	Number
1.	Gold/Silver Ornaments	00
2.	Hard Cash	00
3.	Cupboard	00
4.	TV set	02
5.	Taperecorder/Radio	03
6.	Mobile Phones	00
7.	Beds/Cots	06
8.	Mobikes	00
9.	Live stock	37
10.	Gas Cylinder	00
11.	Kerosene Stove	06

BACKGROUND OF KATKARI CHILDREN AT THE BRICK KILNS

Before getting into the child labour and child rights issues of the Katkari children, it would be appropriate at this juncture to present the background of the Katkari children at the brick kilns. 100 families studied had a population of 110 adult males, 109 adult females, 95 male children and 102 female children amounting to a total population of 416 Katkaris. The details of the total 197 children are given as below.

Age-range Wise Number of Children

As evident from the table 3.43, out of 197 children, 8 per cent of the children belonged to age-range 0 to 1 year, out of these 2 per cent were male and 2 per cent were female children; 79 i.e. 40 per cent between 1 to 5 years, out of these 18 per cent were male and 22 per cent were female children; 57 i.e. 29 per cent between 5 to 10 years, out of these 15 per cent were male and 14 per cent were female children; 41 i.e.21 per cent between 10 to 15 years, out of these 9 per cent were male and 12 per cent were female children and remaining 12 i.e. 6 per cent belonged to age range 15 to 18 years, out of these 9 i.e.5 per cent were male and 3 i.e.1 per cent were female children.

Table 3.43: Age-wise Number of Children

Sr. No.	Age Range	Number		Total
		Male	Female	
1.	Upto 1 yr	04 (2%)	04 (2%)	08 (4%)
2.	1-5 yrs	35 (18%)	44 (22%)	79 (40%)
3.	5 to 10 yrs	29(15%)	28 (14%)	57(29%)
4.	10 to 15 yrs	18 (9%)	23(12%)	41(21%)
5.	15 to 18 yrs	09 (5%)	03 (1%)	12 (6%)
	Total	**95**	**102**	**197 (100%)**

Schooling Status of Children

As evident from table 3.44, out of 197 children 74 i.e. 38 per cent of the children were school going, out of that 20 per cent were male children and 18 per cent were female children; 103 i.e. 52 per cent were non-school going children, out of that 23 per cent were male children and 29 per cent were female children; 20 i.e. 10 per cent children were drop outs, out of these 10 i.e. 5 per cent were male children and 10 i.e.5 per cent were female children. Thus, nearly 62 per cent of the children were deprived from getting education. Those going to school had to compromise with the poor housing conditions and lack of electricity in the place of destination as well as origin.

Table 3.44: Schooling Status of Children

Sr. No.	Schooling Status	Number of Children		Total
		Male	Female	
1.	School going	39 (20%)	35 (18%)	074 (38%)
2.	Non-school going	46 (23%)	57 (29%)	103 (52%)
3.	Drop outs	10 (5%)	10 (5%)	020 (10%)
	Total	**95 (48%)**	**102 (52%)**	**197 (100%)**

Note: Figures in bracket indicate percentage.

Educational Status of Children

As seen in the table 3.45, out of 197 children maximum i.e. 104 (53%) were illiterate, out of these 24 per cent were male children and 29 per cent were female children; 26 i.e.13 per cent attend Anganwadi i.e. pre-primary school, out of these 5 per cent were male and 7 per cent were female children; 49 i.e. 25 per cent studied up to primary school, out of these 13 per cent were male and 12 per cent were female children; 18 i.e. only 9 per cent studied up to secondary school, out of these 6 per cent were male and 3 per cent were female children. Interestingly, not a single child out of total 197 children was found to study up to higher secondary, graduation, post graduation. This certainly proves that daily wage labourer for survival is more essential to Katkari kids than education. This data further proves that daily wage labour and domestic work is more important than education especially for the girl child. The statistics in the table also prove that the Katkari children at the brick kilns are deprived of their Right to Education.

Table 3.45: Educational Status of Katkari Children

Sr. No.	Educational Status	Number		Total
		Male	Female	
1.	Illiterate	46 (23%)	57 (29%)	103 (52%)
2.	Anganwadi (Pre-primary)	12 (6%)	14 (7%)	26 (13%)
3.	Primary (1-4)	26 (13%)	24 (12%)	50 (25%)
4.	Secondary (5-10)	11 (6%)	07 (4%)	18 (10%)
6.	Higher Secondary (11-12)	00	00	00
7.	Undergraduate	00	00	00
8.	Graduate	00	00	00
9.	Post-Graduate	00	00	00
10.	Diploma	00	00	00
	Total	**95 (48%)**	**102 (52%)**	**197 (100%)**

Note: Figures in bracket indicate percentage.

Right to Recreational Facilities

All the 100 re:pondents said that there were no recreational facilities for children at the brick kiln. This proves that the children are deprived of their right to recreation.

Table 3.46: Recreational Facilities

Sr. No.	Status	Number	Percentage
1.	Available	00	00
2.	Not available	100	100
	Total	**100**	**100**

Right to Parental Care

All most all the respondents stated that for 8 to 10 hours their children get neglected. The parents get less time to care for their children. Nursing mothers take off 10 to 20 minutes to feed their children, but over all parental care during the day time is lacking. This certainly proves that the children of brick kiln labourers are deprived of their right to parental care.

Right to Decent Housing

As reported in tables 3.19 and 3.22, the conditions of housing of Katkari labourers is poor both at the place of origin as well as at the place of destination. The children are certainly deprived of right to decent housing.

Nutritional Status of Katkari Children

Out of the total 197 Katkari children, belonging to families of 100 respondents, the researcher was able to get age, height and weight of 178 Children. Nutritional status of these 178 children was plotted in I to IV grades according to International Standards. Table 3.47 presents nutritional status of 178 children.

Table 3.47: Nutritional Status of Katkari Children

Sr. No.	Gradations	Number	Percentage
1.	Normal	34	19
2.	Grade I (Mild Malnutrition)	51	29
3.	Grade II (Moderate Malnutrition)	54	30
4.	Grade III (Severe Malnutrition)	28	16
6.	Grade IV (Severe Malnutrition)	11	06
	Total	**178**	**100**

It is clear from the above table that 144 i.e. 81 per cent of Katkari children are malnourished. This means they are deprived of their right to nutrition and health.

Diet during Pregnancy

As per the table 3.48, 98 per cent of the women do not get special or adequate diet necessary during pregnancy while only 2 per cent of the women get some special food like seasonal fruits, meat etc. during pregnancy. Inadequate and insufficient food during pregnancy leads to the birth of underweight and malnourished children. Apart from this, it also affects health of mother to a great extent.

Table 3.48: Diet during Pregnancy

Sr. No.	Status	Number	Percentage
1.	Get special diet	02	02
2.	Do not get special diet	98	98
	Total	**100**	**100**

Place of Delivery

As per table 3.49 it is clear 92 per cent of the deliveries were conducted at home in the native place of the respondent, while 3 per cent at the work site i.e. at the brick kiln. Only 4 per cent of the deliveries were conducted at Government and Private hospital.

Table 3.49: Place of Delivery

Sr. No.	Gradations	Number	Percentage
1.	Khopi (hut at work site)	03	03
2.	Home at Native Place	92	92
3.	PHC	01	01
4.	Rural Hospital	00	00
5.	Govt. Hospital	03	03
6.	Private Hospital	01	01
	Total	**100**	**100**

Personnel Conducting Delivery

Out of 100, 94 per cent of the respondents stated that the deliveries were conducted by Dai i.e. village Midwife at home while 3 per cent deliveries were conducted by Aged women at worksite and only 3 per cent of the deliveries were conducted by doctor and 1 per cent was by an ANM.

Table 3.50: Personnel who Conducts Delivery

Sr. No.	Gradations	Number	Percentage
1.	Dai/Suine	93	93
2.	ANM	01	01
3.	Trained Midwife	00	00
4.	Doctor	03	03
5.	Gynecologist	00	00
6.	Elderly women at work site	03	01
	Total	**100**	**100**

When do women start working after delivery?

Table 3.49 throws light on number of days after delivery when women start working on Kilns. As per the table given below maximum i.e.60 per cent said that they started working after 30 days of delivery while 17 per cent told that they started working after one and half month i.e. 45 days after the delivery. 18 per cent of the women start working after 15 day while 5 per cent of them start working after 7 days of delivery. This is because of extreme need of earning money for survival.

Table 3.51: Number of Days when Women Start Working after Delivery

Sr. No.	Days	Number	Percentage
1.	After 2 days	00	00
2.	After 7 days	05	05
3.	After 15 days	18	18
4.	After 30 days	60	60
5.	Any other	17	17
	Total	**100**	**100**

Care of Sick Child

Table 3.52 throws light on how brick kiln labourers take care of their sick child. Out of total 100 parents, 28 per cent said that one of the parents take leave and take care of sick child while 24 per cent take leave only if the child is serious. 12 per cent of them said that woman in the house generally take care of sick child and if she is working then she only take leave, instead of her husband; 11 per cent of them keep child with other elder children at the worksite house while 10 per cent of them keep the child with grandparents at the native place so that parents of the child can be tension free. From this we can say that the children of brick kiln labourers are deprived of their right to parental care.

Table 3.52: Care of Sick Child

Sr. No.	Care of Sick Child	Number	Percentage
1.	One of parents take leave	28	28
2.	If serious both take leave	24	24
3.	Keep child with other elder children at work site house	11	11
4.	Woman in the house/if she is working she takes leave	12	12
5.	No child	06	06
6.	Keep the child with grandparents in native village	10	10
	Total	**100**	**100**

Vaccination of Children

It is evident from the table 3.53 that 72 per cent of the Katkari parents have vaccinated their children, while 23 per cent of them have not vaccinated their children. When asked, which vaccines have you given to your children most of them told that they have given polio dose to their children? Hardly any one of them has given other vaccines like Hepatitis B, Hepatitis C, Smallpox, chickenpox, booster etc. to their children. Those who have given their children Polio dose is may be because of Anganwadi workers, PHC nurse, ANM, NGOs are voluntarily going to the brick kilns providing this facility at their doorstep.

Table 3.53: Vaccination of Children

Sr. No.	Vaccination Status	Number	Percentage
1.	Vaccinated	72	72
2.	Not vaccinated	23	23
3.	No child	05	05
	Total	**100**	**100**

CHILD LABOUR AT THE BRICK KILNS

The Katkari respondents revealed through informal interviews, that a girl starts learning household work between the ages 7 to 10 years, as she gets married between 15 to 18 years of age. She must learn all the household work before she gets married. Boys too start helping parents between the age 8 to 10. Table given below portray separately the percentage of male and female children involved in child labour to help the parents meet their brick making targets and work at the kilns to make money. The tables also reveal male and female children engaged in household work, whether or not they are attending school or even working to earn money at the kilns.

Table 3.54: Working Status of Male and Female Children

Sr. No.	Working Status	Number		Percentage
		Male	Female	
1.	Working at the kilns	15 (8%)	05 (2%)	020 (10%)
2.	Not working	20 (10%)	32 (16%)	052 (26%)
3.	Working to help parents	60 (31%)	65 (33%)	125 (64%)
	Total	**95 (48%)**	**102 (52%)**	**197 (100%)**

Note: Figures in bracket indicate percentage.

The table above certainly shows that 10 per cent katkari children are involved in child labour 64 per cent work to help parents meet their work targets. This certainly proves that these unfortunate and helpless children get exploited economically and are forced into child labour, because of the poor socio-economic conditions, bonded labour, indebtedness of their parents. Meeting daily, weekly and monthly brick making target is yet another reason why they pushed into child labour.

CHILD LABOUR AND RIGHTS ISSUES AMONG THE KATKARI BRICK KILN LABOURERS: ANALYTICAL REFLECTIONS

Child labour and rights issues among the Katkari brick kiln labourers cannot be studied in isolation, without understanding their socio-economic background and reasons for migration. The qualitative data presented in the form of 25 case studies in this chapter, along with quantitative data presented, analyzed and interpreted in the form of tables supports the model and the hypothesis developed in this study.

The poor Katkari brick kiln labourers migrate seasonally to the kilns because of the following push factors:

1. **Poverty**: This study revealed that 90 per cent of the Katkari brick kiln labourers were below the poverty line. Tomar Y.P.S and Tribhuwan Robin (2004) in their study on the Katkaris revealed that 100 per cent of the Katkaris studied were Below the Poverty Line. Further, the Bench Mark Survey carried out by the Tribal Research and Training Institute, Pune revealed that 97.14 per cent of the Katkaris in Maharashtra were Below the Poverty Line. In fact, Katkaris are one of the most socially, economically and educationally backward tribes of Maharashtra. The Government of India, Ministry of Tribal Affairs, has clarified the tribe as Particularly Vulnerable Tribal Groups (PVTGs).

   Poverty is no doubt, one of the main push factors that push them to the brick kilns.

2. **Unemployment in the place of origin:** The data revealed that 100 per cent of the migrants were unemployed and hence were forced to migrate to the kilns.
3. **Unskilled Labourers:** 100 per cent of the respondents were unskilled and therefore migrated to the kilns.
4. **Landless Nature:** The data revealed that 67 per cent of the respondents were landless. Those who owned meager land could not produce enough food grains to sustain for the entire year and hence migrated.
5. **Poor housing conditions:** As explained in this chapter the conditions of Katkari houses is very poor in the place of destination.
6. **Illiteracy:** It was observed that 81 per cent of respondents studied were illiterate. The Bench Mark Survey by TRTI, (2001) revealed that 83.62 per cent of the Katkaris were illiterate. High rate among Katkaris is yet another factor that hinders their development. They cannot get jobs in private and Government sectors; hence they migrate to the kilns.
7. **Indebtedness:** The data revealed that 86 per cent of the brick kiln labourers were indebted. They borrow Rs. 10,000/- to Rs. 25,000/- from the brick kiln owners. This amount is repaid in the form of labour, the following year. The kiln owner deducts loan amount, food, medical and other expenses and the remaining money is given to them. The balance money is hardly Rs. 2000 to 5000/-, the labourers are therefore forced to take more loan while returning home and hence get trapped into bonded labour.
8. **Bonded Labour:** Data in this study revealed that 86 per cent of the brick kiln labourers were hooked into bonded labour, for their inability to clear debt.
9. **Economic and hunger crisis:** Economic and hunger crisis in the place of origin is yet another factor that push the Katkaris to the brick kilns. Bhatia Arun and Tribhuwan Robin (2002) stressed these aspects of economic and hunger crisis among the Katkaris in their study captioned, "The Truth about Malnutrition Deaths."
10. **Lack of economic assets:** Other than few vessels, clothes and bed sheets, the Katakari brick kiln labourers do not possess any economic assets both in the place of origin and at the place of destination. This aspect is seen in most nomadic societies. Lack of economic assets is yet another reason for migration among the Katkaris.
11. **Kharchi and Uchal-pull factors : Their hope of survival** – Despite of the long hours of hard work in hot and cold conditions, the poor living conditions at the brick kilns, the exploitation by the owners, indebtedness and bonded labour, the brick kiln owners are the saviors of the labourers. They are ATM machines, finance institutions and debit cards for the Katkaris. They provide money to their labourers any time

during the year. The Katkari labourers get food and expenses for 6 to8 months. The adults and children are able to survive because of the brick kiln owners, who provide them jobs. Hence 'Kharchi' (weekly expenses) and 'Uchal' (Loan) are considered by the respondents as their hope of survival. The researcher rates these two pull factors as the main factors for seasonal migration among the Katkaris.

12. **Lack of Adult Manpower:** The 100 Katkari brick kiln labourer's families studied comprises of 110 adult males (26%),109 i.e. (26%) of adult females and 197 (48%) of children,. On an average every Katkari family had 2 to 5 children living at the kilns. If one analyses the number of adults per family, it comprised mainly of father and mother and in some cases father in law or another member. As compared to the quantum or workload, two or three adults could find it difficult to achieve the same. It is because of this reason, children especially those belonging to the age range 7 to 14 years were forced to participate in activities such as transporting the bricks, mixing clay in water, arranging bricks etc. These children helped their parents to achieve work targets, as well as managed to take care of their younger siblings, managed household work, took care of pets, while some attended school. It was also observed that children between the age 15 to 18 received wages from the brick kiln owner depending on the type of labour and number of hours incurred. Thus, the wages of these teenagers ranged from Rs. 50 to 100 per day. This was also a sought of training to work as adult before getting married and learning how to earn money on one's own.

13. **What is important, survival, child labour or child rights?** – From an etic (outsider's) perspective this question is sensitive, it is linked with human and child rights etc. the emic (insider's) perspective is however contradictory. To the Katkari, the brick kiln labourers, the owners are their saviors, banks, ATM machines and debit cards because the Employment Guarantee Scheme and other Government schemes do not provide them employment, food, clothing, shelter, medicine and other basic necessities of life. Therefore exploitation, bonded labour, child labour, deprivation of child rights to the Katkaris at the brick kilns are not so important as compared to the jobs they get to survive at the brick kilns.

    Given this background, let us look in to child labour and child rights issues among the Katkari brick kiln labourers.

14. **Child Labour Issues:** It was observed that out of 197 children of the 100 families studied 125 i.e. 64 per cent were working at the brick kilns to support their parents so as to achieve their work targets. These children also attended school while some of them were drop outs and a few did not go to school at all. Out of the total number of children who worked to support the parents 60 i.e. 31 per cent were males and

65 i.e. 33 per cent were females. Further, 10 per cent of children were exclusively child labourers, who were paid wages between Rs. 50/- to 100/-. Thus in all out of 197 children belonging to the 100 families studied 145 i.e. 74 per cent can be branded as child labourers. It is also pertinent to note that the remaining 52 i.e. 26 per cent of children who were forced to accompany their parents to the brick kilns were also deprived of child rights.

As mentioned earlier child labour in this study has been classified into following categories:

(a) Child labourers who support the parents to achieve work targets by helping the parents in doing small jobs such as transporting and arranging bricks; loading and unloading baked bricks, charcoal, mud, mixing clay and straw. These children also manage domestic work, attend school. These children do not receive anything in cash from the brick kiln owners. These children belong to the age range between 6 to 10 years.

(b) Child Labourers who are paid by the owners. These are children who are better in making bricks mixing clay with straw, arranging unbaked bricks in the furnace. They are paid daily wages by the owners depending on the type of work per day. In the second category of child labourers the children are mostly drop outs and belong to the age group 15 to 18 years. It is during this period the parents look for suitable mates/spouses so as to get them married.

Nature of Child Labour – The hazardous aspect of child labour as regards to brick making is the exposure of children to heat of the furnace, dust released from the clay and charcoal, extreme hot and cold conditions and finally the long number of working hours at the kilns. Besides this, these children also become victims of the unhealthy environment, unclean drinking water, food exposed to dust etc. The children as well as their parents sometimes become pray to scorpion stings and snake bites.

15. **Child Rights Issues:** Forced migration of the parents due to utter poor economic conditions, indebtedness, bonded labour, lack of employment opportunities in the place of origin, landlessness, unskilled nature of labour etc. factors push them to the kilns. This in turn directly affects the growth and progress of their children who are dependent on them for survival.

Given below are statistics that prove how the children of Katkari brick kiln labourers are deprived of their rights.

(a) **Child Labour:** It was observed that out of 197 children of the 100 families studied 125 i.e. 64 per cent were working at the brick kilns to support their parents so as to achieve their work targets.

Out of the total number of children who worked to support the parents 60 i.e. 31 per cent were males and 65 i.e.33 per cent were females. Further, 10 per cent of children were exclusively child labourers, who were paid wages between Rs. 50/- to 100/-. Thus in all out of 197 children belonging to the 100 families studied 145 i.e. 74 per cent can be branded as child labourers. It is also pertinent to note that the remaining 52 i.e. 26 per cent of children who were forced to accompany their parents to the brick kilns were also deprived of child rights.

(b) **Elementary Education : Right of every child** – As revealed in table number 3.43, that out of 197 Katkari children studied, only 38 per cent children were school going children, 52 per cent were non-school going children while 10 per cent of them were drop outs from the school, that is total 62 per cent of the children studied were out of school. This proves that children of Katkari brick kiln migrant labourers are deprived of their fundamental right to education.

(c) **Right to play and recreation:** The study has revealed that there were no recreational facilities for children. 100 per cent of them stated that there were no recreational facilities for children made available by brick kiln owner. Here again it has been proved that children are deprived of their right to play and recreation.

(d) **Right to Health:**

- *Immunization/Vaccination:* This study has revealed that 72 per cent of the Katkari parents have vaccinated their children while 23 per cent of them have not vaccinated their children. When asked, which vaccines have you given to your children most of them told that they have given polio dose to their children.Hardly any one of them has given other vaccines like Hepatitis B, Hepatitis C, Smallpox, chickenpox, DPT, BCG, etc. to their children, and this is because of unawareness among the parents.
- *Nutrition:* Out of the total 197 Katkari children, belonging to families of 100 respondents, the researcher was able to get age, height and weight of 178 Children. Nutritional status of 178 children is as: 34 i.e 19 per cent - Normal; 51 i.e 29 per cent - Grade I (Mild Malnutrition); 54 i.e. 30 per cent - Grade II (Moderate Malnutrition); 28 i.e. 16 per cent - Grade III (Severe Malnutrition); 11 i.e 06 per cent Grade IV (Severe Malnutrition). Out of 178, 144 i.e. 81 per cent of Katkari children were malnourished. From this statistics it is clear that children of Katkari Brick kiln labourers are deprived of their basic right to nutrition.

- *Day Care & Crèche Facility:* Study has also revealed that facility of day care and Crèche for the children of Katkari brick kiln makers is not provided either by brick kiln owner not by Government.

(e) **Right to Parental Care:** It is clear from the data collected by the researcher that all the respondents work on the brick kilns around 8 to 10 hours daily, sometimes more 10 hours depending on the target of work.The parents get less time to care for their children. Nursing mothers take off 10 to 20 minutes to feed their children, but over all parental care during the day time is lacking. This certainly proves that the children of brick kiln labourers are deprived of their right to parental care because of the busy schedule of the parents.

(f) **Right to shelter/housing:** As already reported previous section of the chapter, in tables 3.19 and 3.22, the conditions of housing of Katkari labourers is poor both at the place of origin as well as at the place of destination. The children are certainly deprived of right to decent housing.

CHAPTER 4

Child Labour and Rights Issues Among the Bhil Sugarcane Cutters

This chapter throws light on five major aspects of Bhil Sugarcane Cutters & their children. These aspects are:

- Brief ethnographic profile of the Bhils.
- Occupational typologies among the Bhils.
- Sugarcane Farms and living conditions scenario.
- Seasonal migration, child labour and child rights issues among the Bhil Sugarcane cutters: Case Studies.
- Socio-economic background of the Bhil Sugarcane cutters.
- Analytical reflections.

Every aspect has been discussed in a logically sequential manner.

BRIEF ETHNOGRAPHIC PROFILE OF THE BHILS

Geographical Distribution in Maharashtra: The Bhils live in the forests, on the hilly areas and on the plains in Maharashtra. The forest is the source of their livelihood. The Bhils are listed at serial number 8, in the Schedule Tribe list of Maharashtra.Accordingly to the census, the predominant districts inhabited by the Bhils are Nandurbar, Dhule, Jalgaon, Nasik, Ahamednagar and Aurangabad. (Shrisalkar, 2004:296).

Population of Bhils in Maharashtra: According to 2001 census the total population of Bhil in Maharashtra is 18,18,792. Infact Bhil population is highest as compared to other tribes in the state.

Dialect: According to Shrisalkar P.R (2004:296) the language of the Bhil is derived from Sanskrit and has great affimity with Gujrati. This gets modified according to the region in which they live. G.S. Thompson found that 84 per cent of the words are derived from Sanskrit, 10 per cent from Arabic and Persian and 6 per cent from uncertain origin. The dialect of the Bhils of the plains differs little, except in pronounciation, from the Marathi spoken by other peasantry. Their dialect is known as Bhili and has no script.

Sub-Tribes: The Bhils as a whole are not single endogamous tribe (Shrisalkar P.R 2004: 297). Ethoven classifies the Bhils of khandesh as the plain Bhils, hills & forest Bhils and mixed Bhils. The most numerous clans (kulis) of the Bhils are those of Valvi, Vasave, Padvi, Mavchi, Gavit, Naik, etc.

Dress Pattern

1. *Adult men:* The Bhil men generally wear a dhoti, a kurta and a turban. Inside the dhoti they always wear a small loin cloth, which is special woven in various designs on the two ends, with plain white cloth in the middle.
2. *Adult women:* Bhil women wear a sari and choli.
3. *Children:* Boys wear a shirt and trousers. Little girls wear skirts & choli.

Clan names: Some of the popular clan names among the Bhils are Valvi, Tadvi, Gavit, Vasave, Padvi, Naik, etc.

Family Types: Both nuclear and joint family types are found among the Bhils, with Patri archy, Patriliny and Patri-local residency as a norm.

Forms of Marriage: Some of the major forms of marriages prevalent among the Bhils are:

1. Marriage by capture.
2. Marriage by trial
3. Marriage by elopement.
4. Marriage by purchase.
5. Marriage by mutual consent.
6. Widow re-marriage.

Monogamy is the principal norm, but polygamy is allowed.

Traditional Occupation: Bhils are small scale cultivators, agricultural labourers, food gatherers & hunters. These days a number of them have got into private and Government services.

Staple Food: The Staple food of the Bhils is dadar (sorghum valghare) a kind of Jowar millet. They also eat bajra, wheat & rarely rice. They are non-vegetarian. The sweet flowers and fleshy petals of Mauha (Bassia latifolia) are fermented & using distillation method mauha liquor is prepared. Liquor plays an important role in their social & religious rituals.

Music & Dance: The Bhils are very fond of music and dance. Their important dances are Dindan, Gaon Diwali, Shikar, Bhongrya, Rodali, Holi and Indar pooja dances. The musical instruments used by them are dhol, jhamlo, biri, deo-dobru, thali and zana.

OCCUPATIONAL TYPOLOGIES AMONG THE KATKARIS

Studies by Shirsalkar P.R (2004); Tribhuwan Robin and Kulkarni Vijaya (1999); Tribhuwan Robin (2010); Tribhuwan Robin and Sherry Karen (2004); Enthoven R.E. (1920); Russel and Hiralal (1975); Census of India – Notes on Scheduled Tribes of Maharashtra (1961); Bhatia Arun and Tribhuwan Robin (2002) reveal that Bhils were involved in following occupational typologies in past as well as present.

(a) **Food Gatherers and Hunters:** 7 to 8 decades ago the Bhils were food gatherers and hunters. This was the time when the depletion rate of forests in India was less. Even today in the forests of Akkalkuwa and Akrani in Nandurbar district of Maharashtra State; Jhabua district of Madhya Pradesh; dense forest areas of Rajasthan and Gujarat, we still come across Bhils who subsist on the forests for their survival and livelihood. Besides gathering fruits, vegetables and other minor forest produce from the forest, the Bhils would hunt animals and birds in order to get meat. Fishing was yet another means of livelihood for those living in inaccessible areas and close to rivers, lakes and streams. (Jain N.S. & Tribhuwan Robin; 1996)

(b) **Marginal Farmers:** As compared to Katkaris, Bhils have land. In fact about 71 per cent of the Bhils are land holders, but most of them have non-irrigated land. Out of 71 per cent of land holders, 31 per cent have land between 1 to 3 acres are marginal farmers. These marginal farmers grow vegetables, chilies, millets etc. on non-irrigated land they posses for 3 to 4 months (Naik T.B.;1965).

(c) **Agricultural Labourers:** There are two types of agricultural laborers among the Bhils. Those who work throughout the year as labourers on the fields of rich farmers and those who work from June to October. 70 per cent of the Bhils work from June to October as agriculture labourers.

(d) **Daily Wage Labourers:** Some of the Bhils work as daily wage labourers from February to June. They work as a cleaner on Lorries, on road construction sites etc.

(e) **Sugarcane Cutters: The Seasonal migrants** – Most of the Bhils in Maharashtra work as Sugarcane cutters. They migrate to the sugarcane fields from October to February, live there in temporary houses made up of bamboo mats or grass or plastic sheets. There are three types of labourers – tire gadi labourers, gadi centre labourers and doki centre labourers. According to Dhamnkar Mona, (2005), Tire Gadi Labourers are those who come with their own bullocks and rent carts from the factories at Rs. 10/- per day. These carts have rubber tires, hence the name tire gadi. Each cart can take up to 2 tons at a time. Gadi centre labourers transport sugarcane directly to the factory in their own bullock-carts; if the fields are far away in the interior areas, they bring into factory trucks for further transportation. Doki centre labourers are those who carry head loads to the trucks or tractor, either in the sugarcane fields or at the main road. (Panjiar Smita; 2007)

SUGARCANE FARMS SCENARIO

This section of the chapter presents a brief journey of the Bhil sugarcane cutters from their native villages to sugarcane fields and back home.

(a) The magnitude of migration

Maharashtra produces about 70 per cent of the sugar in the country, with a total of 186 cooperative sugar factories. Large scale sugarcane cultivation began here in the early 70s after the Koyna dam was built. The seven districts of Western Maharashtra – Nashik, Ahmadnagar, Pune, Satara, Sangli, Kolhapur and Solapur – comprise the sugar belt, which extends into Surat (Gujarat) in the north and Belgum (Karnataka) in south. Five districts of the arid Marathwada region – Beed, Jalgaon, Ahmadnagar, Nashik, and Jalna – send out labour to this sugar belt for six months every year for sugarcane harvesting. (Panjiar Smita;2007:32)

A study commissioned by Janarth, an Aurangabad based NGO, estimates that about 6,50,000 labourers migrate from central to western Maharashtra for sugarcane cutting each year. Of these around 2,00,000 are children in the elementary school age group of 6-14 years. An additional 2,00,000 labourers are received in Surat district of Gujarat for sugarcane cutting every season, of which 75 per cent are from Khandesh region of Maharashtra, and the rest from Dang and other tribal districts in Gujarat. (Panjiar Smita; 2007)

(b) Migration Season

The study revealed that the Bhils migrate seasonally to the sugarcane fieldsfrom October to for a period of 5-6 months. For some it is from October to March or April. The Bhils are generally at the sugarcane camps for a period of 5 to 7 months.

(c) Transportation

Depending on the distance of the native village and number of families migrating to the destined sugarcane farms, they are transported by a tractor or truck. Transportation charges bear by themselves most of the times. Some times mukadam pay the transportation charges. Those who own bullock carts they travel by it.

(d) Who are the sugarcane farm owners?

It was observed that the sugarcane farm owners belong to Gujarati, Jain, Maratha, Sonar and Rajput communities.

(e) Duration of work at the sugarcane fields

As mentioned earlier, the Bhil families are at the sugarcane camps for a period of 5 to 7 months, i.e. in winter and summer season.

(f) Sugarcane crushing operations

The length of the sugarcane crushing season depends upon sugarcane yields and can last anywhere from 160 days to 210 days. During the season, most factories utilize 110-125 per cent of their crushing capacity and the labour requirement is directly proportionate to the number of tons crushed per day, approx 1.5 to 2 tons per labour unit. For Example, in the crushing season of 2001-02 the average capacity utilization was 96 per cent at 2532 tons per day with 2842 adult labour, whereas in 2000-01 the factories utilized 101 per cent of their crushing capacity with 2956 adult labour bringing 2492 tons per day.

The number of accompanying migrant children in the age group 5 to 15 years was estimated at 1307 per factory in 2001-02 and 1359 in 2000-01.

(g) Private and Government Services

Influence of Christianity, Education, Development and Modernity has certainly played an important role among some progressive Bhils, who have got jobs in Government and private sectors. Some economically well off Bhils having leadership qualities have got into politics and are doing well.

It would be appropriate to mention at this juncture, that all the above mentioned categories perform at least two or three types of occupations throughout the year. These are cultivation and daily wage labourer, cultivation and sugarcane cutting, agriculture and daily wage labour, cultivation and agriculture labour including collection of minor forest produce such as firewood, honey, gum, fruits, vegetables etc.

(h) The Migrant Labourers

It has been recognized that seasonal migration is an accepted option in the normal livelihood strategies of the rural poor. For the sugarcane cutters, migration started as a strategy to cope with the worsening situation of dry-land agriculture created by drought, crop failure and poor terms of trade. Sugarcane cutting is a labour intensive activity requiring very high levels of physical stamina and energy. Unless the migrant labour is in desperate need, it would be difficult for him or her to bear the severe weather conditions prevailing throughout the season – extreme cold from October to January, and then hot temperatures up to 45 degrees in the months of March and April.

(i) Types of Labourers

There are three types of labourers – tire gadi labourers, gadi centre labourers and doki centre labourers. According to Dhamankar Mona (2005), Tire Gadi Labourers are those who come with their own bullocks and rent carts from the factories at Rs. 10/- per day. These carts have rubber tires, hence the name tire gadi. Each cart can take up to 2 tons at a time. Gadi centre labourers transport sugarcane directly to the factory in their own bullock-carts; if the fields are far away in the interior areas, they bring into factory trucks for further transportation. Doki centre labourers are those who carry head loads to the trucks or tractor, either in the sugarcane fields or at the main road.

(j) Terms of Work

The wages for cutting ("todani") are fixed and transportation charges are added on the basis of distance and mode of transport by Maharashtra Cooperative Sugar Factories Federation committee and other ministers. Wages are revised every three years. Labourers are contracted by a mukadam, a person either from their own village or from the neighbouring village. Usually one mukadam contracts a toil generally consisting of 8 to 15 koytas (labour units); the number depends upon capacity to mobilize money for additional advances. They earn commission of 15 per cent on each unit's total earnings. All sugar factories use 'advance' as a means to attract labourers. The need for a lump-sum advance for consumption expenditure, to get their children married or pay medical bills, makes the workers approach the contractor. The advance amount is calculated on the basis of a labour unit's capacity to earn and repay within 4 months (120 unit-days), in a crushing season lasting approximately six months. The minimum amount advanced is Rs. 10,000 per unit. Generally, the tire-gadi labourers are paid advances between Rs. 15,000 to 25,000 per family, while the doki and gadi labourers are given up to Rs.15,000/-. Families repay in labour by cutting between one or two tones of sugarcane per day, at the rate of Rs.100 to Rs.115/ - tone for bullock cart-borne workers and Rs. 65 per tonn for tractor-borne/ doki workers. By and large, all labourers try to pay the advances within the same season. However, in case they are not able to earn enough, they negotiate a later date with their respective mukadams. Some mukadams charge upto 48 per cent p.a. interest on the balance, therefore it is in the labourer's interest to repay at the earliest. In order to this, they look for work – EGS or any other work locally. If nothing is available, the men migrate again in search of labour opportunities or they sell their livestock. Thus the family is entrenched in a debt trap and is forced to migrate year after year.

(k) Daily Routine

A typical tyre gadi labourer's day begins with his toil, in the biting cold, around 4.00 am or even earlier depending up on the season. The doki and gadi tolis have to be ready to leave at any time of the night to load the trucks or tractors. Bonfires are the only source of light and warmth as they work at night. In order to be able to repay the advance within the season, each couple must cut between one to two tones of sugarcane per day, at the rate of Rs. 100-115/- per tonn for bullock cart owners and Rs. 65/- for tractor workers. Workers are often given less, as their unpaid loans are offset against the advance. By afternoon, each couple loads its bullock cart with the cane its family has cut, and leaves for the crushing factory. There the man waits in queue for weighment and a bill, while the wife walks back to the adda to cook and complete the household chores. Sometimes they have to wait in line until dawn outside the factory in miserable conditions where there are no proper pathways for the bullock carts, no shade or water to drink. In this routine, the families can barely get two hours of sleep in a day, sometimes even once in 2-3 days.

(l) Facilities at the Sites

Civic amenities and facilities at the sugarcane farms/ camps are below standard and unfit for human habitation. Given below is the description of the same.

- **Toilets:** The Bhils go in open air to defecate on defecation grounds.
- **Bathrooms:** Temporary bathrooms are made up of saris or plastic sheets covered from three sides for women especially. Men take bath in the open or go to a nearby stream, river or lake.
- **Drinking water:** Most Bhils fetch drinking water from bore-wells or from wells or taps in the farm or nearby areas.
- **Cooking facility:** Almost all the Bhils studied were found to cook food on the hearth. They fetch fuel wood from the fields and forests.
- **Housing:** It was observed that the Bhils live in the two types of temporary houses at the farms.

  Grass or bamboo mat hut (Khopi) - Houses made up of grass or bamboo mats provided by factory.

  Plastic walled houses - Yet another category of house type is seen at the sugarcane farms. These houses have plastic walls and plastic roof.

  The doors are small and low. The area of the house is 60 to 100 sq. feet. Extreme heat and cold are typical characteristics of the Bhils huts in the sugarcane farms.
- **Electricity:** Electricity facility was not seen at most addas.
- **Other facilities:** Facilities such as recreation, schools, I.C.D.S. units, first aid boxes, clinics, etc are not there at any sugarcane camp.

(m) Nature of work at the sugarcane farms

The sugarcane cutters are expected to do following jobs:

1. Sugarcane cutting.
2. Making bundles.
3. Carrying them to the truck/tractor/bullock cart.
4. Loading sugarcane in the truck/tractor/bullock cart.

(n) Work targets

On an average every Bhil koyta is expected to cut one to two tonns of sugarcane per day.

(o) Number of hours of work

On an average every Bhil family works for 10-14 hours at the farm. The women folk have to cook as well wash vessels & clothes. It was observed that children, especially the girl child takes up household responsibilities of cleaning vessels, washing clothes, cleaning the house, etc. at an early age of 7 to 8 years, so as to support the working mother.

(p) Kharchi & Uchal concept

In case of Bhil sugarcane cutters, the concept of Kharchi and Uchal is different campared to Katkari brick kiln workers.For sugarcane cutting, the labourers are contracted by a mukadam, a person either from their own village or from neighbouring village. Mukadams select factories based on their relations with the respective factory management and continuity is based on understanding. All sugar factories use 'advance' as a means to attract labourers. The needfor a lump-sum advance for consumption expenditure, to get their children married or pay medical bills, makes the workers approach the contractor. The advance amount is calculated on the basis of labour unit's capacity to earn and repay within four months, in a crushing season lasting approximately six months.The minimum amount advanced is Rs. 10,000 per unit. Generally, the tire-gadi labourers are paid advances between Rs. 15,000 to 25,000 per family, while the doki and gadi labourers are given up to Rs. 15,000/-. The factory's advance is paid in three installment, for example if a family wants 15,000/- advance then first instilment of Rs. 5,000 to 7000 will be given to the family in the month of August, then second installment of Rs. 4000 to 6000 will be given in the month of September and remaining amount will be given in the month of October as 'vat kharch' (travel expenses) just before departure (from their native village) which they have to use for travelling and during the season to fulfill their daily needs. By and large, all labourers try to pay the advances within the same season. However, in case they are not able to earn enough, they negotiate a later date with their respective mukadams. Some mukadams charge upto 48 per cent p.a. interest on the balance, therefore it is in the labourer's interest to repay at the earliest. In order to do this, they look for work – EGS or any other work locally. If nothing is available, the men migrate again in search of labour opportunities or they sell their livestock. Thus the family is entrenched in a debt trap and is forced to migrate year after year.When the sugarcane cutters reach worksite in the month of October each koyta (working unit) is given Rs. 150 to 200/- per day per tonne which amounts to Rs. 4500/- to

Rs. 6000/- per koyta per month. However, the mukadam does not give entire amount to the family, he gives Rs. 2000/- to 2500/- per month twice as kharchi (monthly expenses). The remaining amount is with the mukadam. From the remaining amount which accumulates for 6 to 8, he deducts medical, ration, grocery, rent for the hut and bullock cart etc. while calculating the final payment in April – May. The mukadam takes advantage of the illiterate status of the migrant laboures by showing wrong accounts and amounts. This attitude of the mukadam leaves no or less cash in the final payment of the migrant labourers. This situation forces the migrant family to borrow loan (uchal) with heavy interst per annum while going back to the native village. The consistency of taking advances, uchal and kharchi throughout the year forces the sugarcane cutters to become indebted and bonded labourers, what remains with them is the hard labour with poor pay to compensate for kharchi and uchal. Thus, distress migration has an adverse impact on the lives of the sugarcane cutters both in the place of origin and destinations s. There are two types of mukadams those who have less money and work with sugarcane cutters. The second type are those who have more money and own two wheeler or four wheeler. Their job is to monitor the sugarcane cut by a working unit and loaded into the truck for delivering to the factory. The second type of mukadam is educated and are aware of calculations. They keep a track of the amount of sugarcane cut every day by the koyatas working under them. It was observed that the less educated are more in number as compared to educated. They find it difficult to keep a track of the sugarcane cut every day. The contractors who are at the sugarcane factory are the ones who are aware of the exact amount of sugarcane that comes to the factory. These contractors are true exploiters of illiterate mukadams as well as the migrant labourers. They take advance from the factory and pay to the labourers through the less educated mukadams. Thus, contractors are true exploitators of mukadams and labourers. As rightly pointed out by (Breman, 1996), a system whereby employers advance money to labour contractors for a given amount of work relieves them of any responsibility towards the labour force that produces this work or "frees the owners of capital from the obligation of employer."

(q) Reasons for migration

Group discussion and focused group interviews with the Bhil sugarcane cutters revealed some of the major reasons for migration from their place of origin to the sugarcane farms/camps. These are:

1. Unemployment back home
2. Illiteracy
3. Landless marginal farmer's status

4. Indebtedness and poverty
5. Unskilled labour
6. Poor housing
7. Lack of economic assets
8. Economic & hunger crisis in the native place
9. Bonded labour
10. Hope of survival at the sugarcane fields because of kharchi & loans
11. High wages at sugarcane fields than native villages.

Case studies given in this chapter throw light on the above aspects in detail.

(r) Forms of child labour at the Sugarcane farms

Since both the parents are busy in cutting sugarcane for 10-12 hours the children are neglected. They are forced to take up household responsibilities at an early age. They drop out early from school. In fact most of them do not go to school. At the age of 7-8 they start helping the parents at the sugarcane farms. We classify child labour into two categories, namely:

1. Domestic labour.
2. Commercial labour.

The domestic labour includes children helping their parents by cutting sugarcane, making bundles of sugarcane, carrying sugarcane bundles etc. as well as managing household work. Commercial labour refers to children earning money by working at the sugarcane farms from the tender age of 14 to 17.

(s) Why children are forced into child labour?

Some of the key factors that push the children into labour are:

1. **Seasonal migration:** Since parents migrate, children are forced to migrate.
2. **Poverty, Unemployment, Bonded labour:** Poverty, unemployment, bonded labour, etc. factors push their parents to the sugarcane farms. "Kharchi" & "Uchal" pull their parents to sugarcane farms.
3. **Full time involvement of parents:** Parents have to work for 8-14 hours a day. The children are therefore neglected. They have to manage household work, take care of the young ones, as well as themselves.
4. **Weekly Targets:** Every koyata has to cut one tonn of sugarcane per day. This forces the children to help to take up labour work.
5. **Lack of Adult Manpower:** Lack of adult manpower in the nuclear families, forces children to get into child labour.
6. **Work to survive:** Both the parents and children have to work to survive. No work -no *kharchi*- no *uchal*, no money- no food, no food no survival.

7. **Work to specialize the art of cutting sugarcane:** Both children and parents are aware that after the age of 15 a Bhil child should specialize or master the art of cutting sugarcane. After 15 to 18, the child learns to become a responsible adult & is ready to get married & start another nuclear family. The children therefore work to master the art of sugarcane cutting.

SEASONAL MIGRATION, CHILD LABOUR AND CHILD RIGHTS ISSUES AMONG THE BHIL SUGARCANE CUTTERS: CASE STUDIES

This section of the chapter four presents the various forms of distress migration,starting from mobilization of workforce by labour contractors in villages to its transportation to distant worksites, the scenario at worksites, living and working conditions of migrant Bhils and their children at worksites, child labour and child rights issues. Given below are 25 case studies that threw light in the socio-economic and living conditions of the Bhil sugarcane cutters, the key push and pull factors that force them into distress seasonal migration, and their child labour and rights issues.

CASE STUDY 1

(a) Aim of the case study

To study a typical sugarcane site and the nature of work at the sugarcane sites.

(b) Background

Aavga is a small village in Shahada block of Nandurbar District. On the out skirts of this village, every year sugarcane cutters settlement is established for period of six to eight months beginning from October. The researcher interviewed four Bhil men belonging to this camp to understand the scenario at the settlement.

(c) A typical sugarcane site

The respondents stated that each family is provided with a bamboo mat and poles, which are converted into a small conical hut or 'khopi' (7 to 8 ft. in diameter). Tyre centers or addas have 200 to 500 khopis and gadi centers have 50 to 100 khopis. The khopis are cramped together, and bullocks are parked in front of each. The work units or koytas move in dark hours of the morning to fields where they cut cane throughout the day at the rate of 1to 1.5 tonn per day. The payment rate per tonn varies between Rs. 150 to 200.

The field is divided into strips, and each strip is assigned to one koyta for cutting. The man and the woman cut the cane, remove the stalks and throw it on the ground; the child takes the cane and puts it on a pile. The piles thus made are tied into bundles, carried on the head by men, women and children and put on to the carts. The men drive the cart to the factory, where they may have to wait in a queue for several hours before they get off load the cane. The women mean while, walk several kilometers back to the settlement. In the field interaction, the respondents described how they fight exhaustion all the time.

The mobile sugarcane cutters (the doki centre koytas) work in areas with less intensive cultivation and are, therefore moved, to new locations every 15-20 days by their agents. They do not have their own carts but are dependent on on factory trucks. They also have no shelter and live inopen, unprotected spaces and work in smaller groups of 15-20 as compared to the gadi and tyre centers. Their output is tied to the factory schedule, which works round the clock. The koytas are thus subjected to round the clock loading the trucks that ply up and down all day and night. Often they get sleep once in a two or 3 days. Women and girls in doki centers are more exposed to exploitation.

(d) Analysis

Sugarcane sites are usually far from habitation, in the wilderness, with no basic facilities, not even a road nearby. There are no labour laws at the site. Work hours are long and odd, up to 16 hours daily. Contractors retain control over the workers. After hard days labour, they come back to their khopis to rest. Women and girls have additional responsibility of household work.

CASE STUDY 2

(a) Aim of the case study

To understand the financial arrangement among the Bhil sugarcane cutters.

(b) Background

Jatrya Valvi a male Bhil sugarcane cutter, aged 45, belonging to Avaga sugarcane site was interviewed to understand the financial arrangements among the Bhil sugarcane cutters.

(c) The Financial Arrangements

Jatrya stated that the employers advance money to the contractors to deliver a given amount of work. Contractors in turn recruit labour by advancing money to poor families in the post monsoon harvest period when their need for cash is greatest. In return for this, families pledge their labour for the entire season entering in to debt bondage. With this money they fulfill their urgent family needs like purchase of food grains, medical treatment and bills, marriage, repair, the festival season etc, and then prepare to migrate for 6 to 8 months. The advance amounts are small, in the range of few thousand rupees per (koyta) comprising of two adults and 2 to 3 children.

The financial transactions are unwritten, and controlled entirely by the employers/contractors, with migrants having no negotiating power at all. At worksites payments are made by piece rate, which pulls every family member into work including small children. At the time of final payments taking advantage of their illiteracy the contractors exploit labourers in various ways – by showing a short fall in production, mis-interpreting accounts, with holding or delaying payments – and ultimately pay them way below what their due is.

Moreover several types of deductions are made – travel costs, cost of shelter, and hire charges for implements or carts given by the employers. Migrants also have to make other payments like shop credit. At the end the families are left with hardly any amount to take home.

(d) Analysis

As rightly pointed out by (Breman, 1996), a systemwhereby employers advance money to labour contractors for a given amount of work relieves them of any responsibility towards the labour force that produces this work or "frees the owners of capital from the obligation of employer."

CASE STUDY 3

(a) Aim of the case study

To understand the seasonal migration cycle among the Bhil sugarcane cutters.

(b) Background

Tanu Pratap Valvi, a female, aged 19, unmarried, belonging to the Bhil tribe, a resident of Bijaligavan village from Taloda block of Nandurbar district. Tanu came to the worksite with her sister aged 17, unmarried though. They live together in a khopi at the worksite.

(c) Course of events

Tanu narrated her views regarding the seasonal migration cycle among the Bhil sugarcane cutters. During the months of October-November the contractors come to their village with a tractor or a truck. Those labourers bound to him, sit in the tractors with their belongings and are transported to worksites. The labourers are at the worksites till March-April. They start moving back to their villages from April and are in their villages till October.

(d) Analysis

Seasonal migration among the Bhil sugarcane cutters is not a journey with a destination, but an ongoing process of mobility or labour circulation as rightly revealed by Tanu, the respondent. She and her sister were forced to come to the worksite because their father was suffering from Tuberculosis. He had taken loan with heavy interest from the contractor.

The migration process begins in October-November. The sugarcane cutters are at the worksites from October-November to March-April for a period of 6 to 8 months. They start moving back to their villages from April and remain there till September.

CASE STUDY 4

(a) Aim of the case study

To explore the nature of work sites of the Bhil sugarcane cutters at the place of destination.

(b) Background

Deepak Khanja Tadvi, a male, aged 16 years belonging to the Bhil tribe, a resident of Bijaligavan village from Taloda block of Nandurbar District. Deepak came to the worksite with his elder brother Ishwar. They live together in a Khopi. Their father Khnaja borrowed loan from the contractor, hence he send his sons to replace him. Khnaja went to Gujarat for cutting sugarcane, because the wages there are more.

(c) Nature of worksite

Deepak was interviewed by the researcher to obtain information about the living conditions and facilities at the worksite. Deepak stated that worksites vary from sector to sector. The habitation is usually in the field or outskirts of the village, but close to the sugarcane farm. Sugarcane cutters live in a hut called "Khopi". These huts are made up of a bamboo mat or sugarcane leaves or jowar stems.

Consequently there are no basic facilities like electricity, safe and pure drinking water, a market, a school, health centre, toilet, bathroom etc. Migrant labourers depend on the employers for their needs. If there is a habitation nearby, migrant labourers are usually shunned by the local people, and regarded as bad elements or thieves.

As aptly pointed out by Mosse (2005), local people erect extra fences around their homes to keep the migrants out. They are subject to prejudice and are stigmatized and criminalized. There are no laws at the worksite. Working hours are long and odd, up to 16 hours sometimes. Work norms are set keeping in mind healthy and strong labourers. Children and elderly people have to cope up and adjust to the living conditions.

If working conditions are watched they are wretched and the living space is worse – tiny, unhygienic and inhuman. Most members of the family sleep under the open sky in all weather conditions. The nutrition available is sub-minimal. Health hazards are too numerous to list and range from infection and fevers, contamination and toxicity related diseases, respiratory and gynecological problems, injuries, accidents, malnourishment of children and so on. There are no facilities for medical treatment, and no compensation or insurance, on the contrary, if a worker is ill and cannot work, he gets no pay.

(d) Analysis

In the bargain the health of labourers, their children and weak elderly folk is at risk. The living conditions in the settlement as well as working conditions are worse. All most all the men and women sleep out their huts in the open in all weather conditions. Children and elder sleep in the khopis and sometimes outside too.

CASE STUDY 5

(a) Aim of the case study

To explore the age at which Bhil female children get into domestic work and sugarcane cutting to support the parents to meet their weekly target.

(b) Background

Ranu Atmaram Chavan, a female aged 9 years, a member of Bhil tribe, residing at Avga village camp, in Shahada block of Nandurbar district in the State of Maharashtra. Ranu is illiterate. She was deprived of her child rights as her parents happened to be bonded labourers at the sugarcane farms. Her mother Anitabai as well as sister Manisha stated that girls of her age are into following house hold work and agriculture labour.

House hold activities

At the age of Eleven, Manisha started taking up following house hold activities.

- Cooking food and making tea.
- Fetching fire wood, grocery, minor forest produce etc.
- Washing and drying clothes.
- Cleaning the house.
- Fetching drinking water.
- Taking care of children between the age of 1 to 5 years in the family.
- Bathing children etc.

Activities at the sugarcane farms

Some of the activities in which Ranu is involved at the sugarcane farm are:

- Cutting of sugarcane
- Making bundles of sugarcane
- Making bundles of
- Counting of bundles
- Carrying these bundles to truck

(c) Analysis

Female Bhil children at the sugarcane farms take up house hold work right from the age of 7. These girls start helping the parents in the house hold work when they are between the age of 7 to 9 years. From the age of 9-10 they start working at the sugarcane farms to help their parents achieve weekly & monthly targets.

Thus, house hold work & child labour at sugarcane farms to achieve family targets becomes the prime priority for Bhil female children thereby depriving them of their rights.

CASE STUDY 6

(a) Aim of the case study

To study the recreational activities of the Bhil children at Sugarcane cutting camps.

(b) Background

Sudam aged 7, a male Bhil child residing at Mhasavad village has not been admitted to school yet. He was forced to join his parents, who work at the sugarcane farms. Sudam was interviewed to find out what recreational activities he is into when he is free from domestic work. Sudam narrated following recreational activities.

(c) Recreational activities

- Feeding bullocks and giving them water
- Playing with the clay in farm
- Playing in the stream or flowing water
- Playing with the bicycle tyre
- Learning to use a catapult
- Playing stone marbles
- Climbing on mango trees or other small trees
- Eating sugarcane
- Playing near Khopis in the settlement camps

(d) Analysis

Poverty, bonded labour, illiteracy and ignorance of parents deprives several children like Sudam of their right to recreation. They waste their time and talent growing up as children of the have not's at the sugarcane farms.

Sports such as cricket, foot ball, basket ball, hockey and other recreation activities availed by middle class and rich children in the cities and towns is a dream to the unfortunate – poor Bhil children.

CASE STUDY 7

(a) Aim of the case study

To study the indebtedness among sugarcane cutters with references to Bhils.

(b) . Background

Mr. XY owns a sugarcane farm in the village called Avga, Block Shahada, Nandurbar. There are seven Bhil families working on sugarcane farm. These sugarcane cutters come to the work site in bullock carts in the month of October-November after Diwali. The labourers work till April-May every year. This case study throws light on the aspect of indebtedness among the Bhil sugarcane cutters working as bonded labourers at the sugarcane farms.

(c) Course of events

An informal interview was conducted by the researcher to study the indebtedness among Bhil sugarcane cutters. The respondents stated that, the mukadams visit their native villages in the month of July-August and give them advances in three installments i.e. in the months of August, septmember and October. The third installment is known as 'vat kharch' (travel expenses). On an average each koyta is given Rs. 8,000/ to 10,000/- advance in three installments. After reaching the worksites the amount advanced twice a month to the migrant labourers is called 'kharchi'. This amount is deducted while making the final payment after deducting expenses for ration, grocery, house rent, bullock cart rent etc. after all the deductions are made the migrant families haerdly get 2000/- to 5000/- in their hands. This forces them to take loan (uchal) for survival and other needs while they are at the place of origin. Consistency in taking advances, kharchi and uchal pushes them into indebtedbess and bonded labour. All the respondents of the seven families stated that they were victims of indebtedness.

(d) Analysis

Aavaga sugarcane work site is one example of the many sugarcane worksites that exits in the state of Maharashtra. In fact the rate of indebtedness and bonded labour is very high among the Bhil sugarcane cutters. In the context all the seven families were victim of indebtedness. Each of the seven families had to pay debt ranging from Rs. 20,000/- to 40,000/-.

CASE STUDY 8

(a) Aim of the case study

To study the daily routine of a Bhil Sugarcane cutter's family at sugarcane farms.

(b) Background

Lahu Bapu Ahire, aged 35, a male Bhil Sugarcane cutter is married to Irabai, aged 30. They have three children, two sons Yogesh aged 13 years and Bharat aged 9 years and 11 years old daughter called, Durga. The family is working on the sugarcane field since last 8 years. Their daily routine at the sugarcane field is as given below:

(c) Daily routine

A typical day of sugarcane cutter's family begins with its toil, in the biting cold, around 4.00 am or even earlier depending up on the season.

Lahu is a labourer of doki centre. Therefore he has to be ready to leave at any time of the night to load the trucks and tractors. After completion of their morning duties of going to the defecation ground, brushing, bathing up and cooking by 6.30 am Lahu and Irabai start cutting the sugarcane till 11.30 am. At this time they take a break for lunch for an hour or so and then again go back to work. Lahu's elder son Yogesh and daughter Durga also help them in sugarcane cutting. Durga joins the farm after completing her household work of cleaning utensils, washing clothes and fetching water. Durga and Yogesh make bundles of sugarcane and also separate sugarcane tops. By 5.00 to 5.30 pm they cut the sugarcane, make bundles of it and also load it in the truck or tractor. Lahu goes with truck/tractor to factory to unload the sugarcane at factory while Irabai and children return back to adda to cook and complete the household chores. Sometimes Lahu has to wait in line until dawn outside the factory in miserable conditions where there are no proper pathways for the bullock carts, no shade or water to drink.

(d) Analysis

On an average a Bhil sugarcane worker works at a sugarcane field for 12 to 14 hours (sometimes more than 14 hours a day) to complete, the weekly target of the family. By the time it is evening, the adults and children are tired. Hard work and hard life is a part and parcel of sugarcane cutters.

CASE STUDY 9

(a) Aim of the case study

To unravel the status and awareness of child rights to shelter/housing among the Bhil parents.

(b) Background

Babu Pawar, aged 55, a male Bhil sugarcane cutter, residing at the AAvga sugarcane camp, was interviewed to understand his views about right to shelter and housing.

(c) Views on awareness about child and human rights

On enquiring about human and child rights and the right to shelter/housing, Babu said, "I am hearing about this for the first time in my life, we are so busy with daily labour work, that we hardly know basic rights of tribals.

(d) Analysis

Awareness of human and child rights including to shelter and housing was absent among the Bhil sugarcane cutters. There is an urgent need to free them from poverty, indebtedness and binded labour and then create awareness of human and child rights. Currently, food shelter clothes and regular employment is their priority in life.

CASE STUDY 10

(a) Aim of the case study

To understand the views of Bhil sugarcane cutters about distress seasonal migration and its impact on their lives.

(b) Background

Balu aged 27, a married male Bhil sugarcane cutter, has been working as a bonded labourer for Kantilal Jain for last five years. He goes to Mhadavad village every year along with his wife and three children. The family toils and works hard at the place of destination for 6-7 months just to pay off debts. When they return they have to take loan to survive at the place of origin.

(c) Balu's views on distress seasonal migration

On enquiring what is the impact of distress seasonal migration on the life of his family, Balu with a heavy heart stated that we are living because we are not dying. When we are in our native place we have the problem of unemployment, poor housing conditions, food and economic crisis, lack of economic assets and no social and economic security. Being away from home and village we lead an uprooted life. We do not belong to the places we go and increasingly loose acceptance in our own villages. We are cut off from our own community, culture and traditions and are unable to take part in the festivals, fairs, religious and social functions, which are an important part of our lives.

The vulnerability of people who cross state boundaries is greater as they are unfamiliar with the language and culture of areas they go and find themselves increasingly at the mercy of contractors.

While we the migrating families face hardships, the elderly, ailing family members or children left behind in our villages have difficulty finding for them and are often reduced to destitution. They frequently do not know where we have gone or how to contact us. Dealing with emergencies particularly back home is difficult, especially for those who go long distances. News of injury or death takes a considerable amount of time to reach.

Sometimes people go missing or women and young girls being carried off and people at home are helpless. Further poor and unhealthy conditions ensure that most migrants rapidly decline to ill health. Our children are forced in domestic work and child labour at a early age. The entire family works hard. Most family members take liquor to forget the body pain and daily stress. In the process the children are deprived of education, parental care and right to progress etc.

Some of us mortgage our BPL cards for a meager sum and usually cannot retrieve them on return. We have to forego free health services and schooling for our children. Sometimes the infants do not get covered in immunization drives. We loose opportunities to participate in Panchayat activities back home. We are not eligible for micro-credit intervention and Government schemes, because we are not present in the village.

(d) Analysis

There are thousands of families like Balu's, who suffer due to distress seasonal migration. Such migration lead an uprooted life, belong neither to their villages not the places where they go. As these migrant populations move out for extended periods each year, their links in their native villages weaken. Migrant children face a life of hardship and rootlessness right from infancy. They are deprived of their rights to education, parental care, health, nutrition and development.

CASE STUDY 11

(a) Aim of the case study

To unravel the efforts made by Janarth an NGO in Maharashtra to run the sugar school (Sakhar Shala) program, for the children of sugarcane cutters.

(b) Background

Panjiar Smita (2007:80) has presented a case study of Janarth and its work in running Sakharshalas. The author states that the Marathwada region of Central Maharashtra is highly arid and four or five of its districts send migrant labour to the seven western water rich sugar districts. Nearly 650000 labourers migrate every year for sugarcane harvesting out of which 200000 are children. The State has 186 sugar factories of which on an average 100 become operational every year. Each factory receives 4000-6000 migrants who work in a 25-60 kms radius around the factory.

(c) Sakharshalas – schools for migrant children at sugarcane sites

Janarth was running the Sakharshala program in seven districts covering around 12,000 children of sugarcane cutters. Sakharshalas are alternate schools for children of migrant labour and run at worksites. Their purpose is to achieve universal coverage at these sites.

The initiative began in 2002 in two factories covering around 6000 children. By 2007, Janarth ran 142 Sakhar shalas in 35 factories, reaching out nearly one third of the total operational factories. Sakharshalas are short term schools set up at labourers settlements for six months of migration period. They run in temporary structures made up of bamboo mats and metal pipes. Each school has 75-100 children. There is one classroom and one teacher for every 25 children. Sakharshala follows Government syllabus. 25 per cent of the teachers are women which is an achievement for Janarth.

(d) Analysis

Janarth is one of the pioneering NGOs to start Sakharshalas for migrant labourers. The program is a creation of Janarth and has certainly contributed in catering the educational needs of sugarcane cutter's children. It was however disheartening to note that there were hardly any Sakharshalas in Nandurbar, for Bhil Sugarcane cutter's children, where the research study was conducted.

CASE STUDY 12

(a) Aim of the case study

To unveil the practice of child care of babies below one year, among the Bhil sugarcane cutters.

(b) Background

Aruna aged 23, a married Bhil female, has three.children namely, Sunita (5 years); Anil (3 years) and ganesh one year old. Both Aruna and her husband Ishwar have been working as sugarcane cutters since the last six years. All the three children were born in their native village in Shahada Block of nandurbar District.

(c) Course of events

Aruna's third child namely, Ganesh was born in the year 2009. Soon after one month of the birth, Aruna was back to the sugarcane fields. Since both of them had daily target of sugarcane cutting, loading and unloading the couple was extremely busy.

The busy schedule of the couple had an adverse impact on the care of the new born. The child was fed by the mother in the morning, afternoon and in the evening 3 to 5 times during the work hours. However, the child was left at the mercy of Aruna's elder daughter Sunita. Sunita was instructed if the baby cries continuously, she should summon the mother.

(d) Analysis

Busy schedule of the mother insugarcane cutting to achieve daily target, which is directly linked with daily wages and survival of the family forced the mother to come back to the sugarcane field one month after the delivery. Secondly, her helplessness also forced Aruna's elder daughter to look after her third child. There are several Bhil sugarcane cutters like Aruna, who have to neglect their babies, who are forced to make their grown up children to take care of the younger ones. In the whole bargain of survival, daily wages, bonded labour, indebtedness, the new born babies as well the grown up children are deprived of their right to parental care.

CASE STUDY 13

(a) Aim of the case study

To understand the household responsibilities taken up by female children of Bhil sugarcane cutters.

(b) Background

Sunita a 5 year old girl, studying with her parents and two younger brothers at a sugarcane cutters' camp in Avaga Vasti of Shahada Block in Nandurbar district has been doing several household jobs being the eldest. She had to take up several small scale household responsibilities such as:

- Baby sitting
- Washing utensils
- Sweeping house
- Fetching drinking water
- Getting tea leaves, sugar etc. from the grocery shop.

(d) Analysis

Girl children, as old as 5, like Sunita become victims of household work because their parents are busy in sugarcane cutting work. In the process they deprived of their rights to education, recreation, health, nutrition etc.

CASE STUDY 14

(a) Aim of the case study

To unravel the various types of sugarcane cutting responsibilities taken up by Bhil child labourers while they are at the place of destination.

(b) Background

Ramlal, aged 8, an illiterate boy belonging to a Bhil sugarcane cutting family lives with his parents and three sisters at a sugarcane farm site at Patilwadi, in Shahada block of Nandurbar district. Ramlal along with his elder sisters Ashabai aged 16 years and Ushabai who is 14 years old, work as child labourers and support parents.

(c) Course of events

Ramlal started working as a child labour, when he was seven years old. He mastered in tying sugarcane bundles and learnt t cut sugarcane as well. When enquired about what kind of responsibilities are given to child labourers of ages 8 to 16 years, Ramlal stated that:

- Making sugarcane bundles is an initial task given to children between 7 to 10 years of age.
- Carrying these bundles to the bullock cart, tractor or truck is yet another task assigned.
- Loading and unloading bundles
- Training in sugarcane cutting and handling the knife with sharp blades.

(d) Analysis

At a tender age of 7 to 10 years the children of Bhil sugarcane cutters are forced into child labour and are exposed to hazardous risks of cuts, wounds, rashes, hot climate, snake and scorpion bites etc.

CASE STUDY 15

(a) Aim of the case study

To unravel the various types of wages given to Bhil child labourers, working at the sugarcane field sites.

(b) Background

Ushabai, aged 14, an illiterate girl belonging to a Bhil sugarcane cutting family lives with her parents two other sisters and a brother at Patilwadi sugarcane farm site, in Shahada Block of Nandurbar district. Ushabai along with her elder sister Ashabai and her younger Sudhabai and brother Ramlal have been living at the site since last 3 to 4 years.

(c) Course of events

Ushabai is 14 years old. She started working as a child labourer when she was 10 years old. When enquired what the daily wages are given to child labourers of Bhil sugarcane cutters, she stated that:

1. Male child labourer gets more daily wages than a girl child.
2. Some of the wages given to a male and a female child are as below:

Sr. No.	Type of Job	Wages per day in Rs.	
		Male Child	Female Child
1.	Making sugarcane bundles	15	15
2.	Transporting bundles	25	20
3.	Sugarcane cutting	50	45
4.	Loading and unloading	25	20
5.	All the above mentioned jobs	115	100

(d) Analysis

From the brief case study of Ushabai it is evident that despite of modernization, globalization, technological advancement, post liberalization, gender equality, awareness of human and child rights, unfortunate and unlucky girls like Ushabai are way behind 50 years becoming victims of gender discrimination, child labour and so on.

CASE STUDY 16

(a) Aim of the case study

To understand the health issues of Bhil sugarcane cutters and their children.

(b) Background

Patilwadi is an hamlet located 16 kms away from Shahada block. In all there were 20 families of sugarcane cutters at the site. Out of these 14 families belong to the Bhil tribe. The researcher conducted an informal interview with males and females numbering 12 respondents. The objective of the case studied was to unveil the health issues among the children and migrant workers.

(c) Course of events

Some of the major health issues faced by the respondents were as follows:

1. Absence of First Aid Boxes at the place of destination.
2. Lack of Primary Health Care facilities in the sugarcane settlements.
3. High rate of injuries such as cuts and wounds.
4. Lack of bathroom and toilet facilities.
5. Prevalence of skin, digestive and respiratory disorders among the migrant labourers and their children.
6. Most pregnant women tend to go to their native villages for delivery because of lack of proper facilities at the sites.
7. The Contractors do not make any provisions of maternity leave, medical check-up, nutritional supplements etc.
8. There is hardly any coverage of immunization and vaccination of women and children. Very rarely the sub-centre or PHC staff of a close by village comes to provide polio drops.
9. Lack of drainage and sanitation facilities.
10. Lack of parental care especially of sick children.
11. Negligence of sickness of the elderly people.
12. High incidence of malnutrition among children and women.

(d) Analysis

Patilwadi settlement of Bhil sugarcane cutters is one small example of the thousands of Bhil migrants who are victims of the above mentioned health issues.

CASE STUDY 17

(a) Aim of the case study

To study prevalence of malnutrition among children of Bhil sugarcane cutters.

(b) Background

The researcher measured the height, weight and age of 205 Bhil children. With the help of Dr. Vandana Kakrani, Professor, Dept. of Preventive and Social Medicine, B.J. Medical College, the Body Mass Index of children was derived and their malnutrition. The table given below presents.

Nutritional Status of Bhil Children

Sr. No.	Gradations	Number	Percentage
1.	Normal	57	28
2.	Grade I (Mild Malnutrition)	38	18
3.	Grade II (Moderate Malnutrition)	59	29
4.	Grade III (Severe Malnutrition)	34	17
5.	Grade IV (Severe Malnutrition)	17	08
	Total	**205**	**100**

(d) Analysis

Out of the total 235 Bhil children, belonging to families of 100 respondents, the researcher was able to get age, height and weight of 205 children. Nutritional status of these 205 children was plotted in I to IV gradesincluding the normal grade according to International Standards. It is clear from the above table that out of 205 children only 57 i.e. 28 per cent children were normal while remaining 148 i.e. 72 per cent were malnourished. This clearly indicates their deprivation from their right to nutrition and health.

CASE STUDY 18

(a) Aim of the case study

To study the educational status among the children of Bhil sugarcane cutters.

(b) Background

The researcher studied 100 Bhil sugarcane cutters' families. In these 100 families there were 235 children out of which 126 (54%)were males and 109 (46%) were females. The researcher has noted down the educational status of these 235 children.

Schooling Status of Bhil Children

Sr. No.	Schooling Status	Number of Children		Total
		Males	Females	
1.	School going	59 (25%)	44 (19%)	103 (44%)
2.	Non-school going	43 (18%)	50 (21%)	93 (39%)
3.	Drop outs	24 (10.2%)	15 (6.4%)	39 (16.6%)
	Total	**126 (54%)**	**109 (46%)**	**235 (100%)**

Note: Figures in bracket indicate percentage.

Educational Status of Bhil Children

Sr. No.	Educational Status	Number		Total
		Male	Female	
1.	Illiterate	43 (18.3%)	50 (21.3%)	93 (39%)
2.	Anganwadi (Pre-primary)	12 (5.1%)	08 (3%)	20 (9%)
3.	Primary (1-4)	34 (14.5%)	30 (13%)	64(27%)
4.	Secondary (5-10)	33 (14%)	19 (8%)	52(22%)
6.	Higher Secondary (11-12)	04 (2%)	02 (1%)	06 (3%)
7.	Undergraduate	00	00	00
8.	Graduate	00	00	00
9.	Post-Graduate	00	00	00
10.	Diploma	00	00	00
	Total	**126 (54%)**	**109 (46%)**	**235 (100%)**

(d) Analysis

Out of 235 children 103 (44%) were school going children, 93 (39%) were non school going children and 39 (16.6%) were drop outs. Among the school going children 20 were in pre-primary school i.e. Anganwadi, 64 were in primary school, 52 were in secondary and only 6 were in higher secondary school. The entire non school going children were illiterate. Informal interview with some of the drop children revealed that they wanted to continue the education but because of poor economic conditions, migration of parents and other household responsibilities they left their education and started working. This statistics proves that children of migrant sugarcane cutters are deprived of their right to education.

CASE STUDY 19

(a) Aim of the case study

To study the living conditions at the sugarcane farm sites and assess its impact on children.

(b) Background

Avga Vasti is a settlement of sugarcane cutters comprising of 12 families out of which 7 were Bhil families. The researcher conducted an in depth interviews with the heads of these families to understand living conditions and its impact on the children.

(c) Course of events

The views expressed by the respondents during informal interview about the living conditions at sugarcane farms are as follows:

1. Both the cattle as well as migrant labour live side by side.
2. There is the fear of being beaten by insects, scorpions, snakes etc. as children and their parents have to sleep under the starts on the open grounds.
3. The blades of sugarcane leaves are harmful because they create an itching sensation or feeling. Further, these leaf blades can also cut the skin.
4. The powder of dry leaves can cause breathing problems.
5. Extreme cold and hot conditions have an adverse impact on the health of the migrant labourers and more particularly their children.
6. Lack of proper houses or shades for small children and babies to stay while parents are at work.
7. Lack of recreational facilities for the children of Bhil sugarcane cutters.
8. Lack of ICDS (Anganwadis) centres and ZP schools at the camp sites.
9. Unavailability of pure and safe drinking water.
10. Poor drainage system

(d) Analysis

From the above discussion it is clear that the living conditions at the sugarcane camps do not suit inhabitation of human beings. The child labourers who work at the sites are exposed to the hazardous conditions such as handling of sharp knifes that are used for cutting sugarcane and often become victims of cuts and wounds. It was also observed that children of the bhil sugarcane cutters do not have enough clothing. Most of them move around naked or semi-naked in the field. They are forced to take bath with cold water. The exposure of their bodies to cold water, cold wind and heat including the sharp blades of sugarcane leaves as well as thorns in the field makes them victims of ill health. Lastly, the busy schedule of the parents in achieving daily and weekly targets deprives children of parental care. To sum up, the living conditions at the sugarcane farms definitely have an adverse impact on lives of migrant labourers and their children.

CASE STUDY 20

(a) Aim of the case study

To understand the practice of child marriages among the Bhil sugarcane cutters.

(b) Background

Mr. Kiran Valvi, a male Bhil sugarcane cutter, illiterate, is married living with a wife and two daughters. One of them is 16 years while the younger one is 14 years old Both the daughters having been accompanying the parents since five years i.e. from 2003 to 2008.

(c) Course of events

Mr. Kiran Valvi's friend, who also hails from Mhasavad, asked Kiran if his elder daughter aged 16, could get married to his son. Kiran consulted his wife and his brothers and decided that his daughter will be married to his friend's son. Kiran'srelatives, who knew that would be groom, too gave their consent. They said the girl is getting old and must be married before she turns 17.

(d) Analysis

The Bhils are educated as compared to Katkaris and hence the age at marriage among girls and boys is higher as compared to Katkaris. Girls are married off between the age 16 to 20, while the boys between 17-25. Kiran said, these days the consent of the girl as well as boy is necessary. Modernization and urbanization including education is changing the attitude of Bhil Youth regarding the age at marriage.

CASE STUDY 21

(a) Aim of the case study

To examine the quality of drinking water available to Bhil Sugarcane cutters and their children.

(b) Background

Ms. Geeta, aged 10, a female Bhil child, residing at a sugarcane field in Mhasavad village of Shahada block of Nandurbar District. She was fetching water from a flowing pipe, near the sugarcane field. On enquiring for why was she taking water? , she replied, ' for drinking'. Geeta said the source of the flowing water is from the farm well of the sugarcane farm owner. All the sugarcane cutters use the water for drinking, washing, and more importantly for bathing. There is no dearth of water. It is available in plenty.

(c) Analysis

Sugarcane needs a lot of water. The field owners fix a pumping engine to water fields. The sugarcane cutters have to only switch on the electric pump to get water. As compared to the Katkaris, the Bhil sugarcane cutters get enough and better quality of water. The Bhils do not have to go to the river banks, make pot holes and fetch drinking water. It was however, observed that the Bhils too do not boil water before drinking.

CASE STUDY 22

(a) Aim of the case study

1. To study the birthing practices among the Bhils at the sugarcane farms.
2. To understand the facilities and conditions for a new mother and child, at the sugarcane farms.

(b) Background

Yamunabai, aged 22, a female married Bhil girl, who works as a sugarcane cutter with her husband at a doki centre in Mhasavad village of Shahada block in Nandurbar district. Yamunabai delivered her second son in the Doki center camp in a Khopi near a sugarcane field, without any modern facilities meant for birthing.

The delivery was conducted by a Traditional Birth Attendant (Huvekari) from the Bhil tribe living in the same camp. On the fifth day the "Pachvi Pujan" ritual was performed by the Huvekari, to appease the goddess of fertility – mother earth. The parents and in-laws of Yamunabai offered a chicken, a bottle of liquor and Rs. 50/- to the Traditional Birth Attendant.

(c) Conditions and facilities of maternal and child health care

There were no special health or nutritional care facilities Yamunabai, and the new born. She had the same food consumed by the other family members. There were less bed sheets and clothes for the new mother and child. The six days old baby was wrapped in pieces of old saris. The new born did not have clothes or woolen cap, or nickers etc. It was winter season i.e. December, 2010. The new mother too managed with a old blanket and a quilt (Godhadi). Her husband bought for her a cheap woolen scarf to cover her ears.

The dusty environment, the stagnate water around the hut, the mosquitoes, flies, cold air in the night, hot sun in the afternoon was the kind of situations in which the new mother and child lived. Such an environment is not fit for a new mother and a child. The new mother slept on the floor on a bed sheet and a quilt, without a mattress.

(d) Analysis

It was observed that most mothers who work as sugarcane cutters i.e. 80 per cent prefer to go back to the native place for delivery, as the environment at the sugarcane field camp is not fit for the survival of the new born. However, 20 per cent stay at the settlement camp and deliver their children there, despite of the worse conditions.

CASE STUDY 23

(a) Aim of the case study

To study the co-relationship between education of parents and enrolment of their children in the school.

(b) Background

Mangesh Tadvi, a male Bhil sugarcane cutter, aged 30 years is married with 2 children. Datta has studied up to FYBA and his wife studied up to 9th grade. Though Datta was economically poor, he was educated and was progressive.

His educational background certainly inspired him to see that his children were enrolled in school. His eldest daughter aged 10, studies in 5thgrade, his second son aged 7 years was in 3rd grade.

(c) Course of events

Datta's children did help their parents in household and sugarcane cutting activities. But more importantly they went regularly to school.

(d) Analysis

Educational background of Bhil sugarcane cutters does play a significant role in sending their children to schools. Such parents are conscious about the significance of education of their children in their career.

CASE STUDY 24

(a) Aim of the study

To assess the facilities of the Government at/around sugarcane farms.

(b) Background

Talva is a village in Taloda block of Nandurbar District in the State of Maharashtra. There are four sugarcane camps in Talva. All the 4 camps have around 32 Bhil families, living in there. Visits to all the four camps revealed that all the four camps did not have the following Government facilities:

- Anganwadi (ICDS unit)
- ZilaParishasSchool
- Ration shop
- Electricity
- Clinic/sub-center

(c) Analysis

Observation of all the four sugarcane camps revealed that there are no government schemes implemented at the sugarcane camps studied. Some Bhil women stated that sometimes ANM's and Anganwadi workers from the neighboring villages do come for immunization of children and women.

CASE STUDY 25

(a) Aim of the study

To understand the views of Bhil sugarcane cutters on distressed seasonal migration.

(b) Background

An informal interview of eight Bhil sugarcane cutters was conducted in Mhasavad village of Shahada block of Nandurbar District. The prime objective of the discussion was to get a collective view on distress seasonal migration.

(c) Their views

Labour contractors provide cash advances to poor Bhil families in the villages during the lean post monsoon months, in return for which they pledge their labour for coming season. Migration of Bhil sugarcane cutters begins from October and November. Families spend the next 6 to 8 months at the work sites.

The debt, poverty, hunger crisis, unemployment at the place of origin derives them to worksites. The various poerations of distress migration, starting from mobilization of the workforce by labour contractors in the villages, to its transportation to distant work sites, the production process at worksites, fall in the realm of the illegal.

The imformants said that living and working conditions at worksites are minimal. The work extracted from us is excessive and completely disproportionate to the payments made, which are far below the legal minimum wage. Women and children toil hard. Women and girls cope up aditionally domestic responsibilities as well as psychological insecurity of living conditions. The situation both at native place and at worksites is worse. We are so tired by the end of the dy that both men, women and child labourers drink in order to get good sleep. We are cut off from our people and culture.

(d) Analysis

A major push factor which triggers distress migration is the lack of livelihood options in the place of origin. The consequeses of indebtedness and food insecurity forces large number of poor Bhils to sugarcane cutting sites. The pull factors include high seasonal demand for manual labour in agriculturally advanced areas.

SOCIO-ECONOMIC BACKGROUND OF BHIL SUGARCANE CUTTERS

In order to understand the socio-economic & educational background of the Bhilssugarcane cutters the researcher designed an interview schedule for 100 sugarcane cutters belonging to Bhil Scheduled Tribe. Thus, 100 interview schedules were administered. The main aim was to understand social, economic and educational background, reasons or push factors as well pull factors supported by statistical data that drive them to sugarcane fields.

The earlier section of this chapter has provided description and interpretations of qualitative data related to the conceptual model conceived through this study in the form of 25 case studies. All the case studies scientifically prove the conceptual model right. To support the model scientifically, an interview schedule was developed to gather quantitative data from 200 respondents out of which 100 were Bhils sugarcane cutters. The quantitative variables reported in the research methodology chapter with regards to the socio-economic and the educational status of the Bhils respondents, the push and pull factors that cause seasonal migration; the factors that push the unfortunate and helpless children of the respondents, into child labour, thereby depriving them of their rights, have been reported in this section of Chapter Four. The analysis and interpretation of both qualitative as well as quantitative data support the model as well as the hypothesis scientifically and positively right.

Block-wise Number of Respondents

The researcher selected 100 Bhil Sugarcane cutters as respondents for the study from two blocks of Nandurbar District, namely Shahada and Taloda. Table 4.1 presents details of the same.

Table 4.1: Block-wise Number of Respondents

Sr. No.	Block	Number	Percentage
1.	Shahada	53	53
2.	Taloda	47	47
	Total	**100**	**100**

Sex-wise Number of Respondents

Out of the 100 respondents 94 were males and 6 were females. Table 4.2 gives details.

Table 4.2: Sex-wise Number of Respondents

Sr. No.	Sex	Number	Percentage
1.	Males	94	94
2.	Females	06	06
	Total	**100**	**100**

Village-wise Number of Respondents

Table 4.3 shows that the Bhil respondents interviewed were from 6 different villages of Shahada and Taloda blocks of Nandurbar District.

Table 4.3: Village-wise Number of Bhil Respondents

Sr. No.	Status	Number	Percentage
1.	Avga	7	7
2.	Patilwadi	14	14
3.	Mhasavad	32	32
4.	Amlad	15	15
5.	Amlad Shivar	23	23
6.	Talva	9	9
	Total	**100**	**100%**

Marital Status of Respondents

As evident from table 4.4, 88 per cent of the respondents interviewed were married, 11 per cent were unmarried, and 1 per cent widower.

Table 4.4: Marital Status of Respondents

Sr. No.	Status	Number	Percentage
1.	Married	88	88
2.	Single	11	11
3.	Widow	00	00
4.	Widower	01	01
5.	Separated	0	0
6.	Divorcee	0	0
7.	Deserted	0	0
8.	Others	0	0
	Total	**100**	**100 %**

Age of Respondents

It was observed that 82 per cent of the Bhil Sugarcane cutters studied belonged to the age group 18 to 45 years while 4 per cent of them were below 18. This means that these labourers spend their peak time of adulthood in working as bonded labourers. Table 4.5 gives break-up of age-range and percentage of these labourers.

Table 4.5: Age of the Respondents

Sr. No.	Age Range	Number	Percentage
1.	Below 18	4	4
2.	18-25	26	26
3.	25-30	20	20
4.	30-35	16	16
5.	35-40	13	13
6.	40-45	7	7
7.	45-50	4	4
8.	50-55	8	8
9.	55-60	1	1
10.	Above 60	1	1
	Total	**100**	**100%**

Educational Status of Respondents

As evident from table 4.6, 77 per cent respondents studied were illiterate, 10 per cent studied up to primary, 8 per cent up to secondary school, 2 per cent up to higher secondary school, 1 per cent undergraduate, 1 per cent Post graduate who had done M.A and B.P. Ed and 1 per cent with agriculture diploma after 12th grade. It was however surprising to note that those who have taken education up to higher secondary, graduation, post-graduation and other studies then why they are working as sugarcane cutters, when researcher asked for the reason they said that there is no employment opportunity (Bribe in govt. offices etc.). This data supports the model conceived in this study. Thus, lack of education and unemployment according to the study are seen as a major push factor that is responsible for seasonal migration of Bhils.

Table 4.6: Educational Status of Respondents

Sr. No.	Education	Number	Percentage
1.	Illiterate	77	77
2.	Primary (1-4)	10	10
3.	Secondary (5-10)	08	08
4.	Higher Secondary (11-12)	02	02
5.	Undergraduate	01	01
6.	Graduate	00	00
7.	Post-Graduate	01	01
8.	Diploma	01	01
9.	Others	00	00
	Total	**100**	**100**

Main Occupation

As revealed in table 4.7, 60 per cent of the respondents stated that their main occupation was sugarcane cutting while 35 per cent stated it was cultivation, and 5 per cent were daily wage labour.

Table 4.7: Main Occupation

Sr. No.	Occupation	Number	Percentage
1.	Sugarcane cutting	60	60
2.	Small scale cultivation	35	35
3.	Daily Wage Labour	05	05
	Total	**100**	**100**

Family Size

The study revealed that 46 per cent of the respondents had family size of 4 members; 42 per cent was of 5 to 6 members while 11 per cent of 7 to 8 members.

Table 4.8: Family Size

Sr. No.	Family Size	Number	Percentage
1.	Up to 4	46	46
2.	5-6	42	42
3.	7-8	11	11
4.	Above 8	01	01
	Total	**100**	**100**

Total Population Covered

Total population of 467 Bhils comprising of 129 adult males (28%); 104 adult females (22%); 126 male children (27%)and 109 female children (23%) was covered for the study. Table 4.9 presents details.

Table 4.9: Total Population Covered

Sr. No.	Family Size	Number	Percentage
1.	Adult Males	129	28
2.	Adult Females	104	22
3.	Male Children	126	27
4.	Female children	109	23
	Total	**468**	**100**

Status of Migration to Sugarcane Farms

As revealed in table 4.10, 100 per cent respondents studied, migrated to the sugarcane farms as labourers.

Table 4.10: Status of Migration to Sugarcane Farms

Sr. No.	Status	Number	Percentage
1.	Migrate	100	100
2.	Do not migrate	00	00
	Total	**100**	**100**

Mode of Transportation

It was observed that 41 per cent of the respondent migrated by using their own bullock cart, 40 per cent of the respondents migrated to the sugarcane cutters by using a truck sent by the owner, 13 per cent by bus and 5 per cent by tempo. Table 4.11 presents details.

Table 4.11: Mode of Transportation

Sr. No.	Mode	Number	Percentage
1.	Tractor	01	01
2.	Truck	40	40
3.	Bullock Cart	41	41
4.	Bus	13	13
5.	Train	00	00
6.	Tempo	05	05
7.	Walk	00	00
8.	Other (eg.Autoetc.)	00	00
	Total	**100**	**100**

Payment of Transportation

When asked who bears travel expenses to migrate to the sugarcane fields, it was observed that mukadam i.e. middlemen pay for 26 per cent, 61 per cent pay themselves when they travel by bus or tempo. The sugar factory pay for 13 per cent. Table 4.12 explains it all.

Table 4.12: Bearing of Travel Expenses

Sr. No.	Travel Expenses Paid by	Number	Percentage
1.	Self	61	61
2.	Factory	13	13
3.	Mukadam/Middlemen	26	26
	Total	**100**	**100**

Status of Employment at the Place of Origin

Here again as seen in the table 4.13, 100 per cent of the respondents migrated to the sugarcane fields because of unemployment in the place of origin. Thus, unemployment according to the study is seen as a major push factor that is responsible for seasonal migration of Bhils.

Table 4.13: Status of Employment at the Place of Origin

Sr. No.	Status	Number	Percentage
1.	Unemployed	100	100
2.	Employed	00	00
	Total	**100**	**100**

Type of Labourers

It was observed that 100 per cent Bhil labourers studied were unskilled. Table 4.14 gives details. Thus, unskilled labour according to the study is seen as a major push factor that is responsible for seasonal migration of Bhils.

Table 4.14: Type of Labourers

Sr. No.	Type of Labourers	Number	Percentage
1.	Unskilled	100	100
2.	Skilled	00	00
	Total	**100**	**100**

Land Holding

As clearly shown in the table 4.15, 29 per cent studied are landless while 71 per cent had land. A question was asked to most of the respondents, if you own land, then why are you victim of indebtedness, bonded labour and poverty? Their unanimous and common response was the land owned by them belongs to 3 to 4 brothers and the yield gets distributed in 3 to 4 families, which is not sufficient for 2 to 3 months, hence they are forced to migrate. Meager land holding, poor quality of land and less agricultural yield per family are major push factors in the case of Bhils, who are marginal farmers as well as sugarcane cutters. Details of the same are given in the table 4.16.

Table 4.15: Landholding Status of Respondents

Sr. No.	Status	Number	Percentage
1.	Landholders	71	71
2.	Landless	29	29
	Total	**100**	**100**

Type of Cultivable Land

Out of 71 Bhils Sugarcane cutters who owned land, all of them i.e. 71 per cent owned non-irrigated land.

Table 4.16: Type of Land

Sr. No.	Status	Number	Percentage
1.	Non-irrigated	71	71
2.	Irrigated	00	00
	Total	**71**	**100**

Acre-wise Land Owned

Table 4.17 shows that 44 per cent owned 1 to 3 acres of land, 45 per cent up to 3 to 6 acres, 4 per cent up to 6 to 9 acres and 7 per cent owned land above 9 acres. It was also observed through Focused Group Interviews that most of them do not cultivate jowar on their land as there is no irrigation facility.

Table 4.17: Acre-wise Land Owned

Sr. No.	Area of Land in Acres	Number	Total
1.	1-3 Acres	31	44
2.	3-6 Acres	32	45
3.	6-9Acres	03	04
4.	Above 9 Acres	05	07
	Total	**71**	**100%**

Status of Housing at the Place of Origin

As per table 4.18, 94 per cent of the respondents stated that they have their own house in the place of origin while 6 per cent said that they did not possess own house. Table 4.19, reveals that 62 per cent of the houses were with stick walls and thatched roof, 24 per cent were with stick walls and tiles while 10 per cent were with tiled roof and brick walls. Table 4.20 reveals that 14 per cent of house owners had houses of an area between 100 to 200 sq.ft.; 38 per cent owned 201 to 300 sq.ft.; 42 per cent owned between 301 to 500 sq.ft. while 6 per cent owned an area above 500 sq.ft. who have received the houses through Governent's Gharkul (Housing) Scheme.

Table 4.18: Possession of Own House at the Place of Origin

Sr. No.	Status	Number	Total
1.	Possess	94	94
2.	Do not possess	06	06
	Total	**100**	**100**

Table 4.19: Type of House at the Place of Origin

Sr. No.	Type of house	Number	Total
1.	Stick walls with thatched roof	62	62
2.	Stick walls with tiled roof	24	24
3.	Brick walls with tiled roof	10	10
4.	Home through Gharkul Scheme	04	04
	Total	**100**	**100**

Table 4.20: Area of House at the Place of Origin

Sr. No.	Area of Land in Acres	Number	Total
1.	Less than 100 Sq.ft	00	00
2.	100 to 200 sq.ft.	14	14
3.	200 to 300 sq.ft.	38	38
4.	300 to 500 sq.ft.	42	42
5.	Above 500sq.ft.	06	06
	Total	**100**	**100**

Status of Housing at the Place of Destination

As per table 4.21, 100 per cent of the respondents stated that they do not have their own house at the place of destination. Table 4.22, reveals that maximum i.e. 86 per cent houses made up of grass or bamboo mats, 14 per cent of the houses were made up of plastic sheets. Table 4.23 reveals that 62 per cent of houses were of an area less than 50 sq.ft.while 38 per cent were of an area between 51 to 100 sq.ft.

Table 4.21: Possession of Own House at the Place of Destination

Sr. No.	Status	Number	Total
1.	Do not possess	100	100
2.	Possess	00	00
	Total	**100**	**100**

Table 4.22: Type of House at the Place of Destination

Sr. No.	Status	Number	Percentage
1.	Brick walls with tiled roof	00	00
2.	Stick walls with thatched roof	00	00
3.	Grass/Bamboo mat hut (Khopi)	86	86
4.	Plastic Sheet Tents	14	14
5.	Others	00	00
	Total	**100**	**100**

Table 4.23: Area of House at the Place of Destination

Sr. No.	Status	Number	Percentage
1.	less than 50 sq.ft	62	62
2.	51 to 100 sq.ft	38	38
3.	101 to 150 sq.ft	00	00
4.	151 to 200 sq.ft	00	00
5.	201 to 250 sq.ft	00	00
6.	251 to 300 sq.ft.	00	00
7.	Above 300 sq.ft	00	00
	Total	**100**	**100**

It is clear from tables 4.18, 4.19 and 4.20 that the houses owned by the Bhils in the place of origin are poorly constructed, small in nature and do not have economic value as compared to the houses of economically well off tribes and caste groups. Poor housing conditions of the Bhils at the place of origin have been identified as one of the major push factors of seasonal migration in this study. Similarly, it was observed that the housing conditions in place of destination are still worse as compared to the conditions of the houses at the place of origin. Tables 4.21, 4.22, and 4.23 highlight the conditions of the houses at the place of destination.

Position of Hearth

It is clear from the table 4.24 that maximum i.e. 87 per cent of the respondents were having their hearths outside the house while 13 per cent of them were having the hearths inside their houses. Hearths situated in small houses gives rise to smoke in the houses, which further leads to breathing problems, as carbon-di-oxide is directly inhaled especially by women and children. The main reason for having hearths inside the house as revealed by the respondents was that during winter season live coal in the hearth creates warmth. Respondents having hearths inside the house owned bigger houses. As revealed in table 4.24, 87 per cent had hearths outside the house, because of the danger of house (Khopi) made up of sugarcane leaves and/or bamboo mats can catch fire. Hence they preferred to cook outside the house.

Table 4.24: Position of Hearth

Sr. No.	Status	Number	Percentage
1.	Inside the house	13	13
2.	outside the house	87	87
3.	Both	00	00
	Total	**100**	**100**

Sleeping Place

It is observed that 88 per cent of the respondents sleep inside the house though the area of house is less, to protect themselves from snake bites & scorpion stings. Another reason is to protect them from severe cold. 12 per cent of them sleep either inside or outside the house. However, during the months of April and May i.e. during summer season they sleep outside, with dogs and cats around them.

Table 4.25: Sleeping Place

Sr. No.	Status	Number	Percentage
1.	Inside the house	88	88
2.	outside the house	00	00
3.	Both	12	12
	Total	**100**	**100**

Availability of Electricity

Out of 100 respondents, 98 stated that there is no source of electricity in their houses at the place of destination while only 2 i.e. 2 per cent said that there is availability of the electricity.

Table 4.26: Availability of Electricity

Sr. No.	Status	Number	Percentage
1.	Available	02	02
2.	Not Available	98	98
3.	Common Source	00	00
	Total	**100**	**100**

Facility of Drainage

Table 4.27 shows that 100 per cent of the respondents stated that there is no facility of drainage system in the settlement camps, at the place of destination, as well as at the place of origin.

Table 4.27: Facility of Drainage

Sr. No.	Status	Number	Percentage
1.	Available	00	00
2.	Not Available	100	100
	Total	**100**	**100**

Facility of Bathrooms and Toilets

The most basic and important facilities are availability of bathrooms and toilets. It is evident from the tables 4.28 and 4.29 that 100 per cent of the respondents stated, that there is no facility of bathroom and toilets respectively.

Table 4.28: Facility of Bathrooms

Sr. No.	Status	Number	Percentage
1.	Available	00	00
2.	Not Available	100	100
	Total	**100**	**100**

Table 4.29: Facility of Toilets

Sr. No.	Status	Number	Percentage
1.	Available	00	00
2.	Not Available	100	100
	Total	**100**	**100**

Source of Drinking Water

As evident from the table 4.30, 94 per cent of the respondents get drinking water from bore-well, hand pump, taps, wells while 6 per cent of them get water from small ponds. The water fetched from the ponds is impure and unclean, hence children as well as the sugarcane cutters often suffer from digestive disorders. They are deprived of the right to drink pure and clean water.

Table 4.30: Source of Drinking Water

Sr. No.	Source	Number	Percentage
1.	Well	5	5
2.	Tap	7	7
3.	Stream	0	0
4.	Bore Well	27	27
6.	Water tanker	0	0
7.	Pond	6	6
8.	Hand Pump	55	55
9.	River	0	0
10.	Others	0	0
11.	Pothole near a stream	0	0
	Total	**100**	**100**

Annual Income

One of the most important indicators in this study is annual income of the family. As per the table 4.31, 65 per cent of the families are below poverty line and 35 per cent are above poverty line and their annual income range is minimum Rs. 20,001/- to maximum Rs. 80,000/-. Here it is very important to note that remaining 2 per cent of the families were having income ranging from Rs. -5000/- to Rs. -10,000/- this means these 2 per cent of the respondents still have to repay loan which they will pay in the next season by working with the same contractor.

Table 4.31: Annual Income of the Family

Sr. No.	Source	Number	Percentage
1.	Up to Rs. 20,000/-	63	63
2.	Rs. 20,000 to 40,000/-	29	29
3.	Rs. 40,000 to 60,000/-	05	05
4.	Rs. 60,000 to 80,000/-	01	01
6.	Above Rs. 80,000/-	00	00
7.	Rs. -1,000 to -5,000/-	00	00
8.	Rs. -5,000 to -10,000/-	02	02
9.	Rs.-10,000 to -20,000/-	00	00
	Total	**200**	**100**

Bonded Labourer

It was observed that 76 per cent of the respondents were hooked into the bonded labour. The inability to clear the debt, forced the couple, their brother or any other family members to come and work for the forthcoming years. Table 4.32 reveals it all.

Table 4.32: Bonded Labourer

Sr. No.	Status	Number	Percentage
1.	Bonded Labourers	76	76
2.	Non-bonded labourers	24	24
	Total	**100**	**100**

Borrowing Loan while Returning Home

As aptly shown in tables 4.33 and 4.34 , 76 per cent of the Bhil Sugarcane cutters take loan while returning home. They take Rs. 10,000/- to 25,000/- depending upon their need. The amount rises, if there is a wedding or some ritual in the family.

Table 4.33: Frequency of Borrowing Loan while Returning Home

Sr. No.	Status	Number	Percentage
1.	Borrow	76	76
2.	Do not borrow	24	24
	Total	**100**	100

Source of Borrowing Loan

Majority of the Bhil Sugarcane cutters interviewed i.e. 64 per cent borrowed loan from the Mukadams, while 7 per cent from farm owner, factory contractor or other sources like goldsmith, money lender etc. 24 per cent of them did not borrow loan. It can be concluded that the Mukadams are banks, ATM machines and credit cards for the Bhil labourers. They are the main source of money, food and survival. Our respondents said that they are better off at the sugarcane camps than back home, because they get food and money regularly from the owner for 6 to 8 months.

Table 4.34: Source of Borrowing Loan

Sr. No.	Status	Number	Percentage
1.	Bank	05	05
2.	Farm Owner	02	02
3.	Factory Contractor	02	02
4.	Mukadam	64	64
5.	Other	03	03
6.	N A	24	20
	Total	**100**	**100**

Possession of Livestock

36 per cent of the respondents studied did not possess live stock, while 64 per cent possess livestock. Those who possessed live stock stated they had chickens, goats, sheep, cow and bulls. The Bhil sugarcane cutters require bulls to pull the carts in order to the transport sugarcane to the trucks and to the sugar factory. Those who own cows and buffalos get in advantage of the free fodder within and around sugarcane field. Table 4.35 presents details.

Table 4.35: Possession of Livestock

Sr. No.	Status	Number	Percentage
1.	Possess	64	64
2.	Do not possess	36	36
	Total	**100**	**100**

Collection of Minor Forest Produce

As revealed in table 4.36, 100 per cent of the respondents collected Minor Forest Produce, such as fire wood, fruits, gum, grass, leaves, Karvi sticks etc. from the forest. Table 4.36 gives details.

Table 4.36: Collection of Minor Forest Produce

Sr. No.	Status	Number	Percentage
1.	Collect	100	100
2.	Do not Collect	00	00
	Total	**100**	**100**

Sale of Minor Forest Produce (MFP)

As revealed in table 4.37, only 18 per cent of the respondent sold minor forest produce when asked what they sell. The respondents replied fire wood is sold, both at the place of origin and destination. They sell fire wood to non-tribals and get Rs. 20 to 30 per bundle or head load. This money is used for daily expense.

Table 4.37: Sale/Barter of MFP

Sr. No.	Status	Number	Percentage
1.	Sale	18	18
2.	Do not sale (for self use)	82	82
	Total	**100**	**100**

Hunting

Although hunting is ill-legal, the Bhils do hunt birds, wild boars, hares etc. Hunting is usually carried out in winter and summer.

Snakebite and Scorpion Sting Cases

As seen in table 4.38, 5 per cent of the families of respondents experienced scorpion sting and snake bite problems while working at the brick kilns and staying in temporary houses. Majority of the Bhil Sugarcane cutters keep cats and dogs in their houses at work place, so as to prevent snake bites and scorpion stings. The cats and dogs guard the families from snakes and scorpions while they are in the home or asleep.

Table 4.38: Cases of Snake or Scorpion Bite at Workplace

Sr. No.	Status	Number	Percentage
1.	Yes	05	05
2.	No	95	95
	Total	**100**	**100**

Social, Food, Health and Economic Security

All most all the respondents interviewed unanimously said there is no social and economic security at the place of origin. The Mukadams, the feudal lords are their saviors who provide them social, economic, food and health security at the place of destination.

Number of Working Hours

Since the survival of the Bhil Sugarcane cutters depend a lot on the amount of sugarcane cut by them daily, weekly and monthly to achieve the target given by the Mukadam. They are forced to work for 10 to 12 hours a day and even more. As rightly depicted in table 4.39 it is seen 78 per cent between 12 to 14 hours a day, while 22 per cent work above 14 hours for small financial earnings. Our respondents revealed that they have to cut one or one and half ton sugarcane daily by one Koyta, carry it towards a truck and load it. Sometimes empty trucks come to the fields at 2 am. The couple (Koyta) has to sacrifice their sleep and load sugarcane.

Table 4.39: Number of Working Hours

Sr. No.	Working Hours	Number	Percentage
1.	8-10 hrs.	0	0
2.	10-12 hrs.	0	0
3.	12-14 hrs.	78	78
4.	above 14 hrs.	22	22
	Total	**100**	**100**

Possession of Documents

As compared to Katkaris, the Bhils seem to to possess important documents such as ration card (69%); election card (77%); land documents

(63%); scheduled tribe certificate (55%); house property papers (71%) etc. This certainly reveals that the degree of awareness among the Bhils regarding the significance of important documents is higher than Katkaris. This perhaps due to better literacy (77%) rate as compared to Katkaris.; influence of Missionaries in Nandurbar, network with political party workers and progressive nature of course. Table 4.40, however reveals an important fact, that only 11 per cent of the Bhils studied possessed bank pass book. This indicate that majority of them do not have money to save as they are hooked into debt and bonded labour. Those ones who possessed pass books revealed that they had Rs. 300/- to 4500/- in their bank accounts. These respondents were educated and possessed agriculture land from 7 to 8 acres and above.

Table 4.40: Possession of Documents

Sr. No.	Documents	Number	Percentage
1.	Ration Card	69	69
2.	Election card	77	77
3.	Identity card	05	05
4.	Birth certificate	05	05
5.	Marriage certificate	00	00
6.	Death Certificate	01	01
7.	Bank's Pass Book	11	11
8.	School leaving certificate	26	26
9.	Land documents	63	63
10.	House property papers	71	71
11.	Caste/Tribe certificate	55	55
12.	Any other	00	00
13.	No documents	02	02

Absence of Economic and Financially Valuable Assets

The data revealed in table 4.41 shows that 71 per cent of the respondents studied owned agricultural land. The same table shows that 94 per cent of the them owned houses at the place of origin. However after probing in detail it was observed that 2 to3 families owned agricultural land as a result of which the yield reaped was meager and insufficient, hence agricultural land as an immovable asset possessed by the respondents was not really economically usefully productive. Further, the land possessed by them was non-irrigated. It was also observed that the economic value of this land was far less in the tribal area. Thus as per the conceptual model evolved absence of economic assets or absence of financially valuable assets becomes a key push factor in distress seasonal migration among the Katkari Brick kiln labourers and Bhil sugarcane cutters.

Table 4.41: Possession of Immovable Assets

Sr. No.	Immovable Assets	Number	Percentage
1.	Agricultural land	71 (out of 100 respondents)	71
2.	House	94 (out of 100 respondents)	94

As evident from table 4.42 it was observed that majority of the respondents did not have valuable movable assets such as gold, silver, hard cash, cupboard, TV, tape recorder, radio, utensils, mobile phones, mobikes, beds, cots, etc. except live stock. Few of them who possess movable items like TV set, Bed, Gas Cylinder, Mobike, silver ornaments etc they never carry it to the place of destination but keep in their own house at the place of origin.

Table 4.42: Possession of Movable Assets

Sr. No.	Movable Assets	Number
1.	Gold/Silver Ornaments	06
2.	Hard Cash	00
3.	Cupboard	04
4.	TV set	12
5.	Taperecorder/Radio	08
6.	Mobile Phones	04
7.	Beds/Cots	27
8.	Mobikes	02
9.	Live stock	64
10.	Gas Cylinder	03
11.	Kerosene Stove	08

BACKGROUND OF BHIL CHILDREN AT THE SUGARCANE CAMPS

Age-range Wise Number of Children

As evident from the table 4.42, out of 235 children, 8 per cent of the children belonged to age-range 0 to 1 year, out of these 3 per cent were male and 5 per cent were female children; 67 i.e. 29 per cent between 1 to 5 years, out of these 14 per cent were male and 15 per cent were female children; 62 i.e. 26 per cent between 5 to 10 years, out of these 15 per cent were male and 11 per cent were female children; 61 i.e. 26 per cent between 10 to 15 years, out of these 13 per cent were male and 13 per cent were female children and remaining 27 i.e. 11 per cent belonged to age range 15 to 18 years, out of these 20 i.e.8 per cent were males and 7 i.e. 3 per cent were female children.

Table 4.43: Age-wise Number of Bhil Children

Sr. No.	Age range	Number		Total
		Male	Female	
1.	Upto 1 yr	07 (3%)	11 (5%)	18 (8%)
2.	1-5 yrs	32 (14%)	35 (15%)	67 (29%)
3.	5 to 10 yrs	36 (15%)	26 (11%)	62 (26%)
4.	10 to 15 yrs	31 (13%)	30 (13%)	61 (26%)
5.	15 to 18 yrs	20 (8%)	07 (3%)	27 (11%)
	Total	**126 (54%)**	**109 (46%)**	**235 (100%)**

Note: Figures in bracket indicate percentage.

Schooling Status of Children

As evident from table 4.43, out of 235 children 103 i.e. 44 per cent of the children were school going, out of these 25 per cent were male children and 19 per cent were female children; 96 i.e. 41 per cent were non-school going children, out of that 19 per cent were male children and 22 per cent were female children; 36 i.e. 15 per cent children were drop outs, out of these 23i.e. 10 per cent were male children and 13 i.e.5 per cent were female children. Thus, nearly 56 per cent of the children were deprived from getting education. Those going to school had to compromise with the poor housing conditions and lack of electricity in the place of destination as well as origin.

Table 4.44: Schooling Status of Bhil Children

Sr. No.	Schooling Status	Number of Children		Total
		Males	Females	
1.	School going	59 (25%)	44 (19%)	103 (44%)
2.	Non-school going	44 (19%)	52 (22%)	96 (41%)
3.	Drop outs	23 (10%)	13 (5%)	36 (15%)
	Total	**126 (54%)**	**109 (46%)**	**235 (100%)**

Note: Figures in bracket indicate percentage.

Educational Status of Children

As seen in the table 4.43, out of 235 children maximum i.e. 93 (39%) were illiterate, out of these 18.3 per cent were male children and 21.3 per cent were female children; 20 i.e.9 per cent attend Anganwadi i.e. pre-primary school, out of these 5.1 per cent were male and 3 per cent were female children; 64 i.e. 27 per cent studied up to primary school, out of these 14.5 per cent were male and 13 per cent were female children; 52 i.e. 22 per cent studied up to secondary school, out of these 14 per cent were male and 8 per cent were female children. Educational status of the Bhil children although better off than the Katkaris, but yet they are forced to migrate with their parents due to poverty, unemployment, indebtedness and bonded labour.

Table 4.45: Educational Status of Bhil Children

Sr. No.	Educational Status	Number		Total
		Male	Female	
1.	Illiterate	43 (18.3%)	50 (21.3%)	93 (39%)
2.	Anganwadi (Pre-primary)	12 (5.1%)	08 (3%)	20 (9%)
3.	Primary (1-4)	34 (14.5%)	30 (13%)	64(27%)
4.	Secondary (5-10)	33 (14%)	19 (8%)	52(22%)
6.	Higher Secondary (11-12)	04 (2%)	02 (1%)	06 (3%)
7.	Undergraduate	00	00	00
8.	Graduate	00	00	00
9.	Post-Graduate	00	00	00
10.	Diploma	00	00	00
	Total	**126 (54%)**	**109 (46%)**	**235 (100%)**

Note: Figures in bracket indicate percentage.

Right to Recreational Facilities

All the 100 respondents said that there were no recreational facilities for children in the sugarcane settlements. This proves that the children are deprived of their right to recreation.

Table 4.46: Recreational Facilities

Sr. No.	Status	Number	Percentage
1.	Available	00	00
2.	Not available	100	100
	Total	**100**	**100**

Right to Parental Care

All most all the respondents stated that for 10 to 14 hours their children get neglected. The parents get less time to care for their children. Nursing mothers take off 10 to 20 minutes to feed their children, but over all parental care during the day time is lacking. This certainly proves that children are deprived of their right of parental care.

Right to Decent Housing

As reported in table 4.19 and 4.22, the conditions of housing of Bhil labourers is poor both at the place of origin as well as at the place of destination. The children are certainly deprived of right to decent housing.

Nutritional Status of Bhil Children

Out of the total 235 Bhil children, belonging to families of 100 respondents, the researcher was able to get age, height and weight of 205 children. Nutritional status of these 148 children was plotted in I to IV grades according to International Standards. Table 4.45 presents nutritional status of 148 children.

Table 4.47: Nutritional Status of Bhil Children

Sr. No.	Gradations	Number	Percentage
1.	Normal	57	28
2.	Grade I (Mild Malnutrition)	38	18
3.	Grade II (Moderate Malnutrition)	59	29
4.	Grade III (Severe Malnutrition)	34	17
5.	Grade IV (Severe Malnutrition)	17	08
	Total	**205**	**100**

It is clear from the above table that 148 i.e 72.19 per cent of Bhil children are malnourished. This means they are deprived of their right to nutrition and health.

Diet during Pregnancy

As per the table 4.46, 91 per cent of the women do not get special or adequate diet necessary during pregnancy while only 9 per cent of the women get some special food like seasonal fruits, meat etc. during pregnancy. Inadequate and insufficient food during pregnancy leads to the birth of underweight and malnourished children. Apart from this it also affects health of mother to a great extent.

Table 4.48: Diet during Pregnancy

Sr. No.	Status	Number	Percentage
1.	Get special diet	09	08
2.	Do not get special diet	91	91
	Total	**100**	**100**

Place of Delivery

As per table 4.47 it is clear 82 per cent of the deliveries were conducted at home in the native place of the respondent, while 12 per cent at the work site i.e.in the Khopi (hut) in the place of destination. Only 5 per cent of the deliveries were conducted at Government and Private hospital.

Table 4.49: Place of Delivery

Sr. No.	Gradations	Number	Percentage
1.	Khopi (hut at work site)	12	12
2.	Home at Native Place	82	82
3.	PHC	03	03
4.	Rural Hospital	02	02
5.	Govt. Hospital	00	00
6.	Private Hospital	01	01
	Total	**100**	**100**

Personnel Conducting Delivery

Out of 100, 85 per cent of the respondents stated that the deliveries were conducted by Dai i.e. village Midwife at home while 9 per cent deliveries were conducted by Aged women at worksite and only 6 per cent of the deliveries were conducted by doctor.

Table 4.50: Personnel who Conducts Delivery

Sr. No.	Gradations	Number	Percentage
1.	Dai/Suine	85	85
2.	ANM	00	00
3.	Trained Midwife	00	00
4.	Doctor	06	06
5.	Gynecologist	00	00
6.	Elderly women at work site	09	09
	Total	**100**	**100**

When do women start working after delivery?

Table 4.49 throws light on number of days after delivery when women start working in sugarcane fields. As per the table given below maximum i.e. 65 per cent said that they started working after 30 days of delivery while 35 per cent told that they started working after 15 days.

Table 4.51: Number of Days when Women Start Working after Delivery

Sr. No.	Days	Number	Percentage
1.	After 2 days	00	00
2.	After 7 days	00	00
3.	After 15 days	35	35
4.	After 30 days	65	65
5.	Any other	00	00
	Total	**100**	**100**

Care of Sick Child

Table 4.50 throws light on how Bhil sugarcane cutters take care of their sick child. Out of total 100 parents, 26 per cent said that one of the parents take leave and take care of sick child while 22 per cent take leave only if the child is serious. 14 per cent of them said that woman in the house generally take care of sick child and if she is working then she only takes leave rather than male member; 15 per cent of them keep child with other elder children at the worksite house while 12 per cent of them keep the child with grandparents at the native place so that parents of the child can be tension free. From this we can say that the children of sugarcane cutters are deprived of their right to parental care.

Table 4.52: Care of Sick Child

Sr. No.	Care of Sick Child	Number	Percentage
1.	One of parents take leave	26	26
2.	If serious both take leave	22	22
3.	Keep child with other elder children at work site house	15	15
4.	Woman in the house/if she is working she takes leave	14	14
5.	No child	11	11
6.	Keep the child with grandparents in native village	12	12
	Total	**100**	**100**

Vaccination of Children

It is evident from the table 4.51 that 76 per cent of the Bhil parents have vaccinated their children while 12 per cent of them have not vaccinated their children. When asked, which vaccines have you given to your children most of them told that they have given polio dose to their children. Hardly any one of them has given other vaccines like Hepatitis B, Hepatitis C, Smallpox, chickenpox, booster etc. to their children. Those who have given their children Polio dose is because of Anganwadi workers, PHC nurse, ANM, NGOs are voluntarily going to the sugarcane camps for giving polio dose and providing this facility at their doorstep.

Table 4.53: Vaccination of Children

Sr. No.	Vaccination Status	Number	Percentage
1.	Vaccinated	76	76
2.	Not vaccinated	12	12
3.	No child	12	12
	Total	**100**	**100**

CHILD LABOUR AT THE SUGARCANE FIELDS

The Bhil respondents revealed through informal interviews, that a girl starts learning household work between the age 7 to 10 years, as she gets married between 15 to 18 years of age. She must learn all the household work before she gets married. Boys too start helping parents between the age 8 to 10. Table given below portray separately the percentage of male and female children involved in child labour to help the parents meet their sugarcane cutting targets and work at the sugarcane fields to make money. The table also reveals the status of male and female children engaged in household work, whether or not they are attending school or even working to earn money at the sugarcane fields.

Table 4.54: Working Status of Bhil Male and Female Children

Sr. No.	Working Status	Number		Total
		Male	Female	
1.	Working at the sugarcane fields	39 (17%)	20 (8%)	59 (25%)
2.	Not working	49 (21%)	61 (26%)	110 (47%)
3.	Working to help parents	38 (16%)	28 (12%)	66 (28%)
	Total	**126 (54%)**	**109 (46%)**	**235 (100%)**

Note: Figures in bracket indicate percentage.

The table above certainly shows that 25 per cent of Bhil children are involved in child labour 28 per cent work to help parents meet their work targets. This certainly proves that these unfortunate and helpless children get exploited economically and are forced into child labour, because of the poor socio-economic conditions, bonded labour, indebtedness of their parents. Meeting daily, weekly and monthly brick making target is yet another reason why they pushed into child labour. As compared to the Katkaris, the status of Bhil children who work as child labourers is better though.

CHILD LABOUR AND RIGHTS ISSUES AMONG THE BHIL SUGARCANE CUTTERS: ANALYTICAL REFLECTIONS

Child labour and rights issues of children of the Bhil sugarcane migrant labourers cannot be studied in isolation, without understanding their socio-economic background and reasons for migration. The qualitative data presented in the form of 25 case studies in this chapter, along with quantitative data presented, analyzed and interpreted in the form of tables supports the model and the hypothesis developed in this study.

The poor Bhil sugarcane cutters migrate seasonally to the sugarcane fields because of the following push factors:

1. **Poverty:** This study revealed that 65 per cent of the Bhil Sugarcane cutters were below the poverty line. In his report captioned, "Human Development Indicators among the Scheduled Tribes of Maharashtra",

Tribhuwan Robin (2009), submitted to TRTI, Pune, has revealed that 92.5 per cent of the Bhils were Below Poverty Line. Poverty is no doubt, one of the main push factors that push them to the sugarcane farms.

2. **Unemployment in the place of origin:** The data revealed that 100 per cent of the migrants were unemployed and hence were forced to migrate to the kilns.
3. **Unskilled Labourers:** 100 per cent of the respondents were unskilled and therefore migrated to the kilns.
4. **Meager Landholding:** The data revealed that 71 per cent of the respondents were landholders while 29 per cent were landless. Those who owned meager land could not produce enough food grains to sustain for the entire year and hence migrated. The land gets divided among the 3 or 4 brothers therefore cannot produce enough food grains. In their report captioned, "Malnutrition related deaths of tribal children in Nandurbar District," Bhatia Arun and Tribhuwan Robin (2002:1), revealed that 72 per cent of families owned land less than three acres of which 40 per cent were landless or owned land less than 1 acre.
5. **Poor housing conditions:** As explained in this chapter the conditions of Bhil houses is very poor in the place of destination as well as at the place of origin.
6. **Illiteracy:** It was observed that 77 per cent of respondents studied were illiterate.They cannot get jobs in private and Government sectors; hence they migrate to the sugarcane farms.
7. **Indebtedness:** The data revealed that 76 per cent of the sugarcane cutters were indebted. They borrow Rs. 5,000/- to Rs.25,000/- from the sugarcane contractors. This amount is repaid in the form of labour, the following year. The contractor deducts loan amount, food, medical and other expenses and the remaining money is given to them at the end of season. The balance money is hardly Rs.5000/- to 8000/-, the labourers are therefore forced to take more loan while returning home and hence get trapped into bonded labour.
8. **Bonded Labour:** Data in this study revealed that 76 per cent of the sugarcane cutters were hooked into bonded labour, for their inability to clear debt.
9. **Economic and hunger crisis:** Economic and hunger crisis in the place of origin is yet another factor that push the Bhil to the sugarcane farms. In their report captioned, "Malnutrition related deaths of Tribal Children in Nandurbar District of Maharashtra", Bhatia Arun and Tribhuwan Robin (2002:10), have revealed that 78 per cent of the households had a food deficit of 6 or more months.
10. **Lack of Economic Assets:** Other than few vessels, clothes and bed sheets, the Katakari brick kiln labourers do not possess any economic assets

both in the place of origin and at the place of destination. This aspect is seen in most nomadic societies. Lack of economic assets is yet another reason for migration among the Bhils.

11. **Kharchi and Uchal-pull factors** : **Their hope to survival** – Despite of the long hours of hard work in hot and cold conditions, the poor living conditions at the sugarcane farms, the exploitation by the owners and contractors, indebtedness and bonded labour, the factories & mukadams (contractors) are the saviors of the labourers. They are ATM machines, finance institutions and debit cards for the Bhils. They provide money in advance toto the contractors attract labour.The need for lump-sum advance for consumption expenditure, to get their children married,pay medical bills makes the workers to approach the contractor. The adults and children are able to survive because of the mukadams (contractors), who provide them jobs. Hence 'Kharchi' (fortnightly expenses) and 'Uchal' (Loan) are considered by the respondents as their hope of survival. The researcher rates these two pull factors as the main factors for seasonal migration among the Bhils.

12. **Lack of Adult Manpower:** The 100 Bhil sugarcane cutterrs' families studied compıises of 129 adult males (28%), 104 i.e. (22%) of adult females and 235 (50%) of children. On an average every Bhil family had 2 to 3 children living at the sugarcane fields. If one analyses the number of adults per family, it comprised mainly of father and mother and in some cases father in law or another member. As compared to the quantum or workload, two or three adults could find it difficult to achieve the same. It is because of this reason, children especially those belonging to the age range 7 to 14 years were forced to participate in activities such as making sugarcane bundles, transporting sugarcane bundles etc. These children helped their parents to achieve work targets, as well as managed to take care of their younger siblings, managed household work, while some attended school. It was also observed that children between the age 15 to 18 received wages depending on the type of labour and number of hours incurred. This was also a sought of training to work as adult before getting married and learning how to earn money on one's own.

13. **What is important, survival, child labour or child rights?** – From an etic (outsider's) perspective this question is sensitive, it is linked with human and child rights etc. the emic (insider's) perspective is however contradictory. To the Bhils, the migrant sugarcane cutters, the sugarcane farm owners, factory owners and contractors are their saviors, banks, ATM machines and debit cards because the Employment Guarantee Scheme and other Government schemes do not provide them employment, food, clothing, shelter, medicine and other basic necessities of life. Therefore exploitation bonded labour, child labour, deprivation

of child rights to the Bhils at sugarcane farms are not so important as compared to the jobs they get to survive at the sugarcane farms.

Given this background, let us look in to child labour and child rights issues among the children of Bhil Sugarcane cutters.

14. **Child Labour Issues:** It was observed that out of 235 children of the 100 families studied 125 i.e. 53.19 per cent were working at the brick kilns to support their parents so as to achieve their work targets. Out of these 52 per cent working children 25 per cent children working as Commercial Labourers and remaning 28 per cent were working at sugarcane farms to help their parents without any wages. Out of the total number of working children33 per cent were males and 65 i.e. 20 per cent were females. It is also pertinent to note that here the remaining 110 i.e. 47 per cent of children who were forced to accompany their parents to the sugarcane farms were also deprived of child rights.

As mentioned earlier child labour in this study has been classified into following categories:

(a) Child labourers who support the parents to achieve work targets by helping the parents in doing small jobs such as making bundles of sugarcane tops; counting the number of bundles, making the bundles of sugarcane etc. These children also manage domestic work, attend school. These children do not receive anything in cash from the contractor or farm owner. These children belong to the age range between 6 to 10 years.

(b) Child Labourers who are paid by the owners. These are children who are better in sugarcane cutting, carrying sugarcane bundles from farm to the lorry, loading and unloading the sugarcane bundles in lorry. They are paid daily wages by the mukadams depending on the type of work they do per day. These wages range from Rs. 50 to Rs. 125/-. If a couple (husband and wife is accompanied by a child to work as a unit. This association of three members is called 'did koyta' meaning one and half koyta. In the second category of child labourers the children are mostly drop outs and belong to the age group 13 to 18 years.

Nature of Child Labour – The hazardous aspect of child labour as regards sugarcane cutting is the exposure of children to sharp blades of sugarcane leaves which createitching sensation cuts the skin also,extreme hot and cold conditions, dust and finally the long number of working hours at the sugarcane farms. Besides this, these children also become victims of the unhealthy environment, unclean drinking water, food exposed to dust etc. The children as well as their parents sometimes become pray to scorpion stings and snake bites.

15. **Child Rights Issues:** Forced migration of the parents due to utter poor economic conditions, indebtedness, bonded labour, lack of employment opportunities in the place of origin, landlessness, unskilled nature of labour etc. factors push them to the sugarcane fields. This in turn directly affects the growth and progress of their children who are dependent on them for survival.

Given below are statistics that prove how the children of Bhil sugarcane cutters are deprived of their rights.

(a) **Child Labour:** It was observed that out of 235 children of the 100 families studied 125 i.e. 53.19 per cent were working at the brick kilns to support their parents so as to achieve their work targets. Out of these 52 per cent working children 25 per cent children working as Commercial Labourers and remaning 28 per cent were working at sugarcane farms to help their parents without any wages. Out of the total number of working children33 per cent were males and 65 i.e. 20 per cent were females. It is also pertinent to note that here the remaining 110 i.e. 47 per cent of children who were forced to accompany their parents to the sugarcane farms were also deprived of child rights.

(b) **Elementary Education : Right of every child** – As revealed in table number 4.43, that out of 235 Bhil children studied, only 44 per cent children were school going children, 41 per cent were non-school going children while 15 per cent of them were drop outs from the school, that is total 56 per cent of the children studied were out of school. This proves that children of Bhil migrant sugarcane cutters are deprived of their fundamental right to education.

(c) **Right to play and recreation:** The study has revealed that there were no recreational facilities for children. 100 per cent of them stated that there were no recreational facilities for children available. Here again it has been proved that children are deprived of their right to play and recreation.

(d) Right to Health:

- *Immunization/Vaccination:* This study has revealed that 76 per cent of the Bhil parents have vaccinated their children while 12 per cent of them have not vaccinated their children. When asked, which vaccines have you given to your children most of them told that, they have given polio dose to their children. Hardly any one of them has given other vaccines like Hepatitis B, Hepatitis C, Smallpox, chickenpox, DPT, BCG, etc. to their children, and this is because of unawareness among the parents.

- *Nutrition:* Out of the total 235 Bhil children, belonging to families of 100 respondents, the researcher was able to get age, height and weight of 205 Children. Nutritional status of 205 children is as: 57 i.e 28 per cent - Normal; 38 i.e18 per cent - Grade I (Mild Malnutrition); 59 i.e. 29 per cent - Grade II (Moderate Malnutrition); 34 i.e. 17 per cent - Grade III (Severe Malnutrition); 17 i.e 08 per cent Grade IV (Severe Malnutrition). Out of 205, 148 i.e. 72.19 per cent of Bhil children were malnourished. From this statistics it is clear that children of Bhil sugarcane cutters are deprived of their basic right to nutrition.
- *Day Care & Crèche Facility:* Study has also revealed that facility of day care and Crèche for the children of Bhil migrant sugarcane cutters is not provided either by farm owner not by Government.

(e) *Right to Parental Care:* It is clear from the data collected by the researcher that all the respondents work on the brick kilns around 10 to 12hours daily, sometimes more 12 hours depending on the target of work. The parents get less time to care for their children. Nursing mothers take off 10 to 20 minutes to feed their children, but over all parental care during the day time is lacking. This certainly proves that the children of brick kiln labourers are deprived of their right to parental care because of the busy schedule of the parents.

(f) *Right to shelter/housing:* As already reported previous section of the chapter, in table number 4.19 and 4.22, the conditions of housing of Katkari labourers is poor both at the place of origin as well as at the place of destination. The children are certainly deprived of right to decent housing.

CHAPTER 5

Child Welfare Programmes by Government and NGOs

INTRODUCTION

An attempt has been made by the researcher in this chapter to throw light on some of the programmes by the Government of Maharashtra as well as N.G.Os for the welfare of children of the brick kiln katkari labourers and the Bhil sugar cane cutters. The findings of the study with regards to child welfare programmes are presented in two sections namely programmes by the government and programmes by the N.G.Os. This chapter also throws light on what more needs to be done for the target population.

CHILD WELFARE PROGRAMMES BY THE GOVERNMENT

It was observed that there are no specific Government programmes for the children of brick kiln labourers nor for sugar cane cutters.

There are several programmes implemented for tribal children by various government departments, including the tribal department. It is necessary to note that some of the major schemes implemented by the Government for tribal children. The annual Tribal Sub-Plan of the Tribal Development Department, every year allocates budget as per the major scheme heads. Given below are some of the major schemes for tribal children (Tribal Sub-Plan 2009-2010).

1. Government Ashram schools

The Tribal Development Department is running residential Ashram schools in hilly and remote areas of Maharashtra for social, cultural and educational development of tribal children. In Maharashtra, the Tribal Development Department is running 1078 Ashram schools to cater to the educational, health, nutritional and socio-cultural needs of 4.25 lakh tribal children. An outlay of Rs. 10952.79 lakhs has been provided for this programme during the year 2008-09.

2. Junior Colleges (Attatched to Ashram Schools)

The Government of Maharashtra has attached 67 junior colleges to the secondary Ashram Schools from 1999-2000. As per 2009-10 statistics 9,079 tribal students, i.e. 5343 boys and 3536 girls are beneficiaries of this programme. An outlay of Rs. 394.00 lakhs has been provided under T.S.P. during the year 2009-10.

3. Education in Aided Ashram Schools

There are 556 aided Ashram Schools run by Non Government Organizations, catering educational services to 2,25,576 tribal students, i.e. 1,35,628 boys & 89,948 girls. An outlay of Rs. 3552.06 lakhs has been provided in TSP for the year 2008-09.

4. Junior Colleges (attached to aided Ashram Schools)

25 junior colleges are run by N.G.Os catering services to 3942 tribal students, i.e. 2716 boys and 1326 girls. An outlay of Rs. 78.21 lakhs has been provided under T.S.P. 2009-10 for this programme.

5. Government Hostels for tribal students

343 hostels are being run by the Government that caters lodging, boarding and educational services to 22,733 tribal students i.e. 14,575 boys and 8,158 girls. An outlay of 2701.87 lakhs has been provided under TSP 2009-10.

6. Maintenance Allowance to tribal students of hostels

Since the intake capacity of Government hostels is limited, tribal students are encouraged to stay in hostels, attached to professional colleges. Each student gets Rs. 100/- including Government of India's scholarship. An outlay of Rs. 173.81 lakh is provided under TSP 2009-10.

7. Traveling allowance and scholarship for the Handicapped students who are studying in 8th to 12th grades

A traveling allowance of Rs. 100/- and scholarship of Rs. 500/- per month per student is given. An outlay of Rs. 62.12 lakh has been provided under T.S.P. 2009-10. There is no information on how many handicapped students have benefited from this scheme.

8. Incentives to S.T. girls to reduce dropout rates

The tribal sub-plan (2009-10) states that the dropout rate after 4th grade was 30-35 per cent and after 7th grade it is 60-70 per cent. The census of India, 2001 states that out of the total 353 blocks in Maharashtra, 88 blocks show that the literacy rate of tribal women as below 35. Under this scheme, tribal girls studying in 1 to 4th grade get Rs. 1/- per day as attendance allowance. For girls studying from 5th to 7th grade, get Rs. 50/- per month and for those studying from 8th to 10th grade get Rs. 100/- per month for 10 months. More than 25,000 tribal girls are likely to get benefit from this scheme. An outlay of Rs. 3315.19 lakhs is provided under T.S.P. 2005-10 for this programme.

9. Establishment of model schools for Scheduled Tribe students

Government has started these model schools in Nandurbar and Ahmadnagar districts. An outlay of 10 lakhs is provided in T.S.P. 2009-10.

10. Eklavya English Medium Schools

The Government of Maharashtra with the assistance under article 275(1) of the constitution has established 4 Eklavya English Medium Schools. 850 students i.e. 510 boys and 340 girls are benefited from this programme. An outlay of Rs. 500.00 lakhs is provided for this scheme.

11. Cash awards for meritorious students of 10th& 12th grades

In order to encourage brilliant tribal students, six awards are declared by the government. Three boys and three girls get Rs. 25000/-, 15000/- and 10000/- respectively including Rs. 1000/- per month. An outlay of Rs. 29.00 lakhs is provided under T.S.P. 2009-10.

12. Women and child welfare and nutrition programmes

Although this package is for both women and children, in this section of the chapter, only those programmes that pertain to tribal children are presented. These are as follows:

(a) Child Welfare Programmes

(i) Supply of bicycles to girl students studying in 5th to 10th grades
(ii) Opening of new Balwadis (pre-schools)
(iii) Organizing diagnosis camps for tribal children
(iv) Supply of material/equipments to Anganwadis/Balwadis
(v) Organizing competitions for children
(vi) Purchase of education and sports material/equipments
(vii) Supply of uniforms to tribal students
(viii) Financial assistance to girls belonging to the ecumenically weaker sections for technical education
(ix) Lump sum grants to students for their education for studying in other districts a grant of 205.27 has been provided under T.S.P.

(b) Nutrition programme for tribal children

The I.C.D.S. sponsored programme by the Government of India, provides a packages of services to children below 6 years of age and to pregnant women, nursing mothers and adult women in the age group of 15 to 44 years. The main thrust of this programme is on health, nutrition and nutrition education.

Following services are being provided by I.C.D.S.

(i) Supplementary nutrition
(ii) Immunization
(iii) Health Check-up
(iv) Referral Services
(v) Nutrition and health education
(vi) Non formal education
(vii) Provision of local cereals and pulses

In his study captioned, "Functional Review of Tribal Development Department" Tribhuwan Robin (2006) has stated that, tribals are aware of schemes such as Ashram Schools, hostels, supply of electric and oil engines. However, their level of awareness regarding other schemes is very low.

Tomar Y.P.S. & Tribhuwan Robin (2004: 59-61) revealed following facts about the awareness and benefit level of government schemes among the Katkaris.

(i) **Awareness regarding election constituency**
The study revealed that 100 per cent of the Katkari respondents were unaware of their election constituency.

(ii) **Awareness regarding dates of Gram-sabha**
100 per cent of the respondents were unaware of the dates of Gram-sabhas.

(iii) **Awareness regarding the works taken up by the Gram-sabha**
100 per cent of the Katkaris were unaware of the works taken up by the Gram-sabhas.

(iv) **Awareness regarding tribal development agencies/Departments**
100 per cent were unaware of the same.

(v) **Awareness regarding tribal development schemes**
100 per cent of the katkari respondents were unaware of tribal development schemes.

(vi) **Benefits received from government schemes**
Only 2 per cent of the respondents benefited from government schemes, while 98 per cent did not.

(vii) **Benefits received by the Katkaris from the pen I.T.D.P. since 2001-2003**
100 per cent did not receive any benefit from the pen I.T.D.P.

(viii) **Tribal Identity certificate**
96 per cent of the respondents did not posses scheduled tribe certificates, while only 4 per cent possessed the same.

Informal interviews with the Katkaris as wells as Bhils revealed, that they availed a few schemes of the Tribal Development Department and Zilla

Parishad in the place of origin. Thus, schemes like housing programme, pubic distribution system scheme, goats, etc. are availed by the Bhils and Katkaris, in their native place.

AWARENESS REGARDING GOVERNMENT PROGRAMMES

This section of the chapter throws light on the awareness of the Katkaris and Bhills about few Government programmes for them.

Health Services from the P.H.C. and Sub-Centre

The respondents are very well aware of their rights & services given by the Sub-centre and P.H.C. In times of emergency they avail health services from the sub-centre and P.H.C. Their medical expenses are paid by the brick kiln owners and the contractors. These expenses are deducted while making the final payment. The table given below shows the level of awareness among brick kiln katkari labourers as well as the Bhil sugar cane cutters about P.H.C. & Sub-Centre.

Table 5.1: Awareness about P.H.C. & Sub-Centre

Sr. No.	Awareness Level	Tribe		Total	
		Katkaris	Bhils	No.	Per cent
1.	Aware	68	60	128	64
2.	Unaware	32	40	072	36
	Total	**100**	**100**	**200**	**100**

As evident from the above table, it is clear that 64 per cent of the respondents are aware that they must avail health services from the sub-centre as well as the P.H.C.

Awareness about Anganwadi

As evident from table 5.2, it is seen that 50 per cent of the respondents are aware of the Anganwadi i.e. ICDS (Integrated Child Development Scheme) scheme and its benefits.

Table 5.2: Awareness Regarding Anganwadi Programme

Sr. No.	Awareness Level	Tribe		Total	
		Katkaris	Bhils	No.	%
1.	Aware	47	53	100	50
2.	Unaware	53	47	100	50
	Total	**100**	**100**	**200**	**100**

It was observed that there is no significant difference between the level of awareness regarding Anganwadi among the Bhils & Katkaris.

Awareness Regarding Zilla Parishad Schools

Table 5.3 reveals that 62.5 per cent of the respondents are aware of the Zilla Parishad Schools.

Table 5.3: Awareness Regarding Zilla Parishad Schools

Sr. No.	Awareness Level	Tribe		Total	
		Katkaris	Bhils	No.	%
1.	Aware	56	69	125	62.5
2.	Unaware	44	31	075	37.5
	Total	100	100	200	100

Awareness Regarding Ashram School Programme

Table 5.4 reveals that 63 per cent of the respondents are aware of the Ashram Schools established by the Tribal Development Department, Government of Maharashtra. Ashram Schools take care of educational, nutritional and other needs of tribal children.

Table 5.4: Awareness Regarding Ashram Schools

Sr. No.	Awareness Level	Tribe		Total	
		Katkaris	Bhils	No.	%
1.	Aware	46	80	126	63
2.	Unaware	54	20	074	37
	Total	100	100	200	100

Awareness Regarding Polio drops and Immunization Programme

Both Katkari & Bhil respondents are aware of the Polio drops and immunization programmes implemented by the local P.H.C. and Sub-Centre. Table 5.5 reveals it all.

Table 5.5: Awareness Regarding Polio Drops and Immunization Programme

Sr. No.	Awareness Level	Tribe		Total	
		Katkaris	Bhils	No.	%
1.	Aware	72	76	148	74
2.	Unaware	28	24	052	26
	Total	100	100	200	100

It is evident from the statistics and data presented in section 5.2 and 5.3 of this chapter, that the Katkari brick kiln labourers have:

1. Less or no knowledge of tribal development programmes.
2. That, they do not get benefits of most Government programmes except for ICDS, sub-centre, PHC, public distribution system, Zilla Parishad and Ashram Schools etc.
3. That, the benefits availed by the Katkaris as compared to other tribes is less or meager.

4. That, a few Katkaris have benefitted from the Gharkul (Housing) scheme, in the place of origin.
5. Lack of important documents such as Scheduled Tribe Certificate, ration card, land records, birth/death certificates, school leaving certificate, etc. clubbed with lack of economic assets, become hurdles in availing Government schemes.
6. High percentage of illiteracy and dropout rates too leaves no scope for the Katkari youth to avail programmes for training, self employment, deriving and bus conductor's training etc.

CHILD WELFARE PROGRAMME BY NGOS

The study has revealed that, although a few NGOs were trying to implement welfare programmes for a very negligible percentage of the respondents studied, they have failed to get them out of the bonded system of labour, and their miseries. Two major programmes were observed by the researcher which was being implemented for the children of sugarcane cutters as well as brick kiln labourers. These are:

1. Sugar Schools (Sakhar Shalas)
2. Siren Schools (Bhonga Shalas)

The Sugar Schools (Sakhar Shalas)

The Sakhar Shala programme is implemented through NGO and funded by the Government. Through this programme, the concerned NGO appoints a local teacher, preferably a female, who teaches the children of the sugarcane cutters. It is disheartening to note that majority of sakhar shalas are near sugar mills. One hardly gets to see Sakhar Shala near sugarcane fields. There may be exceptions to this rule. Except for teaching a few slates, note books etc. the students do not receive mid-day meal, recreation and other facilities.

The school building of a Sakhar Shala is a temporary hall made up of bamboo mat walls, a thatched or tin roof. Sometimes the entire hall is made up of tin structure. Facilities like fans, chairs, tables, lights etc are a dream to the children.

Janarth, an Aurangabad based NGO was doing a good job for the sugar cane cutters. Some of the programmes planned and implemented by Janarth for the sugar cane cutters were:

1. Research and Documentation
2. Sakhar Shala Programme for the children of sugar cane cutters.
3. Advocacy Issues etc.

As per the discussion with one of the social worker of Janarth, in the year 2007-08,in Maharashtra there were nine districts namely Ahamdnagar, Aurangabad, Nashik, Nanded, Parbhani, Pune, Satara, Sangli and Kolhapur; in Gujarat Surat and Baroda districts and in Karnataka Belgaon and Vijapur districts where Janarth was running Sakharshalas.

Table 5.6: Awareness Regarding Sugar Schools

Sr. No.	Awareness Level	Number	Percentage
1.	Aware	01	01
2.	Unaware	99	99
	Total	**200**	**100**

It was observed that the concept of sugar schools (Sakhar Shala) was conceived by Janarth, in order to do justice to the educational rights of children of sugar cane cutters – the distressed migrants, belonging to unorganized sector. The study revealed that out of total 2,00,000 children of sugarcane cutters, only 15,000 in the State of Maharashtra only 15,000 i.e. 6 per cent of the children were beneficiaries of Sakhar Shala programme.

Furthermore, it was observed that out of the total number of 236 children, belonging to 100 Bhil sugarcane cutters families studied 143 i.e. 52 per cent attended schools.

The literacy status of the children of Bhil sugar cane cutters belonging to the 100 families is as follows:

1. 39 per cent are ill-literate
2. 27 per cent studied up to primary
3. 22 per cent studied up to high school
4. 3 per cent studied up to Higher secondary
5. Not a single child went to college.

The sugar schools are no more functional. Government is encouraging the children to join Zilla Parishad Schools. NGOs are no more running Sakhar Shalas.

Siren Schools (Bhonga Shalas)

The Shramajeevi Sanghatana, a Thane based NGO, has conceived the concept of Bhonga shala. Shri. Vivek Pandit, an activist turned member of Legislative Assembly, Government of Maharashtra conceived the idea. Some of the programmes implemented by the Shramajeevi Sanghatana are as below :

1. Research and documentation
2. Bhonga shala schools programme
3. Advocacy issues of brick kiln labourers.

Bhonga Shala

Bhonga is a typical hut of the brick kiln labourer's at the site, Shala is School. A School in the temporary hut of the migrant Brick Kiln labourer.A School for the children of the Brick Kiln worker.A School for only six months of the year.A pioneer in addressing the issue of schooling of seasonal migrant labourer's children. (Jayschandran Usha, 2005-06)

According to Shramjeevi Sanghtana, an NGO in Thane, there were 84 siren schools (Bhonga Shalas) in the year 2005-06 in the state of Maharashtra, rendering educational services to 2793 children at brick kilns, belonging to various caste, nomadic groups and tribes. The table given below shows year-wise number of no. of blocks, no. of centers i.e. bonga shalas and students who attended Bhonga Shalas.

Coverage Table – Over the Years

Year	No. of Blocks	No. of Teachers	No. of Centers	No. of Students
1995-96	2	25	15	457
1996-97	2	52	11	1133
1997-98	2	81	22	2093
1998-99	2	82	30	2079
1999-2000	2	115	44	2784
2000-01	2	143	60	3169
2001-02	2	152	62	2956
2002-03	2	145	62	3078
2003-04	9	256	259	5086
2004-05	7	221	208	4265
2005-06	3	125	125	2793

Source: Bhonga Shala Report, 2005-06:12

The siren schools are no more functional. Government is encouraging the children to join Zilla Parishad Schools. NGOs are no more running Bhonga Shalas.

Out of the 100 Katkari respondents interviewed by the researcher in Raigad district only 1 per cent was aware of the Bhonga shala programme. Table 5.7 presents the level of awareness among the Katkari respondents regarding Bhonga Shalas.

Table 5.7: Awareness Regarding Bhonga Shala

Sr. No.	Level of Awareness	Number	Percentage
1.	Aware	01	01
2.	Unaware	99	99
	Total	**100**	**100**

It was observed that the concept of Bhonga Shala was conceived by Shri. Vivek Pandit, in order to justice to the educational needs of the children of brick kiln workers.

With the implementation of *The Right of Children to Free and Compulsory Education Act (No.35 of 2009)*, the Sugar schools and Siren schools have ceased to function. The NGOs and Activists who were involved in implementing these programmes are now encouraging the children of sugarcane cutters and brick kiln labourers to go to Zilla Parishad and Ashram Schools. It was however observed that their efforts have proved futile because children are dependent on their parents who are poor, indebted, bonded labourers, unskilled, landless, and illiterate and hence have no option but to migrate with them and further get forced into domestic work, child labour to support their parents and child labour to earn daily wages. This in turn deprives them of their rights to education, health, parental care etc.

Furthermore, it was observed that out of the total number of 197 Children belonging to the 100 katkari brick kiln laboures studied, only 74 i.e. 38 per cent attended schools regularly. The literacy status of the children of katkari brick kiln labourers studied is as follows:

1. 52 per cent are ill-literate
2. 25 per cent studied up to primary school
3. 10 per cent studied up to High school
4. 0 per cent studied up to Higher Secondary
5. Not a single child went to college.

To sum up both government and NGO programmes have not had a positive impact on the development of the Katkari brick kiln labourers.

WHAT MORE NEEDS TO BE DONE ?

Primary data presented in chapters 3 and 4 on the Socio-Economic background of the brick kiln Katkari labourers and the Bhil sugar cane cutters reveals that utter poverty, landlessness, unemployment and other push and pull factors force these bonded labourers to the kilns and sugar cane fields. They are unaware of their children's rights. The living conditions of both the tribes in the place of destination are poor and not worth for human habitation. A question that arises then, what more needs to be done?

Given below are few suggestions for both Government and Non-Government Organizations. If bonded labour and seasonal migration has to stop, efforts must be made to implement following programmes.

1. Culturally and Ecologically Appropriate Housing

Permanent houses should be built for the Katkaris and bhils in their place of origin ie native place. These houses should as per their cultural traditions and norms. The houses should be ecologically appropriate. The beneficiaries should be involved in planning, implementation and monitoring house construction. They should be permitted to follow their construction rituals.

If they have permanent and strong houses, this will inspire them to live in their native villages.

2. **Self employment**

   Merely giving houses will not solve their problem. They should be given employment during October-May, through Employment Guarantee scheme and National Rural Employment Guarantee Scheme and other programmes.

3. **Agriculture land**

   Each family should be given irrigated land, so that they can cultivate cereals, pulses and vegetables for themselves. This will be a hope for survival.

4. **Live Stock**

   Goats, bulls cows and buffaloes should given to them, so that they earn some money from the same.

5. **Wells and bore wells**

   Wells and bore wells should be installed in or around the hamlets of the Katkaris and Bhils. This will ensure that they get drinking water.

6. **Incentives for education**

   Incentives in kind and cash should be given for both girls and boys so that the rate of enrollment and school attendance goes up.

7. **I.C.D.S. unit**

   Every Katkari and Bhil hamlet, where brick Kiln labourers and sugar cane cutters live should have an Anganwadi.

8. **Legalization of Daily wage labour:**

   The daily wage labour fixed by the government should be strictly implemented by the brick kiln owners and contractors, for both male and female adults.

9. **Provident Fund**

   The brick kiln owners and sugar cane Mukardams should chalk out a provident fund policy for every family working for them.

10. **Educational plans**

    The owners and contractors should also chalkout education policy plan for the children of Katkari brick kiln labourers and the Bhil sugar cane cutters.

11. **Awareness programme**

    NGO's can take up awareness campaigns to educate the target beneficiaries on child rights, education, health, nutrition, development programmes etc.

12. **Recruitment of educated youth**

    Educated boys and girls of the labourers should be employed as peons, sweepers, cooks, watchman, compounders etc in Government departments.

13. Revamping of Bhonga and Sakhare shala programme

In order to prevent child labour the Bhonga and Sakhar shalas should be empowered with more staff, better system of education, mid-day meal facilities, recreation facilities etc. This will attract children there.

14. Hostels

Special hostels should be established in block head quarters for the children of brick kiln labourers and sugar cane cutters.

15. Ashram schools

Parents should be motivated to admit their children in government and aided Ashram schools.

16. Strict prohibition of child labour

Child labour should be strictly prohibited at the brick kilns and sugar cane fields.

17. Free the labourers

It is very necessary to free the brick kiln labourers and sugarcane cutters from indebtedness, poverty, bonded labourer, economic and hunger crisis. The present young generation needs to be educated if progress is the vision of Government and Non-Government Organizations.

18. Strict implementation of The Right of Children to Free and Compulsory Education Act (No. 35 of 2009)

Grass root level Government Agents such as school teachers, head masters, wardens, gram Sevaks, ICDS workers, Tribal Development Inspectors etc. along with sincere, genuine social workers of good NGOs can be given financial incentives to encourage the children of sugarcane cutters and brick kiln labourers to go to school and monitor and follow up their educational progress.

19. National Rural Employment Guarantee Scheme

National Rural Employment Guarantee Scheme is an important scheme which ecsures employment to the rural and tribal people at least for 100 days a year. This scheme is applicable both Bhil sugarcane cutters and Katkari Brick kiln labourers.

CHAPTER 6

Summary of Findings, Conclusions and Recommendations

SUMMARY OF FINDINGS

The subject of movement of populations has occupied a prominent place in social as well as biological sciences. The shifts of physical space and their consequences – economic, social, political and biological – has been the focus of enquiry of many studies (Malhotra K.C., 1976:3). The term migration means movement of an individual, a family, a group or a community from one place to another.

The concept of migration is as old as human civilization. Migration is a process through which people move from one place to residence to another. The change in residence results in redistribution of population, both at its place of origin and place of destination. The process of migration changes the size and structure of population.

Social scientists have defined the concept of migration differently. According to Everett Lee, "permanent or semi-permanent change of residence is migration." Tripathy and Das, define migration as the flow of people over shorter or longer distances from one origin to a destination, either for temporary or permanent settlement. Winberg (1961) defines migration as the change of place permanently or temporarily for an appreciable duration as in case of seasonal labourers.

Concept of migration has been classified in to several types namely:

1. Permanent or temporary migration.
2. Forced or voluntary migration.
3. External or Internal migration.

Social science studies on migration reveal that people migrate from one place of residence to another for following reasons.

1. **Economic Reasons:** For economic reasons such as jobs, business, trade, barter system, collection of Minor Forest Produce etc.
2. **Educational purpose:** For attaining higher education in cities, towns or even abroad.
3. **Political Reasons:** Those who elected has political representatives in the State or National Governments migrate to the capital of the State or to the country to represent the concerned Government.
4. **Due to natural and manmade calamities:** People migrate due to natural calamities such as earth quake, flood, eruption of volcanoes, storm, epidemics etc. and manmade calamities such as riots, wars due to development projects etc.

In the case of Katkari brick kiln labourers and Bhil sugarcane cutters who migrate seasonally (temporarily) to place of destination, are forced due to certain push and pull factors identified through this research study. On the basis of pilot study conducted before the fieldwork and the data collected by administering 200 interview schedules and documenting 50 case studies of respondent, supported with review of literature, a conceptual model was developed and proved scientifically through the data collected analyzed and interpreted.

The child labour and child rights conceptual model is the main contribution of this study. The model will certainly be useful to study various communities that form part of the unorganized labour. Secondly, the research study has also developed an appropriate methodology to study the concept of child labour and child rights issues of two tribal communities. Thirdly, the recommendation given in the study will surely be useful to policy makers for developing appropriate and culturally acceptable programmes for the children of communities that form part of the unorganized labour.

Objectives of the Study

The study aimed at unveiling certain issues of child labour and child rights among Bhil Sugarcane cutters and Katkari brick kiln laboures.

1. To study the socio-economic and living conditions of sugar-cane cutting Bhil labourers and brick kiln Katkari workers of Nandurbar and Raigad Districts respectively.
2. To explore the process and patterns of seasonal migration and among the Bhils and Katkaris.
3. To assess the impact of socio-economic and environmental conditions of the brick kiln workers and sugar-cane cutters on the physical, mental, social, educational and economic growth of their children.
4. To study the impact of seasonal migration and bonded labour on the rights of their children.
5. To understand the factors that give rise to child labour among the brick-kiln and sugar-cane cutting labourers.

6. To document the level of awareness among Bhils & Katkari labourers regarding constitutional provisions, policies, laws and rights of their children.
7. To study the various Government Programmes implemented for these communities and their children at the place of origin and destination.
8. To develop a conceptual model on the issue of child labour and rights among the unorganized tribal labourers.
9. To suggest an action plan for the development of children of brick-kiln and sugar cane cutting tribes and their children.

Hypothesis

1. Extreme poverty, unemployment, landlessness, economic, food and debt crisis, temporary and poor housing, heavy interests on loans, illiteracy, bonded labour, social and economic insecurity, lack of economic assets and unskilled labour status at the place of origin push the Katkari brick kiln labourers and Bhil sugarcane cutters to the kilns and sugarcane fields.
2. Assured *Kharchi* – the weekly expenses, *Uchal* – the loan and employment guarantee at the kilns and sugarcane fields pull the Katkaris and Bhils to the place of destination.
3. Push and the pull factors hook the parents into bonded labour.
4. Poor socio-economic background of the parents, heavy workload targets (i.e. daily, weekly and monthly) and less adult manpower in the family hook children into child labour and deprives them of their rights.
5. Awareness of child rights among the Katkari brick kiln labourers and Bhil sugarcane cutters is absent.

Significance of the Study

Studies by social scientists and more particularly Economists and Social workers are available in abundance on informal sector and allied issues. Among the Sociologists other than Jan Breman's book captioned, "Footloose Labour" (1996), and "Down and Out: Labouring under Global Capitalism" (2000), there are hardly any Sociological studies on informal sector. One of the latest studies by Smita and Prashant Panjiar (2007), highlights the struggle and problems faced by the sugar-cane cutters and brick kiln workers due to migration. However, there are no studies on child rights and child labour among children of brick kiln workers and sugar cane cutters. Hence the findings reported in this study are significant.

This study will certainly give rise to new Sociological theoretical insights. The conceptual model evolved in this study has been proved with the help of statistical data as well as qualitative data presented in the form of case studies. With the help of present model social scientists will be able to study child labour and rights issues among migrant labourers working in other occupational categories of unorganized labour sector. Further, comparative studies on various occupational groups of migrant labourers among the Indian tribes, caste groups and nomadic communities can be carried out so as to test the model. The conceptual model is hence both theoretical as well as methodological contribution.

At the practical level the study will contribute in developing action plans and programmes for the welfare and appropriate policies for the development and empowerment of the brick kiln workers and sugar-cane cutters.

The present study was conducted in 7 villages in the Shahada and Taloda blocks of Nandurbar district and 14 villages in Pen and Khalapur blocks of Raigad district in the state of Maharashtra. Chapter two presents detailed methodology used by the authors to collect, analyse, interpret and present primary and secondary data of the present study.

Major Findings

Given the above background in this section of the chapter major findings of the study are presented. Chapters three and four give separately data of the Katkari brick kiln labourers and Bhil sugarcane cutters. This chapter presents an aggregate sum of the total 200 respondents.

Age of Respondents

It was observed that 88 per cent of the respondents studied belonged to the age group 18 to 45 years, while 2.5 per cent of them were below 18. This means that these labourers spend their peak time of adulthood in working as bonded labourers, without economic, educational, social and health security. Table number 3.5 of chapter three reveals that 94 per cent of the Katkari brick kiln labourers belonged to the age group 18 to 45 year. Similarly, table number 4.5 of chapter four reveals that 82 per cent of the Bhil sugarcane cutters studied belonged to the age group of 18 to 45 years. Generally, married couples of this age group have small children whose life becomes miserable at the worksites, since they are forced to migrate with their parents.

Table 6.1: Age of the Respondents

Sr. No.	Age range	Number	Percentage
1.	Below 18	05	02.5
2.	18-25	53	26.5
3.	25-30	40	20
4.	30-35	33	16.5
5.	35-40	25	12.5
6.	40-45	25	12.5
7.	45-50	07	03.5
8.	50-55	09	04.5
9.	55-60	02	01
10.	Above 60	01	00.5
	Total	**200**	**100%**

Educational Status of Respondents

As evident from table number 6.2, 79 per cent of the respondents were illiterate, 8.5 per cent studied up to primary, 10 per cent up to secondary school, 1 per cent up to higher secondary school, 0.5 per cent were undergraduate, 0.5 per cent were post graduate and 0.5 per cent with agriculture diploma. Table number 3.6 of chapter three revealed that 87 per cent of the Katkari brick kiln labourers studied was illiterate. Table number 4.6 of chapter four revealed that 77 per cent of the Bhil sugarcane cutters studied was illiterate. This data certainly supports the model conceived in this study; illiteracy among the migrant labourers of the unorganized sector is one of the key push factors that force them to migrate seasonally.

Table 6.2: Educational Status of Respondents

Sr. No.	Education	Number	Percentage
1.	Illiterate	158	79
2.	Primary (1-4)	17	8.5
3.	Secondary (5-10)	20	10
4.	Higher Secondary (11-12)	02	01
5.	Undergraduate	01	0.5
6.	Graduate	00	00
7.	Post-Graduate	01	0.5
8.	Diploma	01	0.5
9.	Others	00	00
	Total	**200**	**100**

Main Occupation

As revealed in table number 6.3, 35 per cent of the respondents stated that their main occupation was brick making, 30 per cent stated that it was sugarcane cutting, 23 per cent were small scale cultivators, 6.5 per cent agricultural labourers and 5.5 per cent were daily wage labourers. It is pertinent to mention at this juncture that those having agricultural land cultivate small scale crops or vegetables during the rainy season when they are at home, while the landless work as agriculture or daily wage labourers during the monsoon. However during the months of October to May they work as brick kiln labourers and sugarcane cutting labourers.

Table 6.3: Main Occupation

Sr. No.	Occupation	Number	Percentage
1.	Brick making	70	35
2.	Sugarcane cutting	60	30
3.	Small scale cultivators	46	23
4.	Agriculture Labour	13	06.5
5.	Daily Wage Labour	11	05.5
	Total	**200**	**100**

Family Size

The study revealed 54.5 per cent of the respondents had family size of four members, 37 per cent was of 5 to 6 members while 8 per cent was of 7 to 8 members. Table number 3.8 of chapter three reveals that 63 per cent of the Katkari brick kiln labourers had family size of members up to four further table number 4.8 of chapter four revealed that 46 per cent of the Bhil sugarcane cutters had family size up to four members. This indicates that majority of the Katkari and Bhil families that migrate are nuclear families, hence their small children are forced to migrate with them and get into domestic work and child labour at the worksite at an early age. It was also observed that daily and weekly work targets of the nuclear families force their children to get into domestic work and child labour.

Table 6.4: Family Size

Sr. No.	Family Size	Number	Percentage
1.	Upto 4	109	54.5
2.	5-6	74	37
3.	7-8	16	08
4.	Above 8	01	0.5
	Total	**200**	**100**

Total Population Covered

The total population studied of both the Bhil and the Katkari families comprising of 239 adult males (27%); 213 adult females (24%); 220 male children (25%) and 211 female children (24%) was covered for the study.

Table 6.5: Total Population Covered

Sr. No.	Family Size	Number	Percentage
1.	Adult Males	239	27
2.	Adult Females	213	24
3.	Male Children	220	25
4.	Female children	211	24
	Total	**883**	**100**

Status of Migration to Brick-kilns and Sugarcane Farms

As revealed in table 6.6, 100 per cent of the respondents studied migrated to sugarcane farms as well as brick kiln sites.

Table 6.6: Status of Migration to Brick Kilns and Sugarcane Farms

Sr. No.	Status	Number	Percentage
1.	Migrate	200	100
2.	Do not migrate	00	00
	Total	**200**	**100**

Mode of Transportation

It was observed that 21 per cent of the respondents migrated by using their own bullock cart, 40 per cent by truck, 9.5 per cent by bus, 9.5 per cent by temp, 1.5 per cent by train, 0.5 per cent by tractor, 4.5 per cent by other transportation facilities such as auto while 13.5 per cent of the respondents migrated to the site by walking. From the table given below it is seen that majority of the respondents i.e.50.5 per cent are transported by trucks/tempo or tractors. This means that the brick kiln owners as well as sugarcane cutting contractors bank a lot on the services of the said unorganized labour force.

Table 6.7: Mode of Transportation

Sr. No.	Mode of Transportation	Number	Percentage
1.	Tractor	01	00.5
2.	Truck	80	40
3.	Bullock Cart	42	21
4.	Bus	19	09.5
5.	Train	03	01.5
6.	Tempo	19	09.5
7.	Walk	27	13.5
8.	Other (eg.Auto etc.)	09	04.5
	Total	**200**	**100**

Payment of Transportation

When asked, who bears transportation expenses to go to the work sites? They stated that payment of 32 per cent of the respondents is made by the brick kiln owners, 13 per cent by contractors, 6.5 per cent by sugarcane factory, 35 per cent by the respondents themselves.

Table 6.8: Bearing of Travel Expenses

Sr. No.	Travel Expenses Paid by	Number	Percentage
1.	Self	70	35
2.	Factory	13	06.5
3.	Mukadam/Middlemen	26	13
4.	Brick Owner	64	32
5.	Walk	27	13.5
	Total	**200**	**100**

Status of Employment at the Place of Origin

Out of the total 200 respondents interviewed, it was observed that 100 per cent of them were unemployed at the place of origin. Table 3.13 of chapter three, revealed that 100 per cent of the Katkari respondents were unemployed, so was the case with the Bhil sugarcane cutters as aptly revealed in the table number 4.13 of chapter four. Unemployment in this case is yet another push factor and supports the model conceptualized.

Table 6.9: Status of Employment at the Place of Origin

Sr. No.	Status	Number	Percentage
1.	Unemployed	200	100
2.	Employed	00	00
	Total	**200**	**100**

Type of Labourers

Table 6.10 indicates that 100 per cent of the respondents studied were unskilled. Further, table 3.14 of chapter three and 4.14 of chapter four states that 100 per cent of the Katkaris and Bhils studied were unskilled. Thus, the variable of unskilled workers, becomes a key push factors in seasonal migration and supports the model.

Table 6.10: Type of Labourers

Sr. No.	Type of Labourers	Number	Percentage
1.	Unskilled	200	100
2.	Skilled	00	00
	Total	**200**	**100**

As shown in table number 6.11, 48 per cent of the respondents are landless while 52 per cent owned land. A question was asked to most of the respondents, if you own land then why you are victims of indebtedness, bonded labour and poverty? Their unanimous and common response was, the land owned by them belonged to 3 to 4 brothers or family members, and the yield gets distributed. Meager land holding, poor quality of land and less agriculture yield per family are major push factors that initiate seasonal migration.

Table 6.11: Landholding Status of Respondents

Sr. No.	Status	Number	Percentage
1.	Landholders	104	52
2.	Landless	096	48
	Total	**200**	**100**

Type of Cultivable Land

Out of the total 104 landholders who owned land i.e. 98 per cent owned non-irrigated land. This again indicates the marginal status of farming among the respondents interviewed.

Table 6.12: Type of Land Owned

Sr. No.	Status	Number	Percentage
1.	Non-irrigated	102	98
2.	Irrigated	02	02
	Total	**104**	**100**

Acre-wise Land Owned

As evident in table number 6.13, out of the total 104 respondents, who owned land, 48 per cent had land up to 1-3 acres; 39 per cent up to 3-6 acres; 7 per cent up to 6-9 acres and 6 per cent above 9 acres. The Bhils were found to have more land than the Katkaris.

Table 6.13: Acrewise Land Owned

Sr. No.	Area of Land in Acres	Number	Total
1.	1-3 Acres	50	48%
2.	3-6 Acres	41	39%
3.	6-9Acres	07	07%
4.	Above 9 Acres	06	06%
	Total	**104**	**100%**

Status of Housing at the Place of Origin

As evident from table number 6.14, 92.5 per cent possess their own house. As regards the areas of the house table number 6.15 reveals that 21 per cent of the respondents' houses having an area less than 100 sq.ft; 34.5 per cent between 200 to 300 sq.ft. while 16.5 per cent between 100 to 200sq.ft. This means that 72 per cent of the respondents studied lived in the houses at the place of their origin, having an area less than 300 sq.ft. Further, table number 6.16 revealed that 79.5 per cent of the respondents lived in the houses made up of stick walls with thatched and tiled roofs. This statistics also supports the model that temporary and poor housing conditions at the place of origin is one of the many push factors that force them to migrate.

Table 6.14: Possession of Own House at the Place of Origin

Sr. No.	Status	Number	Total
1.	Possess	185	92.5
2.	Do not possess	015	07.5
	Total	**200**	**100**

Table 6.15: Area of House at the Place of Origin

Sr. No.	Area of Land in Acres	Number	Total
1.	Less than 100 Sq.ft	42	21
2.	100 to 200 Sq.ft.	33	16.5
3.	200 to 300 Sq.ft.	69	34.5
4.	300 to 500 Sq.ft.	50	25
5.	Above 500 Sq.ft.	06	03
	Total	**200**	**100**

Table 6.16: Type of House at the Place of Origin

Sr. No.	Type of House	Number	Total
1.	Stick walls & thatched roof	147	79.5
2.	Stick walls with tiled roof	025	13.5
3.	Brick walls with tiled roof	09	05
4.	Home through Gharkul Scheme	04	02
	Total	**185**	**100**

Status of Housing at the Place of Destination

As evident from tables 6.17 and 6.18, 100 per cent of the respondents do not possess own house at the place of destination. Table number 6.18 reveals that 46 per cent lives in temporary houses having an area less than 50 sq.ft; while 46.5 per cent live in the houses having an area between 51 to 100sq.ft. This means 92.5 per cent of the respondents studied live in the houses having an area less than 100sq.ft. It was observed that their houses are made up of sticks, bamboos, raw brick walls with thatched and plastic sheets' roof. These houses too are substandard as compared to their houses at the place of origin.

Table 6.17: Possession of Own House at the Place of Destination

Sr. No.	Status	Number	Total
1.	Do not possess	200	100
2.	Possess	00	00
	Total	**200**	**100**

Table 6.18: Area of House at the Place of Destination

Sr. No.	Status	Number	Percentage
1.	Less than 50 sq.ft	92	46
2.	51 to 100 sq.ft	93	46.5
3.	101 to 150 sq.ft	11	05.5
4.	151 to 200 sq.ft	02	01
5.	201 to 250 sq.ft	01	00.5
6.	251 to 300 sq.ft.	00	00
7.	Above 300 sq.ft	01	00.5
	Total	**200**	**100**

Table 6.19: Type of House at the Place of Destination

Sr. No.	Status	Number	Percentage
1.	Brick walls with tiled roof	11	05.5
2.	Raw bricks with thatched roof	35	17.5
3.	Stick walls with thatched roof	22	11
4.	Grass/Bamboo mat hut (Khopi)	116	58
5.	Plastic Sheet Tents	14	07
6.	Others	02	01
	Total	**200**	**100**

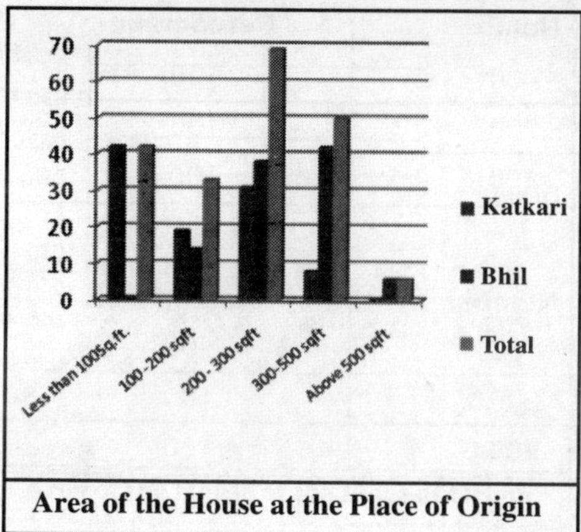

Area of the House at the Place of Origin

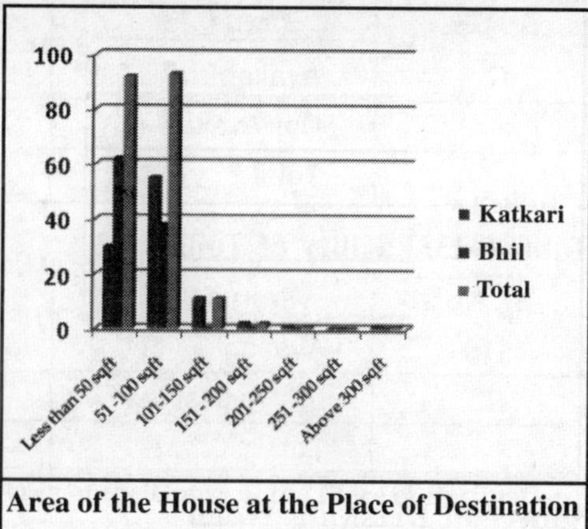

Area of the House at the Place of Destination

Fig. 6.1

Availability of Electricity

Out of the 200 respondents studied 25 per cent had access to electricity provided by the owners or contractors while 75 per cent did not avail this facility.

Table 6.20: Availability of Electricity

Sr. No.	Status	Number	Percentage
1.	Available	50	25
2.	Not Available	150	75
	Total	**200**	**100**

Facility of Drainage

Here again it is seen from the table 6.21, that drainage facility was absent for all the 200 respondents studied.

Table 6.21: Facility of Drainage

Sr. No.	Status	Number	Percentage
1.	Available	00	00
2.	Not Available	200	100
	Total	**200**	100

Facility of Bathrooms and Toilets

Both the Bhil sugarcane cutters as well as Katkari brick kiln labourers did not avail basic facilities of bath-room and toilet. They would bath and defecate in open spaces. Tables 6.21 and 6.23 depicts the picture.

Table 6.22: Facility of Bathrooms

Sr. No.	Status	Number	Percentage
1.	Available	00	00
2.	Not Available	200	100
	Total	**200**	100

Table 6.23: Facility of Toilets

Sr. No.	Status	Number	Percentage
1.	Available	00	00
2.	Not Available	200	100
	Total	**200**	100

Source of Drinking Water

As seen from table 6.23 majority sources of drinking water available were well, bore well, tap and hand pump. These sources were either in the farms of non-tribal farmers or in the nearby villages.

Table 6.24: Source of Drinking Water

Sr. No.	Source	Number	Percentage
1.	Well	26	13
2.	Tap	30	15
3.	Stream	0	00
4.	Bore Well	75	37.5
6.	Water tanker	0	00
7.	Pond	6	03
8.	Hand Pump	55	27.5
9.	River	0	00
10.	Others	0	00
11.	Pothole near a stream	8	04
	Total	**200**	**100**

Annual Income

Table 6.25 clearly indicates that 72.5 per cent of the respondents studied are below the poverty line. Hence, supports the model that poverty is a key push factor that forces them to migrate.

Table 6.25: Annual Income of the Family

Sr. No.	Source	Number	Percentage
1.	Up to Rs. 20,000/-	145	72.5
2.	Rs. 20,000 to 40,000/-	37	18.5
3.	Rs. 40,000 to 60,000/-	06	03
4.	Rs. 60,000 to 80,000/-	02	01
6.	Above Rs. 80,000/-	00	00
7.	Rs. -1,000 to -5,000/-	04	02
8.	Rs. -5,000 to -10,000/-	05	02.5
9.	Rs.-10,000 to -20,000/-	01	00.5
	Total	**200**	**100**

Bonded Labourer

As evident from the table 6.26 that 81 per cent of the respondents studied were bonded labourers. This statistics certainly proves that bonded labour as a variable is a key push factor that pushes the Bhils and Katkaris to migrate seasonally.

Table 6.26: Bonded Labourer

Sr. No.	Status	Number	Percentage
1.	Bonded Labourers	162	81
2.	Non-bonded labourers	038	19
	Total	**200**	**100**

Borrowing Loan while Returning Home

Out of the 200 respondents studied, it was observed that 83 per cent borrowed loan, while returning home during monsoon season. Indebtedness therefore becomes a key push factor in returning to the place of destination the following year.

Table 6.27: Frequency of Borrowing Loan while Returning Home

Sr. No.	Status	Number	Percentage
1.	Borrow	166	83
2.	Do not borrow	034	17
	Total	**200**	100

Source of Borrowing Loan

As revealed in table 6.28, 42 per cent of the respondents borrowed loan from the brick kiln owners while 33.5 per cent from the Mukadams. Mukadams and brick kiln owners play the role bank or ATM machines for these labourers.

Table 6.28: Source of Borrowing Loan

Sr. No.	Status	Number	Percentage
1.	Bank	06	03
2.	Farm Owner	02	01
3.	Brick kiln owner	84	42
4.	Factory Contractor	02	0
5.	Mukadam	67	33.5
6.	Other	05	02.5
7.	N A	34	17
	Total	**200**	**100**

Possession of Livestock

As evident from the table 6.29, 50.5 per cent of the respondents studied possess live stock. Interestingly, maximum the Bhil sugarcane cutters owned live stock, because they need bulls to pull the carts, loaded with sugarcane.

Table 6.29: Possession of Livestock

Sr. No.	Status	Number	Percentage
1.	Possess	101	50.5
2.	Do not possess	099	49.5
	Total	**200**	**100**

Collection of Minor Forest Produce

It was observed that 100 per cent of the respondents collected Minor Forest Produce as needed fuel wood, fruits, seeds, timber, honey, gum etc. for their survival.

Table 6.30: Collection of Minor Forest Produce

Sr. No.	Status	Number	Percentage
1.	Collect	200	100
2.	Do not Collect	00	00
	Total	**200**	**100**

Sale of Minor Forest Produce (MFP)

Both Katkaris and Bhils sold fuel wood to the neighboring villages occasionally, in order to get some cash.

Table 6.31: Sale/Barter of MFP

Sr. No.	Status	Number	Percentage
1.	Sale	039	19.5
2.	Do not sale (for domestic use)	161	80.5
	Total	**200**	**100**

Number of Working Hours

As evident from table 6.33, 23 per cent of the respondents worked for 8 to 10 hours, 35.5 per cent for 10-12 hours, 42 per cent for 12-14 hours and 11 per cent above 14 hours. This proves that these sugarcane cutters as well as brick kiln labourers are exploited maximum by the owners and contractors and have to work for long hours in order to survive.

Table 6.32: Number of Working Hours

Sr. No.	Working Hours	Number	Percentage
1.	8-10 hrs.	23	11.5
2.	10-12hrs.	71	35.5
3.	12-14 hrs.	84	42
4.	above 14 hrs.	22	11
	Total	**200**	**100**

Possession of Documents

As seen in table 6.33, majority of the respondents possessed documents such as ration card, election card and land documents where as documents such as birth, death and school leaving certificates were rarely available.

Table 6.33: Possession of Documents

Sr. No.	Documents	Number	Percentage
1.	Ration Card	109	54.5
2.	Election card	138	69
3.	Identity card	08	04
4.	Birth certificate	18	09
5.	Marriage certificate	01	00.5
6.	Death Certificate	03	01.5
7.	Bank'sPass Book	19	09.5
8.	School leaving certificate	36	18
9.	Land documents	81	40.5
10.	House property papers	126	63
11.	Caste/Tribe certificate	62	31
12.	Any other	00	00
13.	No documents	07	03.5

Absence of Economic and Financially Valuable Assets

The data revealed in table 6.34 shows that 52 per cent of the respondents studied owned agricultural land. The same table shows that 92.5 per cent of them owned houses at the place of origin. However after probing in detail it was observed that 2 to3 families owned agricultural land as a result of which the yield reaped was meager and insufficient, hence agricultural land as an immovable asset possessed by the respondents was not really economically usefully productive. Further, the land possessed by them was non-irrigated. It was also observed that the economic value of this land was far less in the tribal area. Thus as per the conceptual model evolved absence of economic assets or absence of financially valuable assets becomes a key push factor in distress seasonal migration among the Katkari Brick kiln labourers and Bhil sugarcane cutters.

Table 6.34: Possession of Immovable Assets

Sr. No.	Immovable Assets	Number	Percentage
1.	Agricultural land	104 (out of 200 respondents)	52
2.	House	185 (out of 200 respondents)	92.5

As evident from table 6.35 it was observed that majority of the respondents did not have valuable movable assets such as gold, silver, hard cash, cupboard, TV , tape recorder, radio, utensils, mobile phones, mobikes, beds, cots, etc.

Table 6.35: Possession of Movable Assets

Sr. No.	Movable Assets	Number
1.	Gold/Silver Ornaments	06
2.	Hard Cash	00
3.	Cupboard	04
4.	TV set	14
5.	Taperecorder/Radio	11
6.	Mobile Phones	04
7.	Beds/ Cots	33
8.	Mobikes	02
9.	Live stock	101
10.	Gas Cylinder	03
11.	Kerosene Stove	14

Background of Children at the Brick Kilns and Sugarcane Camps

Data presented in table 6.1 to 6.34 clearly indicates the poor socio-economic background of the parents and major push factors such as poverty, unemployment, illiteracy, landlessness etc. which pushes them to the place of destination, thereby depriving their children of their rights and also forces them into domestic work and child labour.

Age-range Wise Number of Children

The data depicted in table 6.36, revealed that there were 432 children at the worksites, i.e. 221 males and 211 females. 91 per cent of these children belonged to age range 1 to 14 years. This is evident from the fact that 91 per cent children were forced to migrate with their parents to the brick kiln and sugarcane farms. The study has revealed that these 91 per cent children were deprived of their rights to survival, education, health, nutrition, recreation and so on.

Table 6.36: Age-wise Number of Children

Sr. No.	Age Range	Number		Total
		Male	Female	
1.	Upto 1 year	11 (2.5%)	15 (3.5%)	26 (6%)
2.	1-5 years	67 (15.5%)	79 (18%)	146 (34%)
3.	5 to 10 years	65 (15%)	54 (12.5%)	119 (27%)
4.	10 to 14 years	49 (11.3%)	53 (12.3%)	102 (24%)
5.	14 to 18 years	29 (7%)	10 (2.3%)	039 (9%)
	Total	**221 (51%)**	**211 (49%)**	**432 (100%)**

Note: Figures in bracket indicate percentage

Schooling Status of Children

Table 6.37 reveals that 46 per cent of the children did not go to school nor Anganwadis; 12 per cent were drop-outs and 41 per cent attended Anganwadis and Zilla Parishad schools. When parents were interviewed they stated, while we are working our children are taken care by the Anganwadi and Zilla Parishad school teachers. Secondly, they get nutrition supplement in the ICDS units and Zilla Parishad schools. The children also receive uniform, books, notebooks and stationary.

Table 6.37: Schooling Status of Children

Sr. No.	Schooling Status	Number of Children		Total
		Male	Female	
1.	School going	98 (23%)	79 (18%)	177 (41%)
2.	Non-school going	90 (21%)	109 (25%)	199 (46%)
3.	Drop outs	33 (7%)	23 (5%)	056 (12%)
	Total	**221 (51%)**	**211 (49%)**	**432 (100%)**

Note: Figures in bracket indicate percentage.

Educational Status of Children

Table 6.38 reveals that 45 per cent of the children studied were illiterate; 10.6 per cent attended Anganwadi; 26 per cent studied in primary school and 16 per cent in secondary school and only 1.4 per cent studied up to higher secondary school. Interestingly not a single student studied in college or post graduate institute. A study after post graduation is a myth and a dream to these children.

Table 6.38: Educational Status of Children

Sr. No.	Educational Status	Number		Total
		Male	Female	
1.	Illiterate	89 (20.6%)	107 (25%)	196 (45%)
2.	Anganwadi (Pre-primary)	24 (5.5%)	22 (5.1%)	46 (10.6%)
3.	Primary (1-4)	60 (14%)	54 (12.5%)	114 (26%)
4.	Secondary (5-10)	44 (10%)	26 (6%)	70 (16%)
6.	Higher Secondary (11-12)	04 (1%)	02 (0.5%)	06 (1.4%)
7.	Undergraduate	00	00	00
8.	Graduate	00	00	00
9.	Post-Graduate	00	00	00
10.	Diploma	00	00	00
	Total	**221 (51%)**	**211 (49%)**	**432 (100%)**

Note: Figures in bracket indicate percentage.

Right to Recreational Facilities

As evident from the table given below 100 per cent of the children studied, were deprived of their right to recreational facilities at the brick kilns and sugarcane cutting camps.

Table 6.39: Recreational Facilities

Sr. No.	Status	Number	Percentage
1.	Available	00	00
2.	Not available	200	100
	Total	**200**	**100**

Nutritional Status of Children

383 children measured for assessing nutritional status out of which 76 per cent were malnourished. This indicates that these children are deprived of their rights to nutrition. The same study revealed that 81 per cent of the Katkari children were malnourished while 72.19 per cent of the Bhil children were malnourished.

Table 6.40: Nutritional Status of Children

Sr. No.	Gradations	Number	Percentage
1.	Normal	91	24
2.	Grade I (Mild Malnutrition)	89	23.2
3.	Grade II (Moderate Malnutrition)	113	29.5
4.	Grade III (Severe Malnutrition)	62	16
6.	Grade IV (Severe Malnutrition)	28	07.3
	Total	**383**	**100**

Diet during Pregnancy

Studies by Bhatia Arun and Tribhuwan Robin (2002); Jain N.S. and Tribhuwan Robin (1996); Tribhuwan Robin (1998); Tribhuwan Robin (2007) revealed that over 80 per cent of the tribal women do not get special diet during pregnancy. This study also revealed that 94.5 per cent of the women do not get special diet during pregnancy.

Table 6.41: Diet during Pregnancy

Sr. No.	Status	Number	Percentage
1.	Get special diet	11	5.5
2.	Do not get special diet	189	94.5
	Total	**200**	**100**

Place of Delivery

Studies by Bhatia Arun & Tribhuwan Robin (2002); Jain N.S. & Tribhuwan Robin (1996); Tribhuwan Robin (1998); Tribhuwan Robin (2007) have revealed that over 95 per cent of the deliveries among the tribals take place at home and are conducted by the Traditional Birth Attendant. This study too has revealed that 92.5 per cent of the deliveries among the Bhil sugarcane cutters and Katkari brick kiln labourers take place at home. The data further reveals that 7.5 per cent deliveries take place in the Khopi – a 40 to 50 sq.ft. hut, among the Bhil sugarcane cutters.

Table 6.42: Place of Delivery

Sr. No.	Gradations	Number	Percentage
1.	Khopi (hut at work site)	15	7.5
2.	Home at Native Place	174	87
3.	PHC	04	02
4.	Rural Hospital	02	01
5.	Govt.Hospital	03	1.5
6.	PrivateHospital	02	01
	Total	**200**	**100**

Personnel Conducting Delivery

As revealed in table 6.43, 89 per cent of the deliveries among the Bhils and Katkaris studied are conducted by traditional midwives, 4.5 per cent by Doctors and 6 per cent by elderly women at the worksites. This certainly indicates that deliveries of tribal children are not conducted by expert gynecologist

Table 6.43: Personnel who Conducts Delivery

Sr. No.	Gradations	Number	Percentage
1.	Dai/Suine	178	89
2.	ANM	01	00.5
3.	Trained Midwife	00	00
4.	Doctor	09	04.5
5.	Gynecologist	00	00
6.	Elderly women at work site	12	06
	Total	**190**	**100**

When do women start working after delivery?

As evident from table 6.44 maximum that is 62.5 per cent of the women stated that women start working after 30 days of delivery, 26.5 per cent work after 15 days while 2.5 per cent of them said that after 7 days of delivery they start working. 8.5 per cent stated that women start working after 45 days or two months of delivery.

Table 6.44: Number of Days when Women Start Working After Delivery

Sr. No.	Days	Number	Percentage
1.	After 2 days	00	00
2.	After 7 days	05	2.5
3.	After 15 days	53	26.5
4.	After 30 days	125	62.5
5.	Any other	17	8.5
	Total	**200**	**100**

Care of Sick Child

As evident from table 6.45, it is seen that 27 per cent of the respondents said one of the parents take leave, 23 per cent said both take leave if the child is serious, 12.5 per cent make elderly children take care of the sick child, 11 per cent keep the child with grandparents in native village, while for 13 per cent of the respondents the question was not applicable because some of them were not having children and some were having married children.

Table 6.45: Care of Sick Child

Sr. No.	Care of Sick Child	Number	Percentage
1.	One of parents take leave	54	27
2.	If serious both take leave	46	23
3.	Keep child with other elder children at work site house	25	12.5
4.	Woman in the house/if she is working she takes leave	27	13.5
5.	No child/Children are married	26	13
6.	Keep the child with grandparents in native village	22	11
	Total	**200**	**100**

Vaccination of Children

It is observed that 74 per cent of the children of Bhil sugarcane cutters and Katkari brick kiln labourers are vaccinated, while 17.5 per cent are not. The dedicated ANMs and health workers of the sub-centre, the Anganwadi teachers and Zilla Parishad School teachers make efforts to reach the kilns and sugarcane cutters' camps.

Table 6.46: Vaccination of Children

Sr. No.	Vaccination Status	Number	Percentage
1.	Vaccinated	148	74
2.	Not vaccinated	35	17.5
3.	No child	17	08.5
	Total	**200**	**100**

While, the migrating families face hardships, the ailing family members, or children left behind in their native villages have difficulty finding for themselves and are often reduced to destitution. Being away from home and village they lead, an uprooted life. They do not belong to the places they go to and increasingly loose acceptance in their won villages. They are cut off from their community, culture and traditions and are unable to take part in their festivals, fairs, religious and social functions, which are an important part of their lives. The vulnerability of Bhil sugarcane cutters and Katkari brick kiln labourers who cross the state boundaries is greater as they are unfamiliar with the language and culture of areas they go o and find themselves increasingly at the mercy of the contractors.

Child Labour at the Brick Kilns & Sugarcane Fields

As evident from table 6.47, 18.28 per cent of the children work as labourers while 44.21 per cent work to help parents in transporting bricks and sugarcane bundle, taking care of the cattle etc. thus 62 per cent of the children are ultimately forced into child labour either to earn small amount of daily wages or help their parents to complete their targets. Most parents stated that the children who help them are gaining experience or learning their job. When they become teenagers they get into child labour to earn small amounts of daily wages.

Table 6.47: Working Status of Male and Female Children

Sr. No.	Working Status	Number		Percentage
		Male	Female	
1.	Working at the kilns/sugarcane fields	54 (12.5%)	25 (5.78%)	079 (18.28%)
2.	Not working	69 (27.31%)	93 (21.52%)	162 (37.5%)
3.	Working to help parents	98 (22.68%)	93 (21.52%)	191 (44.21%)
	Total	**221 (51%)**	**211 (49%)**	**432 (100%)**

Note: Figures in bracket indicate percentage.

The Child Labour – Child Rights : Conceptual Model

Primary data and is interpretation reported in chapter three, four and six supports the conceptual model developed during the pilot study. Given below is the summary of the key push factors supported by statistical data of both the Bhils and Katkaris studied. Considering the main key push factors it is observed that all the respondents studied belonged to the unorganized labour sector. Majority of respondents were poor, landless or marginal farmers, victims of economic and food crisis, victims of indebtedness, unemployed, unskilled labourers and illiterate. Further, most of them lived in temporary houses, having no economic assets and lacked social and economic insecurity. The statistical details of each of the above mentioned key push factor is given below.

Key Push Factors that force Katkari brick kiln labourers & Bhil sugarcane cutters in to seasonal migration.

1. **Poverty:** Out of the 200 respondents studied 72.5 per cent were below the Poverty line. Similarly table 3.31 of chapter three reveals that 82 per cent of the Katkaris were below the poverty line. Further table 4.31 of chapter four reveals that 63 per cent of the Bhil sugarcane cutters were below the poverty line. This statistically proves that povertyis one of the major key push factorsthat force them to the brick kiln and sugarcane farms.
2. **Landlessness:** Out of the 200 respondents studied 48 per cent were landless.Similarly table number 3.15 of chapter three reveals that 67 per cent of the Katkari brick kiln labourers were landless and table 4.15 of

chapter four reveals that 29 per cent of the Bhil sugarcane cutters were landless. Those who possess land are non-irrigated and the yield reaped from the land is insufficient to fulfill the need of whole throughout the year. Therefore landlessness is one of the key push factors for migration of Bhils and Katkaris to the sugarcane farms and brick kilns respectively.

3. **Indebtedness:** Out of 200 respondents 83 per cent was indebted. Table number 3.33of chapter three reveals that 86 per cent of the Katkari brick kiln labourers have taken loan from brick kiln owners or from other sources similarly table 4.33 of chapter four reveals that 76 per cent of the Bhil sugarcane cutters are indebted i.e. they have taken loan from mukadam (contractor), factory owner, bank or from any other source. In case of Bhil sugarcane cutter they have to pay heavy interest (which ranges from 3 per cent to 10 per cent per month) on the loan they have taken from mukadam or from factory contractor or factory owner. Hence indebtedness is one of the key push factor which forces them to the place of destination
4. **Unemployment:** Out of 200 respondents 100 per cent of them were unemployed at the place of origin. Table 3.13 of chapter three and table number 4.13 of chapter four reveals the same. This statistically proves that Unemployment is one of the major push factors in migration of Bhil sugarcane cutters and Katkari Brick kiln labourers to the place of their destination.
5. **Temporary and poor housing:** Out of 200 respondents 79.5 per cent of the respondents are living in the houses made up of stick walls with thatched roof at the place of origin. 58 per cent of the respondents live in khopi i.e. a hut made up of grass or bamboo mat. Thus, temporary and poor housing is also one of the major push factor.
6. **Unskilled labour:** Out of 200 respondents 100 per cent of them are unskilled labourers. Further table 3.14 of chapter three and 4.14 of chapter four reflects the same fact among the Katkaris and Bhils. This proves that unskilled labour status is one of the major push factors responsible for their migration to the places of destination.
7. **Illiteracy:** Out of 200 respondents 79 per cent of the respondents were illiterate. Table 3.6 of chapter three shows that 81 per cent of the katkaris were illiterate while table number 4.6 of chapter four reveals that 77 per cent of the Bhils were illiterate. Illiteracy therefore becomes the key factor to push Katkaris and Bhils into seasonal migration.
8. **Social and economic insecurity:** Out of 200 respondents 100 per cent of them stated that they do not have any social and economic security such as facility of clean and safe drinking water, facility of electricity, toilets and bathrooms, drainage and economic securities such as pension, provident fund, life insurance, medical facilities, facility of maternity

leave etc. Tables 3.26, 3.27, 3.28, 3.39 and 3.30 of chapter three and tables 4.26, 4.27, 4.28, 4.39 and 4.30 of chapter four reflects these facts.

9. **Absence of economic assets:** Out of 200, 52 per cent and 92.5 per cent of the respondents possess immovable economic assets such as agriculture land and own house respectively. Most of them possess non-irrigated land which does not produce sufficient production for the whole year. Table 3.41 and 3.42 of chapter three and tables 4.41 and 4.42 fo chapter four reveals the status of possession of movable and immovable economic assets respectively among Katkaris and Bhils.

Key Pull Factors that attract Kakari brick kiln labourers & Bhil sugarcane cutters to the place of destination.

1. **Kharchi (weekly expenses)**

   All most all the families received weekly expenses i.e. kharchi from their employers, at the place of destination. This was a boon and a hope for survival. The guarantee of getting weekly expenses was assured.

2. **Uchal (Loan)**

   83 per cent of the respondents took loan from their employers. This money was utilized for survival during monsoon back home during the time of crisis.

3. **Labour Guarantee**

   The employers made it sure that the Katkari brick kiln labourers and the Bhil sugarcane cutters received employment.

The study revealed that both push and pull factors complement each other and force the Katkari and Bhil migrant labourers to their respective work sites. In fact through the study it could be concluded that both the pull and push factors mentioned above play significant role in forced distress seasonal migration. The above mentioned push and pull factors hook the migrant labourers into bonded labour. Further, heavy daily work targets and less adult man power in the nuclear families of Bhil sugarcane cutters and Katkari brick kiln labourers force their children into child labour and domestic work, thereby depriving them of their rights. The conceptual model evolved while conducting pilot study was further improvised after collecting primary data on both the tribes so as to scientifically validate it. It can be further, tested by social scientists in other occupational migrant labour groups.

Child Labour Issues

Child Labour: Some Statistical Facts from the Field

This study has revealed that, out of 432 children of the 200 families studied 191 i.e. 44.21 per cent were working at the brick kilns and sugarcane farms to support their parents so as to achieve their work targets. Out of the total number of children who worked to support the parents 98 i.e. 22.68 per cent were males and 93 i.e. 21.52 per cent were females. Further, 18.28 per cent of children were exclusively child labourers, who were paid wages between Rs. 50/- to 125/-per day. Thus in all out of 432 children belonging to the 200 families studied 270 i.e. 62.5 per cent can be branded as child labourers because 18.28 per cent of the children are commercial child labourers and get less wages as compared to adults, however, the other lot includes children who are forced to support their parents in brick making and sugarcane cutting activities so as to achieve daily targets. It is essential to note at this juncture that 62.5 per cent child labourers does not include school going children who help their parents in brick making and sugarcane cutting. It is also pertinent to note that the remaining 162 i.e. 37.5 per cent of children who were forced to accompany their parents to the brick kilns and sugarcane farms were also deprived of child rights.

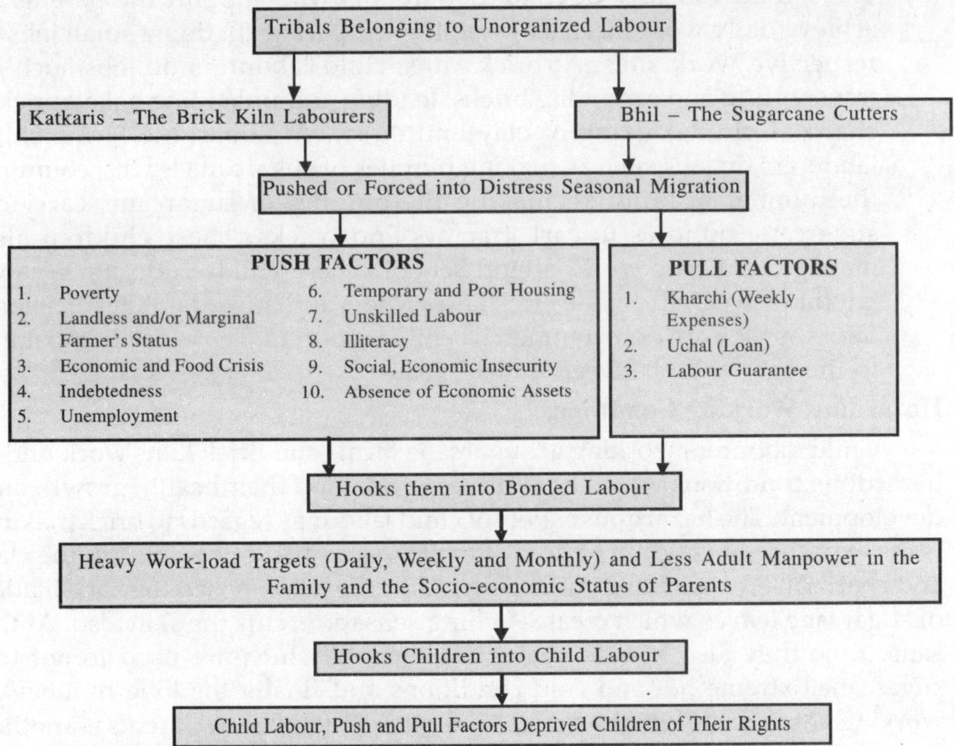

Child Labour & Child Rights: A Conceptual Model

Types of Child Labourers

As mentioned in chapter three and four, child labour in this study has been classified into two categories: (a) commercial child labourers; (b) Child labourers who support their parents.

(a) The first category of child labourers includes those child labourers who are paid by the brick kiln owners and mukadams. Among Katkaris these are children who are better off in making bricks, mixing clay with straw, arranging unbaked bricks in the furnace. They are paid daily wages by the brick kiln owners depending on the type of work they of per day.Among the Bhils these children are trained in sugarcane cutting, carrying sugarcane bundles from farm to the cart, tractor and truck, loading and unloading the sugarcane bundles. They are paid daily wages by the mukadams depending on the type of work they do per day.These wages range from Rs. 50 to Rs. 125/- .If a couple (husband and wife is accompanied by a child to work as a unit. This association of three members is called 'did koyta' meaning one and half koyta.

In the second category of commercial child labourers the children are mostly drop outs and belong to the age group 15 to 18 years.

(b) The second category of child labourers is who support the parents to achieve daily work targets by helping the parents in doing small jobs at respective work sites. At brick kilns, child labourers do jobs such as transporting and arranging bricks; loading and unloading baked bricks, charcoal, mud, mixing of clay and straw. At sugarcane farms child labourers do jobs such as making bundles of sugarcane leaves; counting the number of bundles, making the bundles of sugarcane, carrying sugarcane bundles to cart, tractors and trucks. These children also manage domestic work, attend school. These children do not receive anything in cash from the brick kiln owners and mukadams at sugarcane farms as they are non-commercial child labourers. These children belong to the age range between 6 to 10 years.

Hazardous Working Conditions

Child labourers working at sugarcane farms and brick kilns work under hazardous conditions which have adverse effect on their health, growth and development. The hazardous aspect of child labour as regards to brick making is the exposure of children to heat of the furnace, dust released from the clay and charcoal. At sugarcane cutting sites children are exposed to sharp blades of sugarcane leaves which creates itching sensation, cuts the skin also. At the same time they also handle sharp implements which are used to cut the sugarcane.Extreme hot and cold conditions and finally the long number of working hours at the kilns and sugarcane sites, ignorance by parents is another issue related to child labourers. Besides this, these children also become victims of the unhealthy environment, unsafe drinking water, food exposed to dust etc.

The children as well as their parents sometimes become pray to scorpion stings and snake bites.

Child Rights Issues: Forced migration of the parents due to utter poor economic conditions, indebtedness, bonded labour, lack of employment opportunities in the place of origin, landlessness, unskilled nature of labour etc. factors push them to the kilns and sugarcane fields. This in turn directly affects the growth and progress of their children who are dependent on them for survival. Their children have no choice but to adjust to the socio-economic condition of their parents as well as the living conditions at worksites. In other words, their fate is destined to work as child labourers and get deprived of the child rights.

Given below are statistics that prove how the children of Katkari brick kiln labourers and Bhil Sugarcane cutters are deprived of their rights:

1. **Child Labour:** It was observed that out of 432 children of the 200 families studied 191 i.e. 44.21 per cent were working at the brick kilns and sugarcane farms to support their parents so as to achieve their work targets. Out of the total number of children who worked to support the parents 98 i.e. 22.68 per cent were males and 93 i.e.21.52 per cent were females. Further, 18.28 per cent of children were exclusively child labourers, who were paid wages between Rs. 50/- to 100/-. Thus in all out of 432 children belonging to the 200 families studied 270 i.e. 62.5 per cent can be branded as child labourers because 18.28 per cent of the children are commercial child labourers and get less wages as compared to adults, however, the other lot includes children who are forced to support their parents in brick making and sugarcane activities so as to achieve daily targets. It is essential to note at this juncture that 62.5 per cent child labourers does not include school going children who help their parents in brick making and sugarcane cutting. It is also pertinent to note that the remaining 162 i.e. 37.5 per cent of children who were forced to accompany their parents to the brick kilns were also deprived of child rights.
2. **Elementary Education – Right of every child:** As revealed in table number 6.37, that out of 432 children studied, only 41 per cent children were school going children, 46 per cent were non-school going children while 12 per cent of them were drop outs from the school, that is total 58 per cent of the children studied were out of school. This proves that children ofsugarcane cutters and brick kiln migrant labourers are deprived of their fundamental right to education.
3. **Right to play and recreation:** The study has revealed that there were no recreational facilities for children. 100 per cent of them stated that there were no recreational facilities for children made available by brick kiln owner and sugarcane farm owners. Here again it has been proved that children are deprived of their right to play and recreation.
4. **Right to Health:**
    - **Immunization/Vaccination:** This study has revealed that 74 per cent of the Katkari and Bhil parents have vaccinated their children while 17.5 per cent of them have not vaccinated their children.

When asked, which vaccines have you given to your children?Most of them told that, they have given polio dose to their children.Hardly any one of them has given other vaccines like Hepatitis B, Hepatitis C, Smallpox, chickenpox, DPT, BCG, etc. to their children, and this is because of unawarenessregarding the immunization programme among the parents.

- **Nutrition:** Out of the total 432Bhil and Katkari children, belonging to families of 200 respondents, the researcher was able to get age, height and weight of 383 children. Nutritional status of 383 children is as: 91 i.e 24 per cent - Normal; 89 i.e. 23.2 per cent - Grade I (Mild Malnutrition); 113 i.e. 29.5 per cent - Grade II (Moderate Malnutrition); 62 i.e. 16 per cent - Grade III (Severe Malnutrition); 28 i.e 7.3 per cent Grade IV (Severe Malnutrition). Out of 383, 298 i.e. 76.24 per cent of children were malnourished. From this statistics it is clear that children of Katkari Brick kiln labourers and Bhil sugarcane cutters are deprived of their basic right to nutrition.
- **Day Care & Crèche Facility:** Study has also revealed that facility of day care and Crèche for the children of Katkari brick kiln makers and Bhil sugarcane cutters is not provided either by brick kiln owners, sugarcane farm owners, sugarcane factories and not even by Government.

5. **Right to Parental Care:** It is clear from the data collected by the researcher that, all the respondents work on the work sites around 10 to 14 hours daily, sometimes more than 14 hours depending on the target of work. The parents get less time to care for their children. Nursing mothers take off 10 to 20 minutes to feed their children, but over all parental care during the day time is lacking. This certainly proves that the children of brick kiln labourers are deprived of their right to parental care because of the busy schedule of the parents.
6. **Right to shelter/housing:** As already reported previous section of this chapter, in tables 6.16 and 6.19, the conditions of housing of Katkari and Bhil labourers are poor both at the place of origin as well as at the place of destination. The children are certainly deprived of right to decent housing.

CONCLUSIONS

Based on the primary and secondary data gathered during the period of research following conclusions were drawn. These are as below:

1. The Katkari brick kiln labourers and the Bhil sugarcane cutters are forced to seasonally migrate to the places of destiny. Their migration is forced and not voluntary.

2. While, the migrating families face hardships, the ailing family members, or children left behind in their native villages have difficulty finding for themselves and are often reduced to destitution. Being away from home and village they lead, an uprooted life. They do not belong to the places they go to and increasingly loose acceptance in their own villages. They are cut off from their community, culture and traditions and are unable to take part in their festivals, fairs, religious and social functions, which are an important part of their lives. The vulnerability of Bhil sugarcane cutters and Katkari brick kiln labourers who cross the state boundaries is greater as they are unfamiliar with the language and culture of areas they go and find themselves increasingly at the mercy of the contractors.
3. Landless and Marginal Status versus Labour – In post-colonial India the imperative need to raise agricultural production and productivity precluded any radical land reform. Inspite of repeated pledges that property rights would be handed over to the actual tillers of the fields, policy makers now argued that there was simply not enough surplus land available to include the mass of agricultural labourers in whatever redistribution took place (Breman Jan & Das A,, 2000:30).

   As a result, long –standing inequalities in the village community were hardly touched. To keep intact the social hierarchy and command over natural resources, land and economic assests, the high caste peasant land lords and businessmen in the villages made efforts to safeguard their social and economic interests.

   The landless and marginal farmers continued to be suppressed and dominated by the economically well off peasants and business people in the villages. The Katkari brick kiln labourers and Bhil sugarcane cutters, who get exploited by the feudal landlords and rich peasants at the worksites during October to May, are further exploited by them during the months June to Septemeber at the place of origin.

   The Bhils and Katkari migrant labourers work as agricultural and daily wage labourers for rich peasants and business class castes in their native place of origin. This cycle of labour has become part and parcel of their socio-economic life.
4. Poverty, landless and marginal farmers' status, economic and food crisis, indebtedness, unemployment, unskilled labour, temporary and poor housing, illiteracy, social and economic insecurity and absence of economic assets are major key push factors that force the Bhil sugarcane cutters and Katkari brick kiln labourers to their respective places of destination.
5. Gender, Oldage and Labour Division – As aptly pointed out by Breman Jan and Das Arvind (2000:30), there is a co-relation between grender,

oldage and division of labour within a family. he stated that for one, village after village is today strangely devoid of able-bodied adultmen; they have all gone away to work elsewhere.

The population of the village at the place of origin of the migrant labourers in he case of Katkari brick kiln labourers and Bhil sugarcane cutters, comprise of the old, infirm, the sick and ailing including a few youngsters. Many of these elders have passed through the grinding mills of capital, which has squeezed out their labour power. They live out the reminder of their lives on memories. Other men have been so brutalized by their experiences that they seek to escape the world, through an alcohololic haze. Their drunkenness increases the double burden of women, who true to their reproductive role, try to get the male power back on their feet.

It was observed that both young and old women among the Katkari and Bhil migrant labourers work vigourously by managing commercial labour, household activities as well as the responsibility of reproductive roles. Further, the miseries of hard labour, poor pay; social and financial insecurities force both men and women to indulge in drinking. This paves a way for children to get hooked into child labour and domestic responsibilities.

The women usually have to cope up with a double burden of work. A few hours before starting their paid labour, they are busy with all sorts of domestic activities: preparing meals, washing clothes, caring for children, cleaning utensils etc. They are the first to rise in the moring and the last to go to the bed at night. The men come back tired from their work, demanding rest, food, drinks, care and attention. The women, who are equally tired, are expected as a matter of course to continue their work in the domestic sphere.

As rightly pointed out by Breman J.and Das A. (2000:94), that it is hardly surprising than that the weakest members (women) in their milieu are in turn victimized. There is bitterness behind the sweet taste of sugar.

6. Working Conditions and Poor Health - There is a close relationship between the poor health of Bhil and Katkari migrant labourers and their working condition. Standing, squatting, lifting weight, loading – unloading, bending for long hours on end – they all complain of body and backache. Their lungs become weak by inhaling dust particles and smoke, and begin t suffer from incurable diseases such as TB and Asthma. They suffer from sunstroke, as they have to work in a scorching heat. They suffer from boils, because they sit in dirty and insanitory places. Meidical Doctors of the nearby Primary Health Centres and Private clinics attribute the poor health of majority of migrant labourers studied to the conditions under which they work.

7. Kharchi (Weekly expenses), Uchal (Loan), and labour guarantee at the place of destination is a boon to the migrant labourers and are classified as main key pull factors of distress seasonal migration.
8. The key push and pull factors and poor socio-economic background of the migrant labourers hooks them into bonded labour.
9. Heavy workload targets (daily, weekly and monthly) and less adult man power at the place of destination and poor socio-economic background of the migrating families hook their children in to domestic and child labour at an early age.
10. The poor socio-economic background of the parents, key push and pull factors and bonded labour deprives the children of their right to education, parental care, housing, recreation, health, nutrition and so on.
11. The migrating families, the parents spend their peak time of their adulthood in fighting hardships for survival at the place of destination.
12. Poor, unhealthy, unhygienic conditions at the place of destination ensure that most migrants and children rapidly decline into ill-health.
13. The degree of hardships, food and economic crisis, indebtedness, bonded labour and social and economic insecurity, landlessness, unemployment, illiteracy etc, is higher among the Katkari brick kiln labourers, as compared to the Bhil sugarcane cutters.
14. Child Labour Redefined – The Constitution of India legally recognized a child as a person belonging to the age group 0-14 years of age. Article 24 of the Constitution states that no child below the age of 14 years, shall be employed to work in any factory or men engaged in any hazardous employment. The Census of India defines a child as a person belonging to the age group 6-14 years of age. The United States of America defines a child as an individual below 18 years of age. According to International Labour Organization, 1983, "child Labour includes children prematurely leading adult lives, working long hours for low wages, under conditions damaging to their health and to their physical and mental development, sometimes separated from their families, frequently deprived of meaningful education and training opportunities that could open up for them a better future."

Characteristics of Child Labour

Child labour detracts from the other essential activities for children, such as, education, play and leisure, and hence involves an element of exploitation. It essentially entails deprivations of their rights to health or education or just to childhood (ILO, 1992). Child labour has the following characteristics:

- Working too young
- Working long hours

- Working under strain – physical, social or psychological
- Working conditions unhealthy
- Working for little pay
- Working with little stimulation
- Subject to intimidation (ILO, 1992)

The concept of child labour has been viewed differently by various social scientists. Child labourers have been classified into carious categories such as paid child labourers (Breman Jan:2004).

In the present study the data revealed that child labourers can be classified into two broad categories namely – paid child labourers and unpaid child labourers.

(a) Paid child labourers – Paid child labourers are mostly those children who are within the age range 10 to 14 years of age. These children get a daily wage of rupees ranging from 30/- to 70/- per day, these children work either in industries, agricultur, brick and slat making sectors or any other sector for that matter.

(b) Unpaid child labourers – Data revealed that maximum children of the migrant labourers work to support their parents and help them in achieveing daily, weekly and monthly targets of work. These children are not paid by the owners and the middlemen. Researcher has classified these unpaid children also as child labourer. It was observed that the school going, the dropouts as well as those who have not gone to school at all work with the parents to achieve work targets. Although the study had revealed that 18.28 per cent of the children are paid child labourers and 44.21 per cent are unpaid child labourers. In reality the percentage of paid and unpaid child labourers is between 5 to 14 years at age. Researcher is of the view although children who are paid are legally considered t be child labourers, the study proves that the unpaid children should also be recognized as as child labourers. The policy makers should hence take a note of this finding and work out culturally acceptable and ecologically appropriate programmes for the unpaid child labourers as well. Efforts should also be made to increase budget for this category.

1. Awareness of child and human rights among the migrant labourers studies is totally absent.
2. Most migrant labourers studied, are not eligible for micro-credit intervention, Government schemes and other intervention by NGOs at the place of origin, because they are not in the village.
3. Brick kiln owners and contractors at the sugarcane camps are like ATM machines and finance institutions for the migrating labourers, as their survival depends on them.

4. The interventions of Sakharshala by Janarth and BhongaShala by Shramjeevi Sanghtana – NGOs have had positive impact in the areas where the programmes were implemented. However, the Katkaris of Raigad district and Bhils of Nandurbar district studied were unaware of these programmes.
5. The issue of child labour and child rights among migrant labourers of unorganized sector is inter-twinned with their poor socio-economic background and the key push pull factors identified through the conceptual model that has evolved through this research. Child labour and rights issues therefore, cannot be studied in isolation, as scientifically proved through this research study.
6. Role of State in preventing seasonal migration and welfare of migrant labourers – The concept of State has a special meaning in the social sciences. "It is the institution which mobilizes legimatepower in a territory through the establishment of courts, official leaders, written laws and taxation (Williams 1970:223).

Wallace and Wallace (1945:473) have aptly pointed out that the State is different from the government, in that it is an impersonal institution, while the government consists of those particular personas, who happen to hold office in a state at one point of time.

A State also involves the organization of leadership into authority positions, which are or could be filled in by various incumbents. A State usually has codified norms, which are the rules that have been written and published. Finally, most States exercise the power to raise revenue, through taxation. Perhaps the oldest function of a State is to serve the community as arbiter in disputes which might otherwise threaten both individuals and the community.

In the instant case of Katkari brick kiln labourers and Bhil sugarcane cutters the basic questions that need to be seriously thought of are:

(a) Why do the Katkari brick kiln labourers and Bhil sugarcane cutters continue to be victims of indebtedness, poverty, bonded labour and distress seasonal migration?
(b) What can be done to prevent distress seasonal migration?
(c) What is the role of the State in preventing distress seasonal migration?

Under the Constitution, India is a secular State, a State which observes an attitude of neutrality and impartilality towards its citizens. As er Article 22 of the Constitution of India, the Constitution itself authorizes to make laws providing for "preventive detention" for resaons connected with the security of a State, the maintainance of supplies and services essential to the community.

Further our constitution, lays down certain provisions to prevent exploitation of the weaker sections of the society by unscrupulous individuals and even by the State (Article 23). Special provisions are made for the protection of children is made in Article 24. No child below the age of fourteen years, shall be employed to work in any factory or men engaged in any other hazardous employment.

Part IV of the Constitution (Article 36-51) provides Directive Prinicples of State Policy. The socialisticprinciples stated in some of the articles of the Constitution given below relminds the State of its duty to follow these principles both in administration as wellas in making laws. These articles are:

- Article 38 (a): To secure social order for the promotion of welfare of the people.
- Article 39 (a): The State shall direct its policy towards securing all men and women equally the right to adequate means of livelihood.
- Article 39 (d): Equal pay for equal work to all.
- Article 39 (e): Protection of health of workers.
- Article 39 (f): Protection of children against exploitation.
- Article 41: The State shall within the limits of its economic capacity and development make effective provisions for securing the right to work, to education and public assistance in cases of unemployment, oldage, sickness and disablement.
- Article 43: The State shall endeavaour to secure to all workers a living wage, conditions of work ensuring a descent standard of life.

Well, one can go in quoting articles in the Constitution of India that safeguard the interests of its citizens. In the instant case of the Katkari and Bhil migrant labourers, none of the above provisions made in, the said articles have been effectively implemented for their welfare.

Studies by Jain N.S. and tribhuwan Robin (1996), Bhatia Arun and Tribhuwan Robin (2002), Tribhuwan Robin (2006), Tomar Y.P.S. and Tribhuwan Robin (2004) have revelaed that there is less or no awareness of constitutional provisions, development schemes and human rights among the tribals. Infact, the present study too revealed that the Katkari and Bhil migrants do not avail Government facilities and programme benefits at the place of destination nor, they are aware of human rights. Article 342 of the constitution has made special provisions to safeguards the interests of tribals. The Tribal Development Department has a budget of 3,000 crores per year and over 400 schemes for the welfare of tribals. Agarwal H.O. (2011:*139-139*) in his book captioned, "Human Righs," has presented 16 rights of migrant workers, the implementation procedures and reporting system of the same. These 16 rights provide social, economic, educational, employment and other securities to migrant workers. The study advocated the need to strengthen the role of the state in welfare of moigrant labourers in unorganized sector. The question to be seriously thought of is how much of it goes to the tribals?

RECOMMENDATIONS

Recommendations given in the last section of the thesis are twofold namely, general & occupation specific. The general recommendations are given in the light of the millennium development goals (MDG). There goals very much apply to the labourers of unorganized sector in India.

The Millennium Development Goals were formulated at the Millennium summit in September 2000, based on agreements from world conferences organized by the United Nations in the past decade. The goals have been accepted by many countries as a frame work measuring over all national development progress. The goals focus on the efforts of the world community on achieving significant & measurable improvements in people's lives. They establish yard sticks for measuring results, not just for developing country but for rich countries that help to fund development programmes and for the multilateral institutions that help countries implement them.

The major goals and targets, standards or indicators are the following:

1. Goal one- Eradicate extreme poverty and hunger

   Target One:

   Have halted, between 1990 and 2015, the proportion of people whose income is less than 1 day.

   Target Two:

   Have halted, between 1990 and 2015, the proportion of people who suffer from hunger.

2. Goal Two – Achieve Universal primary Education

   Target Three:

   Ensure that by 2015, children everywhere boys and girls alike, will be able to complete a full course of primary education.

3. Goal Three – Promote Gender Equality & Empower Women.

   Target Four:

   Eliminate gender disparity in primary and secondary education by 2005 and in all levels of education not later than 2015.

4. Goal Four – Reduce child mortality

   Target Five:

   Reduce by two-thirds between 1990 to 2015 the under-five mortality rate.

5. Goal Five – Improve Maternal Health

   Target Six:

   Reduce by three-quarters between 1990 to 2015 maternal mortality ratio.

6. Goal Six – combat HIV/AIDS, Malaria and other diseases.

   Target Seven:

   Have halted by 2015 and begun to reverse the spread of HIV/AIDS.

Target Eight:

Have halted by 2015 and begun to reverse the incidences of malaria & other major diseases.

7. Goal seven – Ensure Environmental sustainability.

Target Nine:

Integrate the principles of sustainable development into country policies and programme and reverse the less of environmental resources.

Target Ten:

Have halted, by 2015, the proportion of people without sustainable access to safe drinking water and basic sanitation.

Target Eleven:

Have halted by 2020 a significant improvement in the lives of at least 100 million slum dwellers.

8. Goal Eight – Develop a global partner ship for development

Target Twelve:

Develop further an open rule base, predictable, non-discriminatory trading and financial system (includes a commitment to good governance, development and poverty reduction both nationally and internationally.)

The above goals apply to India as a developing country and more so to the families of unorganized labour.

Similarly, the widely recognized secular document encouraging the protection for the provisions for children is called. "A world fit for children". At the United Nations a special summit on children held in may 2002, this declaration was signed and adopted by 180 nations. A summary of the 10 principles and objectives of "A world Fit for children," provision is shown below:

1. Put children First – In all actions that affect children, the best interests of the child will be one of the first things, we think about.
2. End poverty- Invest in childrens realize their rights. We promise to end poverty & take actions to stop the worst forms of child labour.
3. Leave no child behind – Every girl & boy is born free and equal in every way. All forms of discrimination against children must end.
4. Care for every Child – Children must get best possible start in life. Take care of children in safe environment so that they can learn to be physically, mentally emotionally & socially healthy.
5. Educate every child-boys & girls should have equal access to education.
6. Protect children from harm & exploitation Children must be protected against any acts of violence, abuse exploitation and discrimination as well as all forms of terrorism and hostage taking.
7. Protect children from war.

8. Combating HIV/AIDS- children and their families must be protected from the terrible impact of HIV/AIDS.
9. Listen to children and ensure their participation – Respect their rights to help them to express themselves and to participate in all matters that affect them, according to their age & maturity.
10. Protect the Earth for children – We must protect the natural environment with its huge variety of life, its beauty and its resources all of which make human life better both new and in future.

The document on, "A world fit for children," basically provides a macro-level recommendations to protect & safe guard the interests of children world over.

Recommendations for the Development of Katkari Brick Kiln Labourers and their children.

The Katkari brick-kiln labourers are victims of poverty, debt hunger & bonded labour; hence they get hooked into brick kiln labour. Given below are a few recommendations to improve them educationally economically & socially.

1. Build permanent Houses
   Build permanent and strong houses with proper ventilation and light in their native villages. This will control semi-nomadism.
2. Provide them Agriculture Land
   Provide them agriculture land so that they could cultivate cereals, vegetables & pulses for their family consumption.
3. Install bore wells & hand pumps
   Install bore wells & hand pumps in katkari hamlets.
4. Plant fruit trees, bamboos & vegetables.
   Plant fruit trees, bamboos & vegetables in Katkari hamlets.
5. Free them from debt
   Free all the Katkaris from debt and interest taken from brick kiln owners and money lenders.
6. Check brick kiln owners
   After freeing the labourers from debts, the brick kiln owners must be strictly warned to pay the labourers as per the Government names child labour at the brick kilns should be discouraged.
7. Compulsory Education
   Special squads should be appointed to check the Katkari children and must help them to get admissions in Ashram Schools and tribal hostels for brick kiln workers children where in their social, educational, emotional and physical needs are met. Primary and secondary education should be made compulsory for the Katkari children.

8. Focus on younger generation and children
An integrated and holistic development plan must be designed for the development of Katkari children. This plan must be implemented monitored and followed up till satisfactory development results are achieved, A separate cell should be established at the I.T.DP's for development of Katkari children.
9. Special I.C.D.S for Katkari hamlets and brick kilns
Speical I.C.D.S (Anganwadis) should be established in every Katkari hamlet and one Anganwadi for 2 to 3 brick kilns. TheseAnganwadis should provide food or at least one meal for children, pregnant women and lactating mothers. These ICDS should be equipped with first aid boxes. They should impart education to Katkari Children. Clothes, blankets, utensils and ration should be kept at the Anganwadis to be sold at subsidized ration to the Katkari families, special ration cards should be given to these families. The Anganwadi teacher and the helper should be from a tribal community.
10. Adiwasi Samaj Sevak
Tribhuwan Robin (2006)has suggested that educated boys and girls preferably from tribal communities should be employed on contract basis to work in the hamlets as Adiwasi samaj sevaks. As on today there is no representative from the Government, Triabl Development Department working in the tribal hamlets like the Anganwadi workers and pada workers. There Samaj Sevak would create awareness among the tribals and this care the Katkaris about development programmes and progressive life. They would help the tribals to fill applications to gete benefit from I.T.D.P's and Zilla parishad schemes. Village level programmes like kitchen garden, road schemes, cleanliness, campaign, income generation programmes etc will be monitered, evaluated and followed by the Adiwasi Samaj Sevak.
11. Brick Kiln Co-operatives
Genuine NGOs should be encouraged to start brick kiln co-operatives for Katkaris near their native villages. Only Katkari families should be employed here. Government should purchase bricks from there kilns so that the co-operative financially sound. In doing so bonded labour, hunger crisis, debt, poverty of the Katkaris will be reduced.
12. Mobile PDS for brick kiln Labourers
Mobile ration shops having food grains, vegetables, pulses, vessels, clothes, bed covers, blankets, oil, soaps etc should be started so that each mobile van covers at least 10 brick kilns per day. The items in the ration shop should be sold to the Katkari labourers at subsidized rates. Tribal youth should be employed on contract basis to manage the mobile ration shops. These shops should be under the control of the I.T.D.P.

13. Mobile clinics

Yet another programme that could help the Katkari labourers and their children is mobile clinic. At lseast two per tehsil should be provided. The clinic should be managed by an N.G.O. The Tribal development department should fund this scheme. The mobile clinic doctor and staff should report to the I.T.D.P through their respective NGO's.

14. Special Incontives to Ethnomedical specialists

Traditional medical practitioners such as bone-setters, herbalists and mid wives in the Katkari communities should be given monthly stipend in the form of cereals, pulses, vegetables and oil, including some cash for the health services they provide to their community members. Tribhuwan Robin (1988) in his book captioned, "Medical world of Tribals" has stated that the ethnomedical specialists have been providing health care services to their tribes men since ages. They receive gifts in cash and kind from their community for the services rendered by them. The Tribal Development Department must formulate schemes to support these practitioners so that they get some thing in kind and cash. In doing so they will also be motivated. These practitioners should be trained to handle first aid boxes. They should be given first Aid boxes, as well.

15. Special cell at the I.T.D.P.

A special cell should be established at the I.T.D.P's Pen, Shahada, Dahanu, Jawahar, Ghodegaon, Goregaon, Rajur, Nasik, Kalwan etc to plan, implement, monitor and follow up development programme for katkari brick kiln laboureres.

16. Hostels for Tribal Child Labourers

One special hostel should be established in tensil head quarters where in Katkari, Dhorkoli and other landless tribal populations inhabit. The children of tribal bonded labourers belonging to the unorganized labour such as brick kiln, sugar cane cutters, salt pan workers, sandworkers, and landless daily wage labourers should be given admissions, to continue their higher studies.

17. Proper Planning and execution of the NREGP

The National Rural Employment Guarantee Programme (NREGP) ensures 100 days employment to the rural poor. Despite of the existence of National Rural Employment Guarantee Scheme, why do the Katkari Brick kiln labourers migrate? How can this indebtedness and bonded labour be stopped? What can be done for the landless and marginal farmers?

These and several questions haunt the mind of an Indian citizen. The Planners and implementators of the NREGA should take a note of this and seriously think over so as to rehabilitate the migrant laboures of unorganized labour.

If the above suggestions are implemented there will certainly be economic, social and educational empowerment and progress among the Katkari brick kiln labourers and their children.

Recommondations for Bhil Sugarcane Cutters and their Children

The Bhil sugarcane cutters are victims of poverty, debt hunger & bonded labour; hence they get hooked into sugarcane cutting. Given below are a few recommendations to improve them educationally economically & socially:

1. **Build permanent Houses**
   Build permanent and strong houses with proper ventilation and light in their native villages. This will control semi-nomadism.
2. **Provide them Agricultural Land**
   Provide them agriculture land so that they could cultivate cereals, vegetables & pulses for their family consumption.
3. **Install bore wells & hand pumps**
   Install bore wells & hand pumps in Bhil hamlets.
4. **Plant fruit trees, bamboos & vegetables**
   Plant fruit trees, bamboos & vegetables in Bhil hamlets.
5. **Free them from debt**
   Free all the Bhils from debt interest taken from contractors, factory owners and money lenders.
6. **Check mukadams**
   After freeing the labourers from debts, the brick kiln owners must be strictly warned to pay the labourers as per the Government norms child labour at the brick kilns should be discouraged.
7. **Compulsory Education**
   Special squads should be appointed to check the Bhil children & must help them to get admissions in Ashram Schools and tribal hostels for sugarcane cutters' children where in their social, educational, emotional and physical needs are met. Primary and secondary education should be made compulsory for the Bhil children.
8. **Focus on younger generation and children**
   An integrated and holistic development plan must be designed for the development plan must be designed for the development of Bhil children. This plan must be implemented monitored and followed up till satisfactory development results are achieved, A separate cell should be established at the I.T.D.P's for development of Bhil children.
9. **Special I.C.D.S for Bhil hamlets and sugarcane field areas**
   Speical I.C.D.S (Anganwadis) should be established in every Bhil hamlet and one Anganwadi for 2 to 3 sugarcane field areas. There Anganwadis should provide food, at least one meal, for children, pregnant women and lactating mothers. There ICDS should be equipped with first aid boxes. They should import education to Bhil Children. Clothes, blankets,

utensils and ration should be kept at the Anganwadis to be sold at subsidized ration to the Bhil families, special ration cards should be given to these families. The Anganwadi teacher and the helper should be from a tribal community.

10. **Adiwasi Samaj Sevak**

Tribhuwan Robin (2006)has suggested that educated boys and girls preferably from tribal communities should be employed on contract basis to work in the hamlets as Adiwasi samaj sevaks. As on today there is no representative from the Government, Tribal Development Department working in the tribal hamlets like the Anganwadi workers and pada workers. These Samaj Sevak would create awareness among the tribals. They would help the tribals to fill applications to get benefit from I.T.D.P.s and Zilla Parishad schemes. Village level programmes like kitchen garden, road schemes, cleanliness campaign, income generation programmes etc. will be monitered, evaluated and followed by the Adiwasi Samaj Sevak.

11. **Mobile PDS for sugarcane cutters**

Mobile ration shops having food grains, vegetables, pulses, vessels, clothes, bed covers, blankets, oil, soaps etc should be started so that each mobile van covers at least 6 to 8 sugarcane cutting sites per day. The items in the ration shop should be sold to the Bhil labourers at subsidized rates. Tribal youth should be employed on contract basis to manage the mobile ration shops. These shops should be under the control of the I.T.D.P.

12. **Mobile clinics**

Yet another programme that could help the Bhil labourers and their children is mobile clinic at least two per tehsil. The clinic should be managed by an NGO. The Tribal Development Department should fund this scheme. The mobile clinic doctor and staff should report to the I.T.D.P through their respective NGOs.

13. **Special Incontives to Ethnomedical specialists**

Traditional medical practitioners such as bone-setters, herbalists and mid wives in the Bhil communities should be given monthly stipend in the form of cereals, pulses, vegetables and oil, including some cash for the health services they provide to their community members.

Tribhuwan Robin, 1988 in his book captioned, "Medical world of Tribals" has stated that the ethnomedical specialists have been providing health care services to their tribes men since ages. They receive gifts in cash and kind from their community for the services rendered by them. The Tribal Development Department must formulate schemes to support these practitioners so that they get some thing in kind and cash. In doing so they will also be motivated. These practitioners should be trained to handle first aid. They should be given first Aid boxes, as well.

14. **Special cell at the I.T.D.P.**

A special cell should be established at the I.T.D.P's Talodaetc.to plan, implement, monitor and follow up development programme for Bhil sugarcane cutters.

15. **Hostels for Tribal Labourers**

One special hostel should be established in tensil head quarters wherein Bhils and other landless tribal populations inhabit. The children of tribal bonded labourers belonging to the unorganized labour such as brick kiln, sugar cane cutters, salt pan workers, sandworkers, and landless daily wage labourers should be given admissions, to continue their higher studies.

16. **Proper Planning and execution of the NREGP**

The National Rural Employment Guarantee Programme (NREGP) ensures 100 days employment to the rural poor. Despite of the existence of National Rural Employment Guarantee Scheme, why do the Bhil sugarcane cutters migrate? How can this indebtedness and bonded labour be stopped? What can be done for the landless and marginal farmers?

These and several questions haunt the mind of an Indian citizen. The Planners and implementators of the NREGA should take a note of this and seriously think over so as to rehabilitate the migrant laboures of unorganized labour.

If the above suggestions are implemented there will certainly be economic, social and educational in empowerment and progress among the Bhil sugarcane cutters and their children.

FURTHER RESEARCH NEEDED

Social science research is an unending process. The broad research area of unorganized labour in India is a vast field to be probed into. This piece of research study has been able to throw light on the child labour and rights issues of children of the Katkari brick kiln labourers and the Bhil sugarcane cutters. Suggested below are few areas of further research in this field.

(a) Testing and validating the child labour and rights model

Social scientists can test and validate the authenticity of the research model evolved through this research study in other migrant occupational groups in unorganized labour sectors of this country.

(b) Impact of Migration

Yet another area of research that needs detailed documentation is the impact of migration on the migrant adults, elderly as well as children, both at the place of origin and at the place of destination.

(c) A survey regarding benefit received by the migrant labourers from national Rural Employment guarantee scheme needs to be conducted.

References

Agarwal H.O., 1970, Human Rights, Central Law Publication, Allahabad.

Ahuja Ram, 2007, Social Problems in India, (2nd Edn), Rawat Publications, Jaipur.

Bajpai Asha, 2003, Child Rights in India, Oxford University Press, New Delhi.

Bajpai Asha, Weiner M., Burra Neera, 2006, Born Unfree, Oxford University Press, New Delhi.

Bhende Asha & Kanitakar Tara, 1978, Principles of Population Studies, Himalaya Publishing House, Mumbai – 04.

Bokil Milind, 2006, Katkari: Vikasache Vyavasthapan, Mauj Prakashan, Girgaon, Mumbai.

Breman Jan and Das Arvind, 2000, Down and Out: Labouring Under Global Capitalism, Oxford University Press, New Delhi.

Breman Jan, 1996, Footloose Labour, Cambridge University Press, Cambridge.

Breman Jan, 1994, Wage Hunters and Gatherers: Search for Work in the Urban and Rural Economy of South Gujarat,Oxford University Press, New Delhi.

Brewer Jonh D., 2010, Ethnography (Indian Edition), Rawat Publication, Jaipur.

Bryman Alan, 2008, Social Research Methods, Oxford Publications, Oxford.

Census Of India, 2001, Government of India.

Desai Mrinalini, 2005, Janarth Sakharshala – the Sending Villages Report.

Enthoven R.E., 1922, The Tribes and Castes of Bombay, vol 1 Reprint Cosmo Publications, New Delhi, 1975.

Everett S. Lee, "A Theory of Migration," In J.A. Jackson (Ed) 'Migration' 1969, Cambridge University Press, Cambridge.

Gaikwad Nancy, 1995, 'Katkaris: A Tribe Seeking an Identity', in Jain N.S. & Tribhuwan Robin (eds.) *'An Overview of Tribal Research Studies'*, TRTI, Pune.

Green J.M, Draper A.K., & Dowler E.A, 2003, Shortcuts to Safety: Risks and 'Rules of Thumb' in Accounts of Food Choice. Health, Risk & Society.

Gupte Suraj, 1995, A Textbook of Peadiatrics, Indian Academy of Peadiatrics, New Delhi.

Haralambos Mike & Holborn Martin, 2000, Sociology: Themes and Perspectives, Collins Publishers, London.

Jhabvala Renana & Subrahmanya R.K.A., (eds)2000. The Unorganised Sector – Work Security and Social Protection, Sage Publications, New Delhi.

JugaleV.B., 1997, "Employment Wages and Industrial Relations: Farm Sector Workers of Sugar Cooperative in Maharashtra", Classical Publishing Company, New Delhi.

Kasar D.V., 1992, Economics and Seasonal Migration", Classical Publishing Company, New Delhi.

Krueger R.A., & Casey M.A., 2000, Focus Groups: A Practical Guide for Applied Research, 3rd Ed. Thousand Oaks, CA/Sage Publication.

Madan G.R., 2009,Indian Social Problems, Volume I (7th Edn), Allied Publishers, Mumbai.

Mishra L, 2000, Child Labour In India, Oxford University Press, New Delhi.

Naidu U.S. and Nakhate U.S., 1985, Child Development Studies in India, Tata Institute of Social Sciences, Mumbai.

Naik T.B., 1956, Bhils: A Study, Bhartiya Adim Jati Sevak Sangh, New Delhi.

Panjiar Smita and Prashant, 2007, Locked Homes, Empty Schools, Zubban, New Delhi.

Paprikar Madhavi, 2002, 'Industries in Maharashtra', in Diddee Jaymala, Jog S.R. , Kale V.S., Datye V.S. (Ed.) *Geography of Maharashtra,* Rawat Publications, Jaipur.

Richardson C.A. & Rabiee F., 2001 "A Question of Access—An Exploration of the Factors Influencing the Health of Young Males Aged 15-19, living in Corbey and their use of Healthcare Services. Health Education Journal.

Rogaly B., and Rafique A, 2003, Struggle to Save Cash: Seasonal Migration and Vulnerabilities in West Bengal, India: Development and Change.

Russell R.V. & Hiralal, 1975, Castes if Central Provinces of India, Vol. II, Tribes and Publications, Delhi.

Sachidanand & Prasad R.R., 1996, Encyclopaedic Profile of Indian Tribes, Discovery Publishing House.

Schenk – Sandbergen Loes (Ed.), 1995, Women & Seasonal Labour Migration, Sage Publications, New Delhi.

Sharma Usha, 2006, Child Labour In India, Mittal Publications, New Delhi.

Siddiqui M.I, 2003, Child Labour: How to Investigate, Deep & Deep Publications, New Delhi.

Sreenivasulu, N.S., 2008, Human Rights: Many Sides to a Coin, Regal Publications, New Delhi.

Singh Surjit, 1994, Urban Informal Sector, Rawat Publications, Delhi.

Tribhuwan Robin and Paranjape S. The World of Tribal Children (Unpublished Book), Discovery Publishing House, New Delhi.

Tribhuwan Robin & Sherry Karen, 2004, Health, Medicine & Nutrition of the Tribes, Discovery Publishing House, New Delhi.

Tribhuwan Robin & Tribhuwan Preeti (Ed.), 1999, Tribal Dances of India, Discovery Publishing House, New Delhi.

Tribhuwan Robin & Jain Navinchandra, 1996, Mirage of Health & Development, Vidyaridhi Publications, Pune.

Tribhuwan Robin, 1988, Medical World of Tribals, Discovery Publishing House, New Delhi.

Tomar Y.P.S. and Tribhuwan Robin, 2004, Development of Primitive Tribes: Status, Continuity & Change, Tribal Research & Training Institute, Pune.

Tripathy S.N. 2006, Dynamics of Tribal Migration, Sonali Publications, New Delhi.

Tripathy S.N., 2005, Tribal Migration, Sonali Publications, New Delhi.

Weston & Burns H. (Ed), 2007, Child Labour and Human Rights, Viva Books,

Williams Robin, 1970, American Society: A Sociological Interpretation (3rd Edition), Alfred Knof, New York.

Wallace R.C. & Wallace W.D., 1945, Sociology, Allan & Bacon inc, London.

Reports and Articles

A Global Alliance Against Forced Labour, 2005, Report I (B), International Labour Conference, 93rd Session, 2005, International Labour Office, Geneva.

Bhatia Arun & Tribhuwan Robin, 2002, Malnutrition Related Deaths of Tribal Children in Nandurbar District of Maharashtra, A Report By Tribal Research & Training Institute, Pune.

Bhatia Arun & Tribhuwan Robin, 2002, Scheme for Financial Assistance to Pregnant Tribal Women, 2002, A Report By Tribal Research & Training Institute, Pune.

Bhatia Arun & Tribhuwan Robin, 2002, Dying Children, 2002, A Report By Tribal Research & Training Institute, Pune.

Bhatia Arun & Tribhuwan Robin, 2002, The Truth about Malnutrition Child Deaths, 2002, A Report By Tribal Research & Training Institute, Pune.

Bose Ashish, 1965, "Internal Migration in India, Pakistan and Ceylon," United Nations, World Population Conference, Belgrade.

By the Sweat and Toil of Children, 1994, A Report, Bureau of International Labour Affairs, U.S. Department of Labour.

Child Labour Statistics, 2008, Report III, 18th International Conference of Labour Statisticians, Geneva, International Labour Office, Geneva, Switzerland.

Desai Mrinalini, 2005, Janarth Sakharshala – the Sending Villages Report, NCAS, Pune.

Deshingkar P., Start D., 2003, Seasonal Migration for Livelihood in India: Coping, Accumulation and Exclusion, ODI Working paper No. 220, Overseas Development Institute: London.

Deshpande A. P.,1976, Estimates of Interstate Migration in India during 1961-71, International Institute of Population Studies, Bombay.

Dhamankar Mona, 2005, Janarth Sakharshala – Documentation Report, Janarth, Aurangabad.

Dorothy S. Thomas,1938, Research memorandum of Migration Differentials, Social Science Research Council Bulletin, New York.

Gaikwad Nancy, 1995, 'Katkaris: A Tribe Seeking an Identity', In Jain N.S. & Tribhuwan Robin (eds.) *'An Overview of Tribal Research Studies'*, TRTI, Pune.

Gambhir Ram & Gurjar Sumedh, 2008, Study of Seasonal Migration and its Impact on the Nutritional Status of Children", YASHADA & Department of Anthropology,University of Pune, Pune.

Guru Gopal, 1989, "Cooperative Sugar Industry and Sugar Workers Movement in Maharashtra – A Study", in Second Maharashtra Rajya Sugar Workers Conference, Nifad, Nashik, on 1st and 2nd October, 1989.

Human Rights Watch, 1996, The Small Hands of Slavery-Bonded Child: Labour in India, Human Rights Watch, New York.

Jayschandran Usha, 2005-06, Bhongashala Report, Shramjeevi Sanghtana, Thane.

Kshirsagar J.B. & Kumar Pawan, (2008), Ashwattha, Vol. 2, Issue No. 1, January-March 2008, YASHADA, Pune.

Kulkarni Sharad (1979), Bonded Labour & Ilicit Moneylending in Maharashtra, Economic & Political Weekly, Vol. XIV. No. 9 March 10, 1979, pp. 561-563.

Mahasveta Devi, 1981, Contract Labour or Bonded Labour, Economic and Political Weekly, June 6, 1981.

Sarada G. & Lakshmanan P., (2007), Ashwattha, Vol. I, Issue No. 3, April-June 2007, YASHADA, Pune.

Schenk – Sandbergen Loes (Ed.), 1995, Women & Seasonal Labour Migration, Sage Publications, New Delhi.

Sharma Shiva, Basnyat B., Ganesh G.C, 2001, Nepal, Bonded Labour Among Child Workers of the Kamaiya System: A Rapid Assessment (ILO, IPEC), International Labour Organization, Geneva.

Shirsalkar P.R., (2004), 'Bhils', in Singh K.S. (ed), People of India Series, ASI, Oxford University Press, New Delhi.

Social Security for Unorganized Workers – A Report, May 2006, National Commission for Enterprises in the Unorganised Sector, New Delhi.

Svedberg Peter, 2010, Estimates of Children Malnutrition in India, Economic & Political Weekly, Vol .XLV No. 12, March 20, 2010, pp. 14-18.

Thomas L., Macmillan J., McColl E.,Hale C. & Bond S., 1995, Comparison of Focus Group and Individual Methodology in Examining Patient Satisfaction with Nursing Care. Social Sciences in Health.

Tribhuwan Robin and Cappel Marcuse, 1999, "Kothmir & Dhamdi Dances of the Katkaris" in Tribhuwan R.D and Tribhuwan P.R (Ed), Discovery Publishing House, New Delhi.

Tribhuwan Robin and Kulkarni Vijaya, (1999) "In Tribal Dances of India" by Tribhuwan Robin & Tribhuwan Preeti(Ed), Discovery Publishing House, New Delhi.

Tribhuwan Robin & Patil Jayshree, 2006, Socio-Economic Status and Development Needs of the Katkaris: A Case Study, A Report Submitted to Women's International Club, Pune.

Tribhuwan Robin (2006), "Functional Review of Tribal Development Department" Report Submitted to YASHADA, Pune.

Tribhuwan Robin, 2006, Socio-Economic Status and Development Needs of the Katkaris: A Case Study, A Report Submitted to Women's International Club, Pune.

Vastala Narain, A. Sebastian and P. Hanumantharayappa, 1970, Rural Migration Patterns in Southern Maharashtra, Demographic Training and Research Centre, Bombay.

Yashmanthan, (Balkamgar Visheshank), Vol. 6, Issue-1 (April June 2005), YASHADA, Pune.

Young P.V.,1960, Scientific Social Surveys and Research (3rd Edn), Prentice Hall Publications, New York.

Unpublished Thesis

Deshpande M, 2008, "Health and Nutritional Status of Women Seasonal Migrant: A Study of Sugarcane Cutters in Kolhapur District" (Unpublished Ph.D., Thesis), Dept. of Sociology, Shivaji University, Kolhapur.

Kendre Balaji, 2009 "Migration and Development : A Sociological Study of Migrant Sugarcane Cutters in Kolhapur District" (Unpublished PhD Thesis), Dept. of Sociology, Swami Ramanad Teerth Marathwada University, Nanded-06.

Patnaik Renuka, 1996 "Patterns of Occupation and Resource Unitlization", Unpublished Ph.D., Thesis, submitted to Department of Geography, University of Pune, Pune.

Shende Sadashiv, 2011 "Exploitation of Chuvalia Koli – Salt Pan Workers: A Sociological Study" (Unpublished M.Phil Thesis), Dept. of Sociology, Tilak Maharashtra Vidyapeet, Pune.

Websites Refered

http://www.hiltonfoundation.org/press/16-pdf3.pdf=Worldwde

http://www.doccentre.net/docsweb/Education/Scanned_material

www.hd-ca.org/pubs/3_5_Child_Ballet_Bhukuth_Radja.pdf

www.ilo.int/public/english/region/asro/.../ipec/.../nepal

Glossary

1. Birhad	:	A term used by the Katkaris to refer to a family
2. Koyta	:	A working unit (consist of two members)
3. Mukadam	:	Contractor or middle-man
4. Ucha	:	Loan taken by the debtor from the brick kiln owner or contractors by the Katkari brick kiln labourers or Bhil sugarcane cutters
5. Kharchi	:	Weekly to the weekly expenses given to the brick-kiln labourers and sugarcane cutters
6. Sakharshala	:	A temporary shade wherein a school is run for the children of sugarcane cutters during sugarcane cutting season
7. Anganwadi	:	A pre-school wherein educational, health and nutritional services are given to children below the age of six years including pregnant and lactating women.
8. Ashram Shala	:	A residential school run by the Tribal Development Department, Government of Maharashtra, for tribal student studying in I to XII grades. The students get food, lodging, uniform, stationary, sports equipments etc. free of charge for 12 years
9. Zilla Parishad School	:	A day school run by the Zilla Parishad for tribal and non-tribal students, belonging to grades I to XII. The students get uniform, books and a mid-day meal free of charge.
10. Bhonga Shala	:	A temporary shade wherein a school is run for the children of brick kiln labourers

11. Khopi	:	A small hut made up of bamboo mat, wherein the sugarcane cutters keep their belongings and use for sleeping. (A temporary hut of sugarcane cutters at sugarcane cutting site)
12. Zopdi	:	A temporary small hut in which the Katkari brick kiln labourers live
13. Vit Bhatti	:	Brick – kiln
14. Vit	:	Brick
15. Lugde	:	Sari worn by women
16. Bandi	:	Sleeveless shirt worn by men
17. Wadi	:	Hamlet
18. Dhol	:	Drum
19. Mahua Daru	:	Liquor prepared from the Mahua (Basia Latifolia) flowers, using fermentation and distillation method.
20. Tyre Gadi Center	:	Tyre Gadi centers migrants bring their bullocks and are provided technologically improved carts (with rubber tyres) to transport sugarcane, they live in large settlements closer to the factory. These settlements are called as Tyre Gadi Centers.
21. Gadi Center	:	Gadi canter migrants bring their own wooden bullock carts and animals and live further away from the factory. Their settlements are called as Gadi Centers.
22. Doki Center	:	The Doki center migrants are mobile, they have no assets, they cut cane and load it into factory trucks, stay farthest away, work in groups of 15-20, and are shifted from site to site depending on cane availability and factory schedule. Their settlements are known as Doki centers.

Index

S